Programming in Oberon

ACM PRESS

Editor-in-Chief **Peter Wegner** Brown University
International Editor **Dines Bjørner** Technical University
(Europe) of Denmark

SELECTED TITLES

Advances in Database Programming Languages *François Bancilhon and Peter Buneman (Eds)*

Algebraic Specification *J.A. Bergstra, J. Heering and P. Klint (Eds)*

Software Reusability (Volume 1: Concepts and Models) *Ted Biggerstaff and Alan Perlis (Eds)*

Software Reusability (Volume 2: Applications and Experience) *Ted Biggerstaff and Alan Perlis (Eds)*

Object-Oriented Concepts, Databases and Applications *Won Kim and Frederick H. Lochovsky (Eds)*

Performance Instrumentation and Visualization *Rebecca Koskela and Margaret Simmons (Eds)*

Distributed Systems *Sape Mullender (Ed)*

The Programmer's Apprentice *Charles Rich and Richard C. Waters*

Instrumentation for Future Parallel Computer Systems *Margaret Simmons, Ingrid Bucher and Rebecca Koskela (Eds)*

User Interface Design *Harold Thimbleby*

The Oberon System: User Guide and Programmer's Manual *Martin Reiser*

Programming in Oberon

Steps beyond Pascal and Modula

Martin Reiser
IBM Research Division
Zürich Research Laboratory
Säumerstrasse 4
8803 Rüschlikon

and

Niklaus Wirth
Institut fur Computersysteme
ETH Zentrum
8092 Zürich

ACM Press
New York, New York

Addison-Wesley Publishing Company
Wokingham, England · Reading, Massachusetts · Menlo Park, California
New York · Don Mills, Ontario · Amsterdam · Bonn
Sydney · Singapore · Tokyo · Madrid · San Juan · Milan
Paris · Mexico City · Seoul · Taipei

Copyright © 1992 by the ACM Press, A Division of the Association for Computing Machinery, Inc. (ACM).

All rights reserved. No part of this publication may be reproduced, stored in a retrieval system, or transmitted in any form or by any means, electronic, mechanical, photocopying, recording or otherwise, without prior written permission of the publisher.

The programs in this book have been included for their instructional value. They have been tested with care but are not guaranteed for any particular purpose. The publisher does not offer any warranties or representations, nor does it accept any liabilities with respect to the programs.

Many of the designations used by manufacturers and sellers to distinguish their products are claimed as trademarks. The publisher has made every attempt to supply trademark information about manufacturers and their products mentioned in this book. A list of the trademark designations and their owners appears on p. x.

Cover designed by Hybert Design and Type, Maidenhead
and printed by The Riverside Printing Co. (Reading) Ltd.
Typeset by Keyword Publishing Services Ltd
Printed in Great Britain by Mackays of Chatham, Kent

First printed 1992.

British Library Cataloguing in Publication Data
A catalogue record for this book is available from the British Library

Library of Congress Cataloging in Publication Data
Reiser, Martin.
    Programming in Oberon : steps beyond Pascal and Modula / Martin Reiser and Niklaus Wirth.
       p.   cm.
    Includes bibliographical references and index.
    ISBN 0-201-56543-9 : $30.00 (est.)
    1. Operating systems (Computers) 2. Oberon. I. Wirth, Niklaus.
II. Title.
QA76.76.063R46   1992   92-12597
005.13'3—dc20   CIP

Preface

The most amazing fact about the computing industry is the dramatic improvement in the performance of computing machinery – a trend observed for three decades and projected to continue unabated. Not only is this trend exponential – a doubling of the power every two to four years – it also takes place at costs that are roughly constant for each machine class, CPU, minicomputer, PC or workstation. In other words, the price-performance drops the same way as performance increases.

In contrast to the hardware, the programs that make computers useful do not show anything close to steady advancement – let alone exponential progress. Historically, innovation took place in short intensive spurts, interrupted by long plateaus during which armies of programmers struggled to embody new concepts in useful software. In the field of personal computing, such a surge took place during the seventies, lead by the famous Palo Alto Research Center (PARC). The eighties, in contrast, are a rather dull period characterized by a predominant product orientation.

As the industry tries to implement the personal computing paradigm, more and more difficulties emerge. The operation systems that became standards fail even to capitalize on the 'software engineering principles' available at the time. The premature rush into standards froze innovation in that area and led to the phenomenon of grafting layer upon layer of code onto a dated base system.

A critical eyewitness may conclude that software is well on its way to neutralizing the phenomenal gains of the hardware. The reasons are many, and there is no single patent answer. We observe, however, that despite claims of doing 'software engineering,' the most basic of engineering principles is rarely practiced: to strive for economy of means and simplicity of solutions. 'Software engineers' are still beating the lather, rather than using the razor of Occham!

It is precisely at this point that one of us started research: to build a system from scratch – led by the quote by Albert Einstein: *'make it as simple as possible, but not simpler.'* The result of that research is Oberon: a language and an operating system for a personal computer or workstation.

This book is one of three. It describes the *language Oberon* (the others being Reiser, 1991; Wirth and Gutknecht, 1992). Its concept follows *Programming in MODULA-2* (Wirth, 1982):

- It is a language reference.
- It is a programming tutorial, exhibiting modern programming concepts.
- It implements these concepts in Oberon.

The book should therefore serve the professional programmer as well as university professors and students. The text is composed of reference sections and examples.

Writing a book on programming poses many challenges, in particular how to choose the order in which concepts and constructs are introduced and how to choose examples that are exciting and realistic, yet rely solely on material explained earlier in the text. Our approach is distinguished in two ways: the procedure and module are introduced early, right after the control structures, and the examples share a common theme: simulation. In the end, a complete and realistic simulation package is obtained.

The Oberon language was purposefully designed to serve as an implementation tool for the *Oberon system*, an efficient, concise operating system founded on object-oriented programming. The language, however, is not tied to the system – compilers can be provided for any machine under most current operating systems. *Programming in Oberon* therefore requires no knowledge of the Oberon system, and digresses only minimally into a discussion of Oberon system concepts.

The book is organized into three parts as follows.

Part I: Tokens, basic types, assignment, control structures, procedures, modules

Part I is about basic programming constructs. At the end, all knowledge is available to write complete Oberon modules that use scalar variables only.

The syntax of Oberon is introduced rigorously using the well-known EBNF[1] notation. The semantics of the assignment and the control structures are *formally defined* using transformation rules of predicates that define the state of the computation prior and after execution of a

---

[1] Extended Backus Naur formalism.

statement. The formalism, due to Dijkstra, is introduced by means of easy examples and presented in a notation close to that of Oberon.

The early introduction of the procedure and the module is made possible by using a stimulating example: drawing a fractal fern. To complete the example, the *basic concepts of input and output* are introduced through the *notion of the stream* and a module providing graphic output. Oberon takes the view that input and output are not parts of the language, but are provided by modules that can be considered extensions of the operating system.

Part II: Arrays, records, pointers, dynamic data, stepwise refinement, data abstraction

Part II introduces classic programming. At the end, roughly the scope of Modula-2 is covered.

The array and dynamic data structures are the turf of 'data structures and algorithms' – a classical topic of computer science. This text is not in competition with the many excellent textbooks in that area. Nevertheless, searching in arrays (but not sorting), the list and the tree are discussed. The list processing procedures lay the foundation for the completed examples that will follow.

Part II ends with Chapter 10, which introduces the important programming techniques of *stepwise refinement, abstract data structures* and *abstract data types*. These programming concepts are introduced by developing a simulation package composed of several modules.

Part III: Type extension, procedure types, object-orientation

Here starts the new and exciting material that sets Oberon aside from its predecessor Modula-2. The goal is a programming technique that makes programs *extensible and reusable*. Type extension in combination with procedure variables lay the foundation. Chapter 11 is a reference for Oberon type extension and procedure types.

Object-orientation as a programming technique, together with object-oriented programming languages, is a fashionable topic. Oberon is true to its spirit: a minimal language extension – namely extension of record types – suffices. This is in contrast to other approaches that introduce a wealth of new concepts many simply renaming established notions.

Chapter 12 introduces object-orientation, the Oberon way. The example of a graphics editor is used to avoid talking in abstract terms only.

Chapter 13 restates the simulation program of Chapter 10 using an object-oriented approach. A fully functional package is presented that is actually fit to serve in the practice of discrete event simulations.

Oberon objects differ from those defined by other languages (such as C++) by the fact that procedures (methods) are bound to instances, not to the type of objects. Chapter 14, finally, describes Oberon-2, a small and fully upward compatible extension of Oberon proper (Mössenböck and Wirth, 1991). The major addition of Oberon-2 is the *type-bound procedure* that implements dynamic binding to the type.

Appendices

A revised version of the original report on the programming language Oberon is found in Appendix A (Wirth, 1988). Appendix B gives an ASCII table and lists common extremal values of the basic types. Throughout the book, we make use of certain input/output abstraction that are provided by three modules, *In, Out* and *XY plane*. The source text of these modules is given in Appendix C.

On the examples and exercises

We conclude this preface with some remarks about the examples used and the exercises suggested in this text. The selection of examples and exercises is always important – but it is crucial in the area of programming. Every teacher of programming also knows from experience that this choice is also burdened by an inherent dilemma. Obviously, this book cannot banish it. On the one hand, every extensive and complex subject must be taught in steps, and in each step exercises should be confined to the concepts presented. They have to be reasonably small and concentrate on the essentials. On the other hand, true mastery of programming requires experience in the construction of large, non-trivial designs. Such experience, however, cannot be acquired only by study, nor through solving small exercise problems. It requires active involvement in projects, and is earned through years of deep involvement. But it finally rests on certain basic rules of discipline, and these rules may very well be taught – in fact should be taught – in introductory courses. The irony lies in the fact that such rules are largely considered as irrelevant in the solution of typical course exercises. They are ridiculed by most students, if they are mentioned at all, as idiosyncrasies and expressions of the pedantry of the teacher. Their basic value is recognized only when large projects are undertaken and fail

– which happens long after the introductory course has been completed successfully. We must accept this dilemma and muster the courage to stress the importance of details, even if pedantic insistence on discipline is mistakenly interpreted as hindrance to creativity. Pedantry in programming is not a luxury, but a necessity.

Students on most programming courses are given the impression that the essence of programming is to concoct code that causes a computer to operate in a specific fashion. While this may be true for typical commercial endeavors, we maintain that ultimately a program is worthless if it cannot be understood by other human beings. Its formulation must be chosen with the goal of providing the conviction to human beings that it satisfies its purpose. Every program should be a *publishable design*. This is a far cry from the usual goal that the 'program runs'!

We can at least assure the reader that a notation which encourages the programmer to be precise and explicit is indispensable for approaching this goal. *Oberon is such a notation.*

Oberon system implementations

It is self-evident that this book will be most useful if the reader has an Oberon compiler at his or her disposal. Besides the original Oberon version running on the *Ceres* workstation built at the Swiss Federal Institute of Technology (Eberle, 1987), many implementations are currently available as freeware, in particular for

- RS/6000 (IBM)
- Sparcstation (SUN microsystems)
- Macintosh II (Apple)
- DECStation/3100 and 3500 (DEC).

How to get Oberon

Oberon can be obtained via anonymous internet file transfer ftp (at no charge) or on floppy disks (for a fee of 50 Swiss Francs per implementation, which is about 35 US Dollars). We accept payment via Eurocard/Mastercard or VISA. To order by credit card, specify your card number, expiry date and your name exactly as it appears on the card. Please remember to specify your type of machine when ordering.

         FTP Hostname: neptune.inf.ethz.ch
         Internet Address: 129.132.101.33
         FTP Directory: Oberon

For further information, please contact

The Secretary, Institut für Computersysteme ETH, 8092 Zurich, Switzerland
Telephone (+41−1) 254 7311. Facsimile (+41−1) 261 5389.

Sample Programs from *Programming in Oberon*

Various sample programs from within this book are also available in Source form from the ETH Server via anonymous internet file transfer ftp (at no charge).

Acknowledgements

The authors thank Peter Mössenböck for many helpful suggestions and a careful manuscript reading.

References

Eberle H. (1987). Development and analysis of a workstation computer. Ph. D. Thesis, Swiss Federal Institute of Technology, ETH Nr. 8431.
Mössenböck H. and Wirth N. (1991). The programming language Oberon-2. *Structured Programming*, **12**, 179–95.
Reiser M. (1991). *The Oberon System: User Guide and Programmer's Manual*. Wokingham: Addison-Wesley.
Wirth N. (1982). *Programming in Modula-2*. Berlin: Springer-Verlag.
Wirth N. (1988). The programming language Oberon. *Software–Practice and Experience*,**18**, 671–90.
Wirth N. and Gutknecht J. (1992). *Project Oberon*. Wokingham: Addison-Wesley.

Trademark notice
Apple[TM] and Macintosh[TM] are registered trademarks of Apple Computer, Inc.
DECstation[TM] is a trademark of Digital Equipment Corporation
IBM RISC System/6000[TM] is a trademark of International Business Machines Corporation
Smalltalk[TM] and Smalltalk-80[TM] are trademarks of Xerox Corporation
MC 68030[TM] and MC 68882[TM] are trademarks of Motorola Corporation
Series 32000R[TM] is a trademark of National Semiconductor Corporation
SUN Sparcstation[TM] is a trademark of Sun Microsystems Incorporated

Contents

		Preface	v
1		**Why Oberon?**	1
	1.1	The Algol family	1
	1.2	The Oberon system	5
2		**A first Oberon program**	9
	2.1	A notation to describe the syntax of Oberon	17
	2.2	Exercises	18

Part I   Tokens, Basic types, Assignment, Control structures, Procedures, Modules

3		**Tokens and basic types**	23
	3.1	The vocabulary of Oberon	23
		3.1.1 Identifiers	24
		3.1.2 Numbers	24
		3.1.3 Character constants	25
		3.1.4 Strings	25
		3.1.5 Operators and delimiters	25
		3.1.6 Predeclared identifiers	26
		3.1.7 Rules for blanks and carriage-returns	26
	3.2	Basic types	27
		3.2.1 The types SHORTINT, INTEGER and LONGINT	27
		3.2.2 The types REAL and LONGREAL	28
		3.2.3 Hierarchy of the numeric types	28
		3.2.4 The type BOOLEAN	28
		3.2.5 The type SET	29
		3.2.6 The type CHAR	39
4		**Declarations, expressions and assignments**	30
	4.1	Declarations	30
		4.1.1 Constant declarations	31
		4.1.2 Variable declarations	31

xi

	4.2	Expressions	32
		4.2.1 Syntax and general semantics	32
		4.2.2 Type rules	34
		4.2.3 Relations	35
		4.2.4 Arithmetic expressions	36
		4.2.5 Boolean expressions	37
		4.2.6 Set expressions	38
		4.2.7 Predeclared functions	39
	4.3	The assignment statement	39
		4.3.1 Type rules	40
		4.3.2 Formal definition, pre-condition and post-condition	41
		4.3.3 Statement sequence	42
		4.3.4 Special assignment statements as predeclared procedures	44
	4.4	Summary	44
	4.5	Exercises	45
5	**Control structures**		**47**
	5.1	Conditional statements	48
		5.1.1 The if statement	48
		5.1.2 Formal definition of the if statement	49
		5.1.3 The case statement	52
		5.1.4 Formal definition of the case statement	53
	5.2	Repetitive statements	53
		5.2.1 The while statement	54
		5.2.2 Formal definition of the while statement	54
		5.2.3 The repeat statement	57
		5.2.4 Formal definition of the repeat statement	58
		5.2.5 The loop statement	58
	5.3	Summary	59
	5.4	Exercises	60
6	**Procedures and modules**		**63**
	6.1	The procedure: a statement sequence with a name	66
	6.2	The concept of locality	67
		6.2.1 Scope	68
		6.2.2 Nesting of scopes	68
		6.2.3 Advantage of locality	69
	6.3	Modules	69
		6.3.1 The scope defined by a module declaration of global variables	70
		6.3.2 The statement sequence of a module	71
		6.3.3 Export and import of declarations	71

6.4		Function procedures and parameters	73
	6.4.1	The function procedure heading	74
	6.4.2	Formal parameters and the return statement	75
	6.4.3	Actual parameters, the function call	76
6.5		Proper procedures	77
	6.5.1	Syntax, the call statement	77
	6.5.2	Value and variable parameters	78
6.6		More on function procedures	80
	6.6.1	Side-effects	80
	6.6.2	Recursion	81
6.7		Compiler hints	82
6.8		Summary	83
6.9		Exercises	84

7 Input and output 87

7.1		Sequential input and output, modules *In* and *Out*	88
7.2		Graphics output	90
7.3		The fractal fern, completion of the example	92
7.4		The Oberon system: a short digression	95
	7.4.1	Execution of commands	95
	7.4.2	The role of texts	96
	7.4.3	Modules *In* and *Out*	98
	7.4.4	Module *XYplane*	100
7.5		Summary	100
7.6		Exercises	101

Part II Arrays, Records, Pointers, Dynamic data, Stepwise refinement, Data abstraction

8 Type declarations, array and record types 109

8.1		Type declaration	110
8.2		Arrays	112
	8.2.1	The array type and the array declaration	112
	8.2.2	The array designator, assignment and expressions	113
	8.2.3	Parameters of array type	115
	8.2.4	The open array parameter	117
	8.2.5	The array as a table	119
	8.2.6	Strings and the type ARRAY n OF CHAR	122
8.3		Records	126
	8.3.1	The record type and the record declaration	126
	8.3.2	The record designator, assignments and expressions	128
	8.3.3	Use of records	130
8.4		Summary	131
8.5		Exercises	132

9 Dynamic data structures and pointer types — 134
- 9.1 Pointers — 136
  - 9.1.1 The pointer type and pointer declarations — 136
  - 9.1.2 Creation of variables referenced by pointers — 137
  - 9.1.3 Dereferencing a pointer — 137
  - 9.1.4 Memory management — 139
- 9.2 Lists — 140
  - 9.2.1 Simple or linear lists — 140
  - 9.2.2 FIFO lists — 144
- 9.3 Trees — 146
  - 9.3.1 Inherently recursive procedures — 148
  - 9.3.2 Searching in trees — 151
- 9.4 Other dynamic data structures — 153
- 9.5 Summary — 154
- 9.6 Exercises — 155

10 Stepwise refinement and data abstraction — 158
- 10.1 Discrete event simulation of a waiting line — 158
- 10.2 Putting the operation of the queue into Oberon terms — 161
  - 10.2.1 Data representation of the system state — 161
  - 10.2.2 A first round of refinement of the queueing algorithm — 162
- 10.3 Hiding of details — 164
  - 10.3.1 Implementation of module *Calendar* — 164
  - 10.3.2 Computing statistics: module *Paths* — 167
- 10.4 Completion of the simulation example — 170
- 10.5 More on program structuring and abstraction — 173
  - 10.5.1 Decomposition into modules, data hiding — 173
  - 10.5.2 Module *Out*: an example of an abstract data structure — 174
  - 10.5.3 Module *Files*: an example of an abstract data type — 176
  - 10.5.4 Textual structure and naming — 179
- 10.6 Summary — 181
- 10.7 Exercises — 182

Part III Type extension, Procedure types, Object orientation

11 Type extension and procedure types — 187
- 11.1 Extension of record types — 190
  - 11.1.1 Declaration of an extended type — 190
  - 11.1.2 Record designators and assignments — 191
- 11.2 Pointers, type guards and type tests — 194
  - 11.2.1 Extension of pointer types — 194
  - 11.2.2 Static and dynamic type, type guard, type test — 195
  - 11.2.3 With statement, regional type guard — 197

	11.3	Procedure types	199
		11.3.1 The procedure type and procedure variables	199
		11.3.2 Expressions and assignments	200
		11.3.3 Call of procedure variables	201
		11.3.4 Formal parameters of procedure type	202
		11.3.5 Up-calls	203
	11.4	Summary	204
	11.5	Exercises	205
12	**Object-orientation**		**208**
	12.1	Generic modules	210
	12.2	Heterogeneous data structures	212
	12.3	Objects, dynamic binding of procedures	215
	12.4	Objects and modules	220
		12.4.1 Module *Graphics*	221
		12.4.2 Shape-specific modules	223
		12.4.3 Creation of a new figure	224
		12.4.4 Redefining a dynamically bound procedure	227
		12.4.5 Summary	229
	12.5	Message and handlers	230
		12.5.1 Message and handler	231
		12.5.2 Message broadcast	233
		12.5.3. Generality of handlers	234
		12.5.4 Summary	235
	12.6	Conclusions and outlook	236
		12.6.1 Two categories of Oberon objects – a comparison	236
		12.6.2 On the object-oriented programming paradigm	238
	12.7	Exercises	239
13	**A simulation example**		**245**
	13.1	Generic module *Qs*	245
		13.1.1 Definition	246
		13.1.2 Implementation	247
	13.2	An object-oriented simulation calendar	250
		13.2.1 Data type *Actor* and basic module structure	250
		13.2.2 Module *Sim*: an abstract simulation	251
	13.3	A simulation based on module *Sim*	254
		13.3.1 Data types and module structure	256
		13.3.2 Definition of module *Stations*	257
		13.3.3 Implementation of module *Stations*	258
		13.3.4 Implementation of module *Model*	260
	13.4	Summary	262
	13.5	Exercises	263

14 Oberon-2 — 265

- 14.1 Type-bound procedures — 265
  - 14.1.1 Syntax and general semantics — 267
  - 14.1.2 Example: graphics editor — 270
- 14.2 For statement — 273
- 14.3 The open array variable — 274
- 14.4 The Oberon-2 with statement — 275
- 14.5 Read-only export — 276
- 14.6 Summary and discussion — 277
- 14.7 Exercises — 278

Appendix A The programming language Oberon — 281

- A.1 Introduction — 281
- A.2 Syntax — 281
- A.3 Vocabulary and representation — 282
- A.4 Declarations and scope rules — 284
- A.5 Constant declarations — 285
- A.6 Type declarations — 285
- A.7 Variable declarations — 289
- A.8 Expressions — 290
- A.9 Statements — 294
- A.10 Procedure declarations — 299
- A.11 Modules — 303
- A.12 The Module SYSTEM — 304

Appendix B ASCII Character set and extremal values — 306

Appendix C Modules *In*, *Out* and *XYplane* — 308

Index — 315

1 Why Oberon?

This is a book about programming, and in particular about programming in the language *Oberon*. Why should the reader be interested in learning to program in Oberon instead of one of the widely known languages? The answer is because it is a language that is defined in terms of relatively few, fundamental programming concepts, because it is rigorously structured, and because it is efficiently implemented on modern computers. These are essentially the same reasons that 20 years ago spoke for the language *Pascal*. These properties encourage a systematic approach to the design of programs, and are the prerequisites for using the essential technique of modular design based on abstractions. Oberon is a 'small' language, which makes it particularly suited as notation for an introduction to programming. Yet its concepts are general and powerful, making it equally appropriate for the construction of large software systems. These claims have been substantiated by the use of Oberon both in teaching and in the design of the Oberon system itself.

1.1 The Algol family

Oberon is both new and old. It is new, because it is not merely an extension of another language. And it is old in the sense that most of its concepts have been taken over from existing languages. Oberon is the latest descendant in the family of languages whose root is Algol 60 (1960), and whose other members are Pascal (1970), Modula-2 (1979) and Oberon (1988). It is therefore appropriate to comment on these members and thereby to explain the family's evolution and the 'philosophy' behind it.

Algol 60   Algol 60 was designed by a a committee of 13 experts from many countries (Naur, 1963). The goal was to establish a common notation for the formulation of algorithms (programs), for the purpose of having them not only interpreted by computers, but also studied and understood by programmers. A necessary condition for approaching this latter goal was that the language be rigorously defined without reference to any specific computer or abstract mechanism. The goal was splendidly reached with regard to syntax. Algol 60 was the first language where it was easily decidable whether or not a sequence of symbols formed a (syntactically) correct program. The influence of this rigor had a tremendous impact on defining, explaining and implementing languages. With regard to defining the semantics of various language constructs, the goal of a mechanism-independent static definition still remains elusive. Nevertheless, much progress has been made – all based on the prerequisite that a language's syntax be clearly structured.

However, Algol 60 was a mixture of elegant, fundamental constructs and of strangely baroque features. Not surprisingly, the latter turned out to be largely unsuccessful and quite superfluous. We mention the overly general for statement, the own variables, and the name parameters. At the same time, facilities that emerged as indispensable for certain applications, such as record and pointer variables were entirely missing. Algol 60 had been designed by mathematicians for the formulation of their numerical algorithms, and its designers had little background in other areas.

Pascal – structured programming

Many descendants of Algol 60 were proposed and even implemented. The most successful was Pascal (Wirth, 1971; Hoare and Wirth, 1973), which is still in wide use at the present time. It followed the Algol tradition of being a structured language well suited for practicing *structured programming*. Algol's oddities had been left out, and a few facilities for widening its range of applications had been added. The single most important innovation was to apply the same approach to the definition of data as was introduced by Algol for executable statements: *recursive structuring*.

Algol 60 featured the basic data types of integers, real numbers, and Boolean truth values, and it allowed the programmer to define arrays of variables of these types. Pascal provides, in addition to further basic types, the array, record, set and file structures. User-defined structures can be given names and can be used as types of components of other structures. Hence it is possible to define nested structures, such as arrays of records and records with arrays as components. Records, in particular, extended the range of applications beyond that of numerical computation.

Of special importance was the introduction of pointers and dynamic allocation. This facility opened the door to all sorts of applications requiring dynamic data structures; that is, structures that grow and shrink during the computation. In contrast to address manipulation as it is used in assembler coding, pointer manipulation provides much greater safety against mistakes, because every pointer variable is, by virtue of its declaration, bound to point to an object of a given type. Therefore a compiler is capable of guarding against violations, and the error can be detected while the program is still being developed and in its designer's hands. To extend the notion of static type checking to dynamic variables was indeed a significant achievement.

But Pascal too suffered from deficiencies. They are perhaps not significant in the context of exercises in an introductory course, but certainly are relevant in the realm of programming larger systems. Whereas Pascal encouraged structured design, in the meantime *modular design* had become important in software engineering. This notion has at least two aspects. The first became known as *information hiding*. Any large system is composed of modules that are to be designed in relative isolation. This implies that definitions of interfaces exist that specify all properties accessible to partner modules and that hide all others. The second aspect is of a technical nature: separate compilation of modules. It implies that in every module all modules to which references occur (so-called imports) be explicitly specified and that a compilation proceed under the availability of the interface definitions of those imports.

Modula-2 – modular programming

The principal innovation of the language Modula-2 (Wirth, 1982) with respect to Pascal was indeed the module concept, incorporating information hiding and separate compilation. In contrast to independent compilation known from assemblers and other language's compilers, separate compilation enables a compiler to perform the same type-consistency checks across module boundaries as within a module. The explicit definition of interfaces and the retention of full type safety turned out to be a tremendous benefit.

Modules exporting one or several data types, typically record or pointer to record types, together with a set of procedures operating on variables of these types, represented the notion of *abstract data type*. In these cases, only the names of the types appear in the module's interface, whereas the structure of the records remains hidden in the module's implementation. This guarantees that access to the record's fields is possible via exported procedures only, which can therefore rely on the validity of certain invariants governing the abstract types.

Furthermore, Modula-2 removed one of the most aggravating handicaps introduced by strong typing: it introduced dynamic arrays as parameters of procedures. Also noteworthy were the introduction of procedure types for variables, and facilities for concurrent processes and for low-level programming. The latter allow a programmer to refer directly to specific machine facilities, such as interface registers for controlling input/output operations. Once again, these features contributed to the widening of the language's range of applications, particularly into the areas of system design and process control. And last but not least, certain unfortunate syntactic properties of Pascal were remedied, notably the open-ended if, while and for statements. These were precisely the structures that were adopted from Algol 60 and left unchanged in order to maintain tradition and to avoid alienating the Algol community – a mistake in hindsight.

Several years of experience of practicing modular design with Modula-2 and other system programming languages revealed that the ultimate goal was *extensible design* and that structured programming and modular programming were merely intermediate steps towards that goal. The introduction of abstractions represented by modules and the use of procedures calling procedures declared at lower levels of the abstraction hierarchy embodies extensibility in the procedural domain. Equally important for a successful design, however, is extensibility in the domain of data definition. In this respect, Modula-2 is inadequate, because types cannot be extended and at the same time remain compatible.

In this respect, so-called *object-oriented languages* provided a viable solution, and became the wave of the 1980s. They offer a facility to define subtypes $T1$, called subclasses, of a given type (class) $T0$ with the property that all operations applicable to instances of $T0$ are also applicable to instances of $T1$. We recognize at this point that the ultimate innovation was data type extensibility, which unfortunately remained obscured behind the much less expressive term 'object-oriented.' Rather unfortunately, this term was accompanied by a whole new nomenclature for many already familiar concepts with the aim of perpetrating a new view or metaphor of programming at large. Thus types became classes, variables instances, procedures methods and procedure activations messages.

Oberon – extensible programming

The primary merit of the language Oberon (Wirth, 1988a, b), defined in 1986, lies in the provision of data type extensibility on the basis of the established, well-understood notions of data type and procedure. The consequence is that no break with traditional programming technique is necessary and no familiarization with a whole new class of concepts and notions is required. The only new facility is that for extending a record type. Oberon thereby unifies the traditional concepts of procedural programming with the techniques required to obtain data extensibility.

This single new facility might well have been added to Modula-2. Why was yet another new language to be created? The reason was the desire to have a language available that upholds the principle of programming at a truly machine-independent level, in contrast to creating programs that appeared to be machine-independent, yet where too many interspersed uses of system-dependent low-level facilities in fact rendered programs highly implementation-dependent. Indeed, Modula-2's low-level facilities had become far too frequently misused in order to overcome the lack of extensible types. Modula-2 also had become rather too large: it contains features that can be ignored without loss of generality and expressive power. Oberon thus became not only a modest extension, but also a strongly streamlined descendant of Modula-2. The result is manifest in the form of its defining report of only 16 pages. This figure compares well with the Modula report's 45 pages.

Simplification and *unification* mark genuine progress and are particularly appreciated in teaching the fundamentals of a scientific subject. Oberon's design truly follows the spirit of Algol 60.

1.2 The Oberon system

The development of the language Oberon was only a part of a more comprehensive project. In 1985, while visiting the Xerox Palo Alto Research Center, J. Gutknecht and N. Wirth decided to design and implement a new operating system (Wirth and Gutknecht, 1989, 1992). In order not to be hindered by imposed constraints, they decided to design the Oberon system from scratch. The ultimate goal was to create a system for personal workstations that was not only powerful and convenient for practical use, but also *describable and explicable in a convincing way*. Since there exists relatively little published literature explaining how a system *was* designed – in contrast to how it *could be* designed – this was felt to be not only a formidable challenge but also a worthwhile endeavor.

A driving force behind the project was a deep dissatisfaction with widespread practices in software development. It appears that systems are – with few exceptions – unnecessarily bulky and their design contorted. One reason for this is the lack of extensibility of existing software, invariably leading to innumerable additions that usually include and duplicate functions that are already there but deeply embedded in some part of the existing system. These parts, however, can seldom be re-used – either because they need to be slightly modified or simply because they are inaccessible in their original place due to fixed linking and packaging strategies. It is now quite common that operating systems on workstations require several megabytes of memory and hundreds of megabytes of secondary store in order to be functional. Even though there is no intrinsic necessity for such bulkiness, the situation is unfortunately tolerated by users, because the tremendous advances of semiconductor technology have made large memories affordable at reasonably modest expense – modest at least by the standards of a decade ago.

The much deeper problem, however, is not the need for large stores, but the unreliability and unadaptability (called unmaintainability) of large software systems. Certainly, the size of a program alone is only a crude measure for the number of mistakes it contains. But it is an established fact that the number of errors grows rapidly with a system's increasing size. It should be recognized that the single most important contribution towards a design's reliability is the *elimination of superfluous features and facilities, and the containment of its complexity*. One is left with the nagging impression that many systems have grown into gigantic monsters not because their complexity is inherent in the desired functionality, but rather because of inadequate design and because of chosen structures that later could not be corrected. And even more disconcerting is the circumstance that many customers are impressed by complex designs more than by economical engineering. After all, impenetrable software may still hide some promises and surprises. We call this psychological phenomenon – which is surprisingly common in the world of computing – 'gigalomania.'

It is of course much easier to design a *large* system than an *economical* one. The latter requires experience, much careful planning and minute attention to details – in short, more time from its designers. Project Oberon has driven this knowledge home with indubitable clarity. The object-code size of the so-called *outer core* of the Oberon system is less than 200 kBytes, and comprises

- a kernel;
- a dynamic loader and a garbage collector;
- a file system;
- drivers for disk, diskette, mouse, keyboard, asynchronous and synchronous communication, printer and a bitmapped display;
- local area network services;
- support for texts and fonts;
- a window subsystem;
- a text editor;
- the Oberon compiler.

Even allowing for the fact that the National Semiconductor 32000 series processor produces denser code than many other popular microprocessors, Oberon is easily an order of magnitude smaller than system of comparable (or even lesser) functionality.

The Oberon system is a hierarchy of modules, most of which export one or a few abstract data types. Each user is encouraged to extend the system – extensions are created by simply adding new modules. There is no boundary between 'the system' and 'the application program.' Figure 1.1 shows the modules that comprise the so-called outer core of Oberon. Except for modules *Kernel* and *Display*, the entire Oberon system is expressed in the programming language Oberon (for a system reference see Reiser, 1991).

Much emphasis is nowadays placed on the use of sophisticated *tools*. We warn the reader against putting too much hope and trust in the potential of tools. None can produce miracles, and none has ever replaced careful and competent designers. But good tools certainly increase the designer's productivity. In fact, the better the designer, the higher is the gain of using appropriate tools.

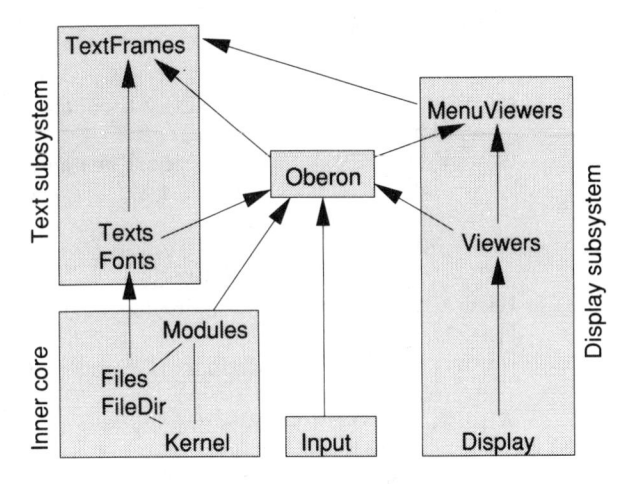

Figure 1.1 Module hierarchy of the outer core of the Oberon system. Arrows depict import relations; for example, module *Oberon* imports module *Input*. Note that only the major import relations are shown, and several driver and command modules are omitted for clarity.

Among all possible tools, we find that the programming language plays by far the most important role. In Project Oberon, it was initially planned to use Modula-2 because of its support of structured and modular program construction. But it was soon realized that the same principle of economy in design that was declared fundamental for the system should also be applied to the language. The design of the Oberon language evolved in parallel with a large software project. Modula-2 was stripped of features that did not genuinely contribute to its power of expression. The principal concept that was added – type extension – was, on the other hand, the sorely needed missing part in the otherwise most important asset of Modula-2: in its strict, static typing of variables and functions. Thus Oberon is not another design conducted in the abstract with the attitude 'let's invent another nice feature.' It is purposefully tuned to be an efficient, convenient and safe instrument to express programs in the large.

The result, the language Oberon, is presented in this book. A detailed account of Project Oberon is found in Wirth and Gutknecht (1992). Not surprisingly, an economically designed language is particularly suitable as a basis for teaching the subject of programming. After all, programming is inherently difficult, and hence a student must be protected from having to carry the additional burden of a complex language.

References

Hoare C.A.R. and Wirth N. (1973). An axiomatic definition of the programming language Pascal. *Acta Informatica*, **2**, 335–55.

Naur P., ed. (1963). Revised report on the algorithmic language Algol 60. *Communications of the ACM*, **6**, 1–7; *Computer Journal*, **5**, 349–67; *Numerical Mathematics*, **4**, 420–53.

Reiser, M. (1991). *The Oberon System: User Guide and Programmer's Manual*. Wokingham: Addison-Wesley.

Wirth N. (1971). The programming language Pascal. *Acta Infomatica*, **1**, 35–63.

Wirth N. (1982). *Programming in Modula-2*. Berlin: Springer-Verlag.

Wirth N. (1988a). From Modula to Oberon. *Software–Practice and Experience*, **18**, 662–70.

Wirth N. (1988b). The programming language Oberon. *Software–Practice and Experience*, **18**, 671–90.

Wirth N. and Gutknecht J. (1989). The Oberon system. *Software–Practice and Experience*, **19**, 857–93.

Wirth N. and Gutknecht J. (1992). *Project Oberon: The Design of an Operating System and Compiler*. Wokingham: Addison-Wesley.

2 A first Oberon program

In this chapter we will follow the steps of writing a simple program, technically speaking a *module*, and thereby explain some of the fundamental concepts of programming and of the facilities of Oberon. The task is to provide a *random number generator* – a program that 'throws dice' and produces successive unpredictable numbers. Such random number generators are an important utility in a computer. We will frequently use it ourselves in subsequent examples.

The concepts of randomness and algorithm – a recipe for computation – are of course irreconcilable. All one could hope for is an algorithm capable of producing a very long sequence of numbers in such a way that no pattern becomes discernible.

The non-specialist might expect that the more ingeniously random such a program would be, the better its results. Knuth (1971) gives an example of such a 'super random numbers generator' that produced periodic sequences of very short length (a few thousands). Says Knuth: 'The moral to this story is that *random numbers should not be generated with a method chosen at random*. Some theory should be used.' A method proposed by D. H. Lehmer some 40 years ago – the multiplicative linear congruential algorithm – withstood the test of time (see Box 2.1).

The basic recipe – the so-called *algorithm* – is contained in Equations (1) – (2) of Box 2.1. We have to put this prescription into terms of Oberon. A first attempt leads to

   z := (a*z) MOD m;
   "Return the real value z/m as result"

This piece of text is yet far from being a program. However, an attempt to make one on its premise would be doomed. It is not difficult to see that the product *a*z* may easily exceed the range of integers that can be represented with 32 bits. There is a clever trick due to Schrage that

Box 2.1
Linear congruential random number generator

> The mathematical foundation is a beautiful example of the elegance of simplicity. All that is needed is a judicious choice of two integer parameters – the modulus m and the multiplier a – in the simple recurrence formula
>
> $$z_{n+1} = az_n \bmod m \qquad (1)$$
>
> The sequence must be started with an initial value z_1 called the *seed*. It turns out that the choice of m and a is critical. With $m = 2^{31} - 1 = 2\,147\,483\,647$ and $a = 7^5 = 16\,807$, all numbers between 1 and m appear exactly once in the sequence defined by Equation (1) – there will be over 2 billion random numbers that passed stringent statistical tests. For a discussion of random number generators, see the survey paper by Park and Miller (1988).
>
> In practice, one seldom needs random integers as large as 2 147 483 647. We therefore normalize:
>
> $$r = z_n/m \qquad (2)$$
>
> The real random numbers r_n are now from the interval $0 < r_n \leq 1$.

circumvents this difficulty. Select new constants $q = \lfloor m/a \rfloor = 127\,773$[1] and $r = m \bmod a = 2\,836$ and compute

```
gamma := a*(z MOD q) – r*(z DIV q);
IF gamma > 0 THEN
    z := gamma
ELSE
    z := gamma + m
END;
```
"Return the real value z/m as result"

The meaning of these Oberon statements should be quite obvious. Less obvious is that the modified computation is the same as (1). For our example, the mathematical detail is not essential. We refer the interested reader to Park and Miller (1988).

Declaration

The quantities z and *gamma* are variables; m, a, q and r are constants. Many programming languages require that the variables and constants

---

[1] $\lfloor x \rfloor$ denotes the largest integer not greater than x.

be explicitly defined and their type (such as integer or real) specified. Also, we need to express formally the fact that our program is a function that returns real values.

Procedure Groups of statements that have a name and may be invoked from other locations in a program are called *procedures*. Constant, variable and procedure declarations read as follows:

```
PROCEDURE Uniform(): REAL;
CONST  a = 16807;  m = 2147483647;  q = m DIV a;  r = m MOD a;
VAR gamma: LONGINT;
BEGIN
   gamma := a*(z MOD q) – r*(z DIV q);
   IF  gamma > 0  THEN
      z := gamma
   ELSE
      z := gamma + m
   END;
   RETURN  z*(1.0/m)
END Uniform;
```

The first line expresses the fact that the procedure *Uniform*[1] is a function procedure (without arguments) which returns a real value when invoked. The procedure statement is followed by the *declarations* of the constants and the variable *gamma*. Note that q and r are declared in the form of constant expressions that can be evaluated without the need to actually run the program. The operator DIV denotes the integer division and MOD the modulus. Constants and variables thus declared are local to the procedure. Therefore the variable z, which needs to retain its value from execution to execution, must be declared in a larger context.

Module This larger context is the *module*. A module is a text unit that is accepted by the Oberon compiler and translated into machine executable code. But a module is more than that. It provides mechanisms for:

(1) structuring of a program into independent units;
(2) the declaration of variables that keep their value for the duration the module is active (that is, in memory) – these variables are called *global* to the module;
(3) *export of variables* and procedures to be used in other modules.

---

[1] The name *Uniform* suggests that the random numbers all have the same probability – they are uniformly distributed.

The module therefore provides the facilities for abstractions – *abstract data types* – which we will explore in detail in Chapter 10 and Part III. A module, *RandomNumbers*, encapsulating our procedure *Uniform* reads

```
MODULE RandomNumbers;
VAR z: LONGINT; (* global variable *)

PROCEDURE Uniform*(): REAL;
CONST a = 16807; m = 2147483647; q = m DIV a; r = m MOD a;
VAR gamma: LONGINT;
BEGIN
   gamma := a*(z MOD q) – r*(z DIV q);
   IF gamma > 0 THEN
      z := gamma
   ELSE
      z := gamma + m
   END;
   RETURN z*(1.0/m) (* value of the function *)
END Uniform;

PROCEDURE InitSeed*(seed: LONGINT);
BEGIN
   z := seed
END InitSeed;

BEGIN
   z := 314159 (* initial value of seed *)
END RandomNumbers.
```

Export The *asterisk following the procedure name marks that procedure for export*. In other words, it may be used in other modules that *import* module *RandomNumbers*. Similarly, a module may export variables.

Body The statements between BEGIN and END at the trailing of the program text are called the module's *body*. They are executed when the module is loaded into the computer's primary memory. In our example, the body consists of a single statement that is initializing the global variable z. Initialization of variables is a typical task for the statements comprising a module's body.

A random number generator is a utility to be used in other programs. Module *RandomNumbers*, independently compiled and available in object form in the system's program library, makes the utility available to procedures contained in other modules. These modules are *clients* of module *RandomNumbers*. Let us illustrate the concept with a further example. Module *ListRN* prints a table of 100 random numbers. We realize that we need to specify an action that makes results visible. For this purpose, we should actually know the computer's facilities to communicate with its user. Since we do not wish to refer to a specific system running Oberon programs, we introduce *abstractions* that we postulate to be available. We stress, however, that they are not part of the language.

```
MODULE ListRN;
IMPORT Out, RandomNumbers;

PROCEDURE List* ;
VAR i, max: INTEGER;  rn: REAL;
BEGIN
    max := 100;  i := 0;
    WHILE i < max DO
        rn := RandomNumbers.Uniform();
        Out.Real(rn, 14);    (* print random number *)
        Out.Ln;              (* skip line *)
        i := i + 1
    END
END List;

END ListRN.
```

Import, qualified name

The procedure *Out.Real(x, n)* writes a real variable *x* to a suitable output medium, for example a display window (*n* measures the total number of characters). Similarly, *Out.Ln* appends a line break. The *import statement* specifies which modules should become accessible within the scope of *ListRN*, namely module *Out* and module *RandomNumbers*.

Procedures and variables from those imported modules appear with *qualified identifiers*. For example *Out.Real (x)* means call the procedure *Real (x)* from module *Out*. Similarly, *RandomNumbers.Uniform()* invokes the function *Uniform()* exported by module *RandomNumbers*.

Client module

We say that module *ListRN* is a *client* of modules *Out* and *RandomNumbers*. Thus the module is also a *package of data and functions to be reused by other modules*. To *ListRN*, both module *Out* and module *RandomNumbers* are utilities. They can be used without recompilation or access to the source texts.

We trust that even though the Oberon statements used so far were not defined rigorously, the reader – even if he or she has little prior exposure to programming – could easily grasp their meaning. One thing, however, remains mysterious: *where is the main program*? Module *ListRN* has no body and comprises a procedure declaration only. How then can *ListRN* be run?

Command The answer is that Oberon departs from the notion of a main program that can be run and procedures that are constituents of such a main program. An exported Oberon procedure is called a *command*.[1]

The system that runs Oberon must provide facilities to start commands. Procedure *List* in module *ListRN* is such a command that can be executed from the computer's controls and as a result, lists 100 random numbers.

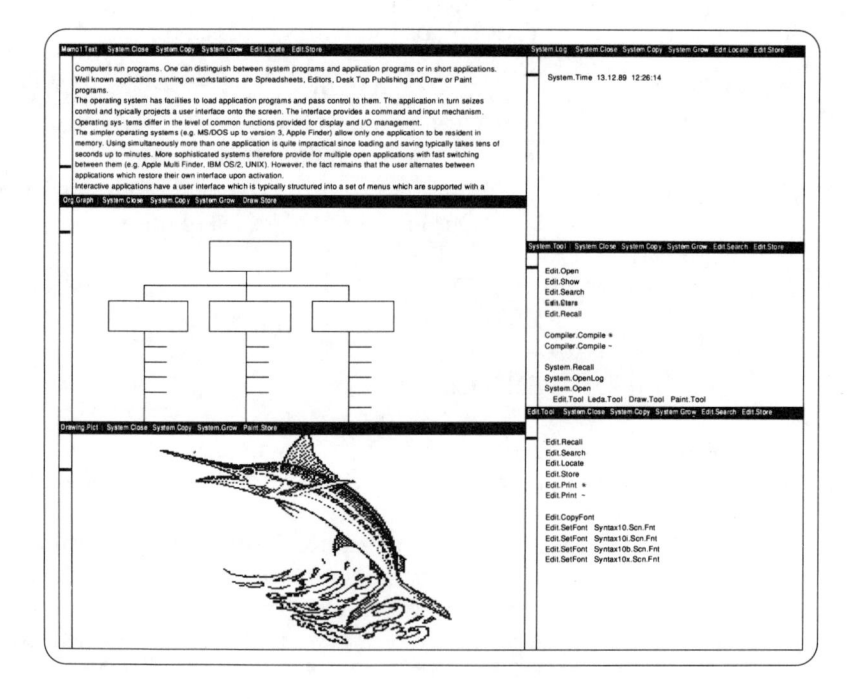

Figure 2.1 Display screen of an Oberon system.

Oberon system Let us provide an example of a system running commands written in the Oberon programming language: the Oberon operating system

---

[1] To be precise, a procedure without formal parameters.

(Reiser, 1991). The display of a workstation running Oberon is portrayed in Figure 2.1.

The screen is exhaustively tiled into non-overlapping rectangles called *viewers*, which display documents such as texts, graphics and pictures. If the name of a command appears anywhere in a text viewer, it can be activated by pointing at it with the mouse cursor and clicking the (middle) mouse key.

Figure 2.2 shows a close-up view of two text viewers with titles *System.Log* and *ListRN.Tool*. *System.Log* is the name of a special viewer where commands display progress or error messages. The procedure *Out.Real* exported by module *Out* is assumed to write into that viewer. The viewer *ListRN.Tool* shows the command name *ListRN.List*. It was typed into this viewer using a text editor. The command can be executed by pointing at it with the mouse cursor. Thus the viewer *ListRN.Tool* operates like the menus of a conventional system. In our example, the command was executed and 100 random numbers are written into the viewer with name *System.Log*.

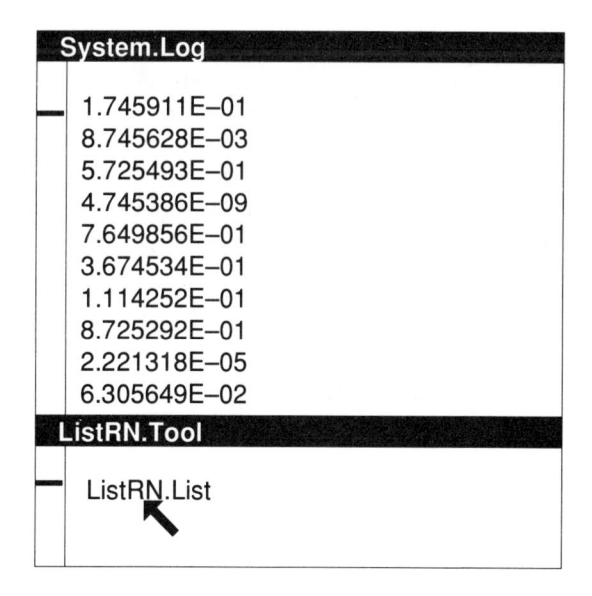

```
System.Log
  1.745911E-01
  8.745628E-03
  5.725493E-01
  4.745386E-09
  7.649856E-01
  3.674534E-01
  1.114252E-01
  8.725292E-01
  2.221318E-05
  6.305649E-02
ListRN.Tool
  ListRN.List
```

Figure 2.2 Output produced by the command *ListRN.List*.

A few more comments to our example are in order. The command *List* produces an editable text as output that is displayed in the viewer *System.Log*. From the 100 items, we see only 10. The others are accessible by scrolling, which is done in the usual manner using the scroll bar located at left.

This concludes the discussion of our example. We remind the reader that the short excursion into the Oberon operating system was meant to illustrate one of many environments that could support commands written in the Oberon language.

Summary

In summary, we have learned

- Oberon 'programs' are texts composed of procedural statements that specify an algorithm.
- The *procedure is the executable unit*. The texts that specify procedures are contained in modules, which are accepted by the compiler for translation.
- All variables used in procedures are defined in *declaration* statements. Variables may be local to a procedure or global to a module.
- Besides data declarations and procedure texts, *modules have a list of statements* that is executed when the module is loaded into the computer's memory.
- The module selectively *exports* procedures and variables. It serves as a utility for other modules that import that module. Hiding the implementation details of data structures in a module and providing access through procedures only is an important tool to structure large systems.[1]
- The notion of a main program, a mainstay of traditional languages, is absent in Oberon. Oberon 'programs' are *families of commands*. The system running Oberon code provides facilities to execute commands, which are procedures exported by modules.

Lastly, the example of random number generation has taught important lessons about program design. Let us conclude with another quote from Knuth: '...look at the subroutine library of each computer installation in your organization, and replace the random number generators by good ones. Try to avoid being too shocked at what you find.' Our advice to readers is to use another generator only if you have positive evidence that it is better than the standard generator discussed in this section. Many in current use are worse!

---

[1] Called abstract data structure or abstract data type – see Chapter 10 and Part III.

2.1 A notation to describe the syntax of Oberon

The discussion of the last section was kept quite informal. This was permissible for an introductory example. However, programming is creating new programs. For this purpose, only a precise formal description is adequate.

Formal language A *formal language* is a set of sequences of *symbols*. Elements of this set are called *sentences*. The term 'sentence' is more reminiscent of the applications of formal languages in linguistics. In the case of a programming language, these sentences are *programs* – in Oberon technically termed *modules*.

The symbols originate from a finite set called the *vocabulary*. The set of programs (which is infinite) is defined by rules of their composition. Sequences of symbols that are composed by these rules are said to be syntactically correct or well formed. The set of rules is the *syntax* of the language. The program (or sentence of the formal language) consists of parts called *syntactic entities*, such as declarations, statements or expressions.

Syntactic factors If a construct *A* consists of *B* followed by *C* – that is, the concatenation *BC* – then we call *B* and *C* syntactic *factors* and describe *A* by the syntactic formula

$A = BC.$

Syntactic terms If, on the other hand, *A* is composed of a factor *B* or, alternatively a *C* we call *B* and *C* syntactic *terms* and express *A* by

$A = B \mid C.$

In addition to concatenation and choice, it is convenient to have a notation for *option* and *repetition*. If a construct *A* may be either *B* or nothing, this is expressed as

$A = [B].$

If *A* consists of the concatenation of any number of *B*s, including none, this is denoted by

$A = \{B\}.$

Parentheses may be used to group factors or terms. One should note that A, B and C denote syntactic entities whereas |, =, [,] { , }, (,) and the period are symbols of the meta-notation describing our syntax. Obviously, they are termed *meta-symbols,* and the notation introduced here is known as *Extended Backus-Naur Formalism (EBNF).*

A few examples show how sets of sentences are defined by EBNF formulas:

(A | B)(C | D)	AC AD BC BD
A[B]C	ABC AC
A{BA}	A ABA ABABA ABABABA ...
{A	B}C	C AC BC AAC ABC BAC BBC ...

Besides syntactic entities denoted by identifiers, we have a need to substitute elements – also called *tokens* – taken from the formal language's vocabulary. We will adopt the widely used conventions for programming languages, namely: *an identifier consists of a sequence of letters and digits, where the first character must be a letter; a string consists of any sequence of characters enclosed by quote marks.*

2.2 Exercises

2.1 Provide an EBNF definition of identifiers and strings as defined above.

2.2 The production A = T {"+" T} defines the sentences T, T+T, T+T+T and so on. The braces are only a convenient abbreviation. List two production rules, not involving braces or brackets, that define the same language.

2.3 Consider the EBNF syntax

E = ["+" | "–"] T {ao T}.
ao = "+" | "–".
T = F {mo F}.
mo = "*" | "/".
F = nu | id | "(" E ")".
nu = digit {digit}.
id = letter {letter | digit}.

The entities *letter* and *digit* have their usual meaning. Construct sentences E of this language. What are these sentences? Reformulate the grammar using more suggestive names for the nonterminal symbols.

2.4 Clearly EBNF is itself a formal language. If it suits its purpose, it should at least be able to describe itself. Construct such a description. Use the following names for entities:

syntax:	a sequence of statements
statement:	a syntactic equation
expression:	a list of alternative terms
term:	a concatenation of factors
factor:	an identifier, a string or a parenthesized expression

The terminal symbols are identifiers, strings and the following symbols: | = [ ] . { } ( ).

References

Knuth D. E. (1971). *The Art of Computer Programming*, 2nd edn. Reading, MA: Addison-Wesley.

Park S. K. and Miller K. W. (1988). Random number generators, good ones are hard to find. *Communications of the ACM*, **31**, 1192–1201.

Reiser M. (1991). *The Oberon System: User Guide and Programmer's Manual*. Wokingham: Addison-Wesley.

Part I

Tokens
Basic types
Assignment
Control structures
Procedures
Modules

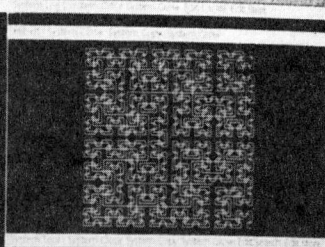

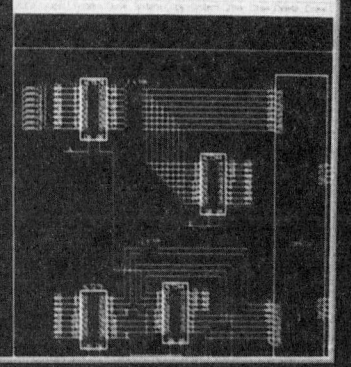

Synopsis

Part I introduces the fundamental concepts of programming: the basic types, the assignment statement, control structures and procedures and modules.

An extended Backus–Naur formalism is used to describe the *syntax*. The *semantics* of the control structures, namely the if statement, the case statement, and the loop expressed by while, repeat and loop statements are defined formally by means of predicates and their transformations.

Input and output operations are introduced as service modules, based on the notion of the *stream*. The part ends with a complete module, drawing a fractal fern.

3 Tokens and basic types

The formal definition of a programming language must eventually be given in terms of the characters available from the computer's keyboard. The creation of an intermediate level of representation by symbol sequences, called *tokens*, provides a useful decoupling between the language and its ultimate representation. Examples of tokens are

- 1024, 3.1415   Numbers
- gamma, a, pi   Identifiers
- +, –, *   Operators
- BEGIN, END, IF   Keywords.

The introductory example taught us that Oberon programs – more precisely Oberon modules and procedures – contain variables (designated by identifiers) that are bound to a *type* by means of a declaration. This data type represents information about the variable that is permanent, in contrast, for example, to its value. The *type* of a variable determines its set of possible values together with the operations that may be applied to it. Data types may be declared in the program (see Section 8.1). Such constructed types are usually based on composition of basic types. There exists a number of most frequently used *elementary types* that are basic to the language and need not be declared. In Oberon, these types are SHORTINT, INTEGER, LONGINT, REAL, LONGREAL, BOOLEAN, SET and CHAR. Since Oberon programs will execute on computers, the basic types have a close association with facilities of contemporary hardware.

3.1 The vocabulary of Oberon

The tokens of the Oberon vocabulary are divided into the following classes:

(1) identifiers
(2) numbers

(3) character constants
(4) strings
(5) operators and delimiters.

The rules governing their representation in the standard character set are as follows.

3.1.1 Identifiers

> ident = letter {letter | digit}.
> letter = "A" | "B" |...| "Z" | "a" | "b" |...| "z".
> digit = "0" | "1" | "2" |...| "9".

Upper and lower case letters are considered distinct. Examples of well-formed identifiers are:

> List list a12 nextItem Viewers SR101

Examples of words that are not identifiers

> List element   blank space not allowed
> List-element   neither is a hyphen
> List_element   nor an underscore
> 2N   first character must be a letter

3.1.2 Numbers

> number = integer | real.
> integer = digit {digit} | digit {hexDigit} "H".
> hexDigit = digit | "A" | "B" | "C" | "D" | "E" | "F".
> real = digit {digit} "." {digit} [ScaleFactor].
> ScaleFactor = ("E" | "D") ["+" | "–"] digit {digit}.

Numbers are unsigned integers or unsigned real numbers. Decimal integers are sequences of digits. Hexadecimal integers must start with a digit followed by a sequence of hexadecimal digits and trailed by the suffix "H". Real numbers always contain a decimal point and a fractional part. A scale factor may optionally be appended. It starts with a "E" or a "D" which reads 'times ten to the power of.' The prefix "E" or "D" in the scale factor determines the *type* of the real number, either REAL or LONGREAL.

Examples of well-formed numbers are

1024		an integer in decimal notation
1AFH		an integer in hexadecimal notation (=431)
3.1416	2.99792458D8	real numbers

The following character strings are not recognized as well-formed Oberon numbers:

FFFFH   3,14159   .665;   1.35–43

3.1.3 Character constants

CharConstant = """" character """" | digit {hexDigit} "X".
character = digit | letter | " " | specialChar.

Special characters are all the printable characters on the computer's keyboard that are not digits, letters or a blank. The following special characters are common to the ASCII character set: ! " # $ % & ' ( ) * + , - . / : ; < = > ? @ [\ ] ^ _ ` { | } ~.

A character constant may, instead of enclosing the character in quote marks, be specified by its ordinal number[1] in hexadecimal notation, followed by the letter X.

Examples of character constants are "a", "b", "1", "@" and 61X. Both "a" and 61X denote the same character, namely 'lower case A' (if the ASCII code is assumed).

3.1.4 Strings

string = """" {character} """".

A string is a sequence of printable characters, including blanks and special characters, enclosed in quote marks. In order that the closing quote mark be recognized unambiguously, the string cannot contain such a quote mark. Example: "This is a string".

3.1.5 Operators and delimiters

Delimiters and operators are either special characters (or pairs thereof) or reserved words written in capital letters. They serve as terminal

---

[1] A character's ordinal number is defined by the encoding scheme. In most contemporary personal computers and workstations, this is the standard ASCII code.

symbols in the Oberon syntax – their meaning will be explained throughout subsequent chapters. A complete list is found in Appendix A, Section A.3, page 283.

Examples include:

- + − * / < <= > >=   Operators
- ( ) [ ] : ; :=   Delimiters
- BEGIN END PROCEDURE MODULE   Reserved words

The term *reserved word* means that these letter sequences must not be used as identifiers.

3.1.6 Predeclared identifiers

Besides the set of reserved words, which act as separators and are part of the vocabulary of the Oberon definition, there is a list of predefined or standard identifiers. Syntactically, they appear at places where user-defined identifiers may also apply.

Predeclared identifiers are used as:

- *truth values*: TRUE, FALSE;
- *type identifiers*, for example INTEGER, REAL, SET, CHAR;
- *standard functions and procedures*, for example ABS, LEN, INC.

The predeclared identifiers can be visualized as if declared in a context that encompasses the module being created by the programmer. Therefore they are also called *pervasive* since they are valid in all parts of the module's text. A completed list is found in Appendix A, Section A4, page 284.

3.1.7 Rules for blanks and carriage returns

Oberon programs are sequences of the tokens defined above. The syntactic rules governing these sequences will be the object of the following chapters. There is one further rule, which will not be expressed formally: *blanks, tab and carriage return characters may be added or removed from the program text, except where a token's identity would be lost.* An example will make the point:

　　　　IF x = y THEN...

The space before *x* and after *y* is essential. If omitted, *IFx* and *yTHEN* will be parsed as identifiers. On the other hand, the spaces enclosing the equal sign "=" are optional.

Blanks and tabs should be used liberally to make program texts more readable. For example, the spaces enclosing the equal sign above improve the appearance of a program text. Similarly, in the introductory example, *indentation* was used to enhance the structure of programs.

Comments At any point in the program's text, *comments* may be interspersed. A comment is any sequence of characters enclosed in the brackets "(*" and "*)". Comments may also contain *instructions for the compiler*.

3.2 Basic types

There are eight basic types in Oberon. They are identified by the predeclared identifiers SHORTINT, INTEGER, LONGINT, REAL, LONGREAL, BOOLEAN, SET and CHAR (see also Appendix A, Section A.6.1).

For the basic types, the set of admissible values is bounded by extremal values, which may be accessed in Oberon programs through the (predeclared) functions

MIN(T):	The minimum value of type T
MAX(T):	The maximum value of type T

For example, if SHORTINT is represented by 8 bits, then MAX(SHORTINT) = 127 and MIN(SHORTINT) = –128. Typical extremal values are listed in Appendix B. For obvious reasons the first five types are called the *numeric types*. They form a set hierarchy (see Section 3.2.3).

3.2.1 The types SHORTINT, INTEGER and LONGINT

The three types comprise the *integer types*. They represent the integer numbers and differ by the cardinality of the set of numbers represented by each type. The need for different types arises from the architectures of machines, which – for reasons of efficiency – provide various word formats with corresponding machine instructions. It is the responsibility of the programmer to insure that the result of a computation again lies within the set of numbers represented by each type. Otherwise, an *overflow* is said to have occurred, leading in general to a termination of the program that caused the overflow.[1]

3.2.2 The types REAL and LONGREAL

The real types approximate the real numbers. Each element from the set of REAL or LONGREAL is representative of an interval of genuine real numbers. Variables of a real type are represented by pairs of integers, a *mantissa* and an *exponent*. This is called *floating-point* representation. The two types are distinguished by the number of digits of the mantissa (the fractional part) and the exponent. As with the integer types, *overflow* may occur and result in termination of the program.

Floating-point numbers are only an approximation to the real numbers of mathematics. As a consequence, computations involving floating-point values are inexact because each operation may be subject to truncation. The resulting problems have been investigated in detail, and are treated in every text on numerical mathematics.

3.2.3 Hierarchy of the numeric types

The *numeric types* are comprised of the integer and real types and form a set hierarchy.

$$\text{LONGREAL} \supseteq \text{REAL} \supseteq \text{LONGINT} \supseteq \text{INTEGER} \supseteq \text{SHORTINT}$$

The range of the larger type includes the ranges of the smaller types. For example, REAL *includes* LONGINT...SHORTINT. The smaller type is said to be *compatible* with the larger one in the sense that it can, without danger of loss of leading digits, be converted. In most cases, such a conversion is also exact.[2] In assignments and in expressions, the conversion of internal representations is automatic.

---

[1] Some implementations allow trapping of overflow to be switched on and off.
[2] The typical exception is REAL $\supseteq$ LONGINT, where truncation may occur.

3.2.4 The type BOOLEAN

A Boolean value is one of the *logical truth values*, which are represented in Oberon by the standard identifiers TRUE and FALSE.

3.2.5 The type SET

The values belonging to the type SET are *elements of the power set of* {0, 1, ..., N} where N = MAX(SET). N is a constant defined by the implementation. It is typically the word length of the computer (or a small multiple of it). In fact, sets are efficiently implemented as bit operations.

The *notation for sets* follows the mathematical convention:

> set = "{" [element { "," element}] "}".
> element = expression [".." expression].

If *expression* is an integer constant (or a constant expression, see Section 4.1), we speak of a *set constant*. The double period is a shorthand notation for a range of integers, for example {0, 2..4, 8} = {0, 2, 3, 4, 8}.

Examples of set constants are

$$\{\}\quad \{1, 6, 10\}\quad \{0, 2..4, 8\}$$

where { } denotes the empty set.

3.2.6 The type CHAR

A major portion of the input and output of computers is in the form of strings of numerals, characters from the roman alphabet and a small set of special symbols such as punctuation marks and symbols used frequently in commerce and mathematics. This set consists the value range of the type CHAR. For the computing machine, each symbol must be represented by a binary value that *encodes* the symbol. Different brands of computers may use different character sets. However, there is a strong trend towards the so-called ASCII code (of ISO) which defines a set of 128 characters, 33 of which are so-called control characters. The remaining 95 are printable characters (see Appendix B).

ordinal numbers The set representing the type CHAR is ordered, and each character has a fixed position or *ordinal number*. This is reflected in the notation for character constants, which may be written as "a" or 61X, the first form denoting the value of a variable of type CHAR by the representation, the second by the (hexadecimal) ordinal number.

4 Declarations, expressions and assignments

Computers execute sequences of machine instructions, each one transforming the machine's state, which is defined as the contents of memory and registers. A programming language is an abstraction of such a machine instruction sequence. The basic unit is the *statement*, which – when interpreted or executed – specifies an *action*.

The most elementary action is the *assignment* of a value to a variable. Let us introduce a few examples of assignment statements:

```
i := 1
i := i + 1
x := a1 * X + b1 * Y + e1
det := b * b - a * c
r1 := (ABS(b) + sqrt(det))/a
```

We observe that the assignment statement consists of a variable on the left and an expression on the right of the assignment symbol ":=". The expression is evaluated, and its result replaces the value that the variable had prior to the assignment.

In this chapter, we will introduce form and semantics of expressions and of the assignment statement. Since all variables have to be declared, the topic of constant and variable declarations is considered first. The declaration binds an identifier to properties of the object that it represents. These properties are expressed by the object's type. The type defines the set of values and the operations that are applicable.

4.1 Declarations

In Oberon, every object of the language such as constants, variables, procedures and even types must be declared. The declaration creates the object and defines its type.

4.1.1 Constant declarations

The constant declaration binds an identifier to a constant or a constant expression. It observes the syntax:

ConstDeclaration = ident ["*"] "=" ConstExpression.
ConstExpression = expression.

The simplest expression is a number, a character, a truth value or a set constant. More complex expressions are treated in the next section. The evaluation of a constant expression must be possible by a mere textual scan without actual execution of the program – the operands are restricted to constants.

The asterisk is called the *export mark*. Identifiers thus marked will be visible outside the module containing the declaration. We will say more about this in Chapter 6. A sequence of constant declarations, separated by semicolons, is preceded by the symbol "CONST", for example

CONST a = 16807; m = 2147483647; q = m DIV a; r = m MOD a;

Constants with suggestive names help make a program readable. The use of identifiers declared as constants rather than their value has the additional benefit that if the constant value should change, there is *only one place where the program text need be updated*. This avoids a common mistake that one or a few instances of an explicit constant, spread throughout the program, remain unrevised.

4.1.2 Variable declarations

The state of an Oberon computation is defined by a set of *variables*. Such variables have two properties:

- a *type* that defines the set of values it may assume as well as the operations applicable to it;
- a *value*.

The variable declaration *defines a variable* and binds an identifier and a type to it. The value of the variable however, remains undefined. We say that the variable *is an instance of its type* and that the identifier *denotes* (or *represents*) the variable. In the computer implementation, a variable of the basic types is a byte, a word or a double word of memory; the identifier can be visualized as its address.

The syntax of the variable declaration is

> VarDeclaration = IdentList ":" type.
> IdentList = ident ["*"] {"," ident ["*"]}.

At this point, type stands for one of the predefined identifiers representing standard types, namely SHORTINT, INTEGER, LONGINT, REAL, LONGREAL, BOOLEAN, CHAR and SET. Again the asterisk is the export mark. More types will be introduced in Chapters 8 and 11.

Variables of the same type may be grouped in the same declaration; a sequence of variable declarations, separated by semicolons, is preceded by the symbol "VAR"; for example,

```
VAR
    i, m, n: INTEGER;  index: LONGINT;
    a, b, time* : REAL;
    ch: CHAR;
```

The identifier *time* is marked for export.

4.2 Expressions

4.2.1 Syntax and general semantics

An expression is, in general, composed of several operands and operators. Its *evaluation* consists in applying the operators to the operands in a prescribed order, in general from *left to right*. Parentheses are used to modify this left-to-right rule. The operands may be constants, variables or functions.

Terms An expression consists of consecutive *terms*:

$$T_0 \oplus T_1 \oplus \ldots \oplus T_n. \tag{1}$$

The symbol $\oplus$ stands for an *add operator* such as + or − from ordinary arithmetic. Parentheses are used to indicate precedence, that is, the order in which the expression is evaluated. Using parentheses, the left-to-right order of evaluation in (1) is made explicit:

$$(\ldots((T_0 \oplus T_1) \oplus T_2)\ldots) \oplus T_n. \tag{2}$$

Factors

Each term of the expression similarly consists of *factors*:

$$F0 \otimes F1 \otimes \ldots \otimes Fn. \tag{3}$$

where (3), like (1), is evaluated from left to right, that is, is parenthesized like (2). The symbol $\otimes$ stands for a multiplication operator. As is usual in mathematics, multiplication operators take precedence over add operators, a fact that we express symbolically as $\otimes \rightarrow \oplus$.

In EBNF notation, an expression is defined by

```
expression = SimpleExpr [relation SimpleExpr].
relation = "=" | "#" | "<" | "<=" | ">=" | ">" | "IN" | "IS"¹.

SimpleExpr = ["+" | "–"] term {AddOperator term}.
AddOperator = "+" | "–" | "OR".
term = factor {MulOperator factor}.
MulOperator = "*" | "/" | "DIV" | "MOD" | "&".
factor = number | CharConstant | string | set | NIL²
       | designator | FunctionCall
       | "(" expression ")" | "~" factor.

FunctionCall = designator "(" [ActualParameters] ")".
ActualParameters = expression {"," expression}.

designator = ident.
```

As the term suggests, a *designator* designates a variable or a constant. For the time being, it is simply an identifier. More complex designators will be introduced later. For example, a designator may represent an array element *a*[*i*] or a field *f* of a record *r* expressed as *r.f*.

A *function call* looks like the familiar mathematical function notation, for example

sin(x)   cos(omega∗t)   sqrt(b∗b – 4∗a∗c).

Function calls as factors act exactly as one would expect from ordinary mathematics. They stand for a result that is obtained through a prescribed operation on the arguments.

---

[1] Explained in Chapter 11.
[2] See chapter 9.

Examples

It is instructive to study a set of examples. In fact, we encourage the reader to parse the following expressions into their syntactic constituents:

a + b − c + d	(a + b) − (c + d)
b∗b − 4∗a∗c	−y + ABS(x)
a = b	(NextString = "END") OR flag
(−b + sqrt(b∗b − 4∗a∗c))/(2∗a)	(i DIV j) − 3.14159
~(a∗a < b) & ~ (a = 4.0) OR c & d	61X = "a"

The meaning – or *semantics* – of the examples is straightforward. They are either numerical expressions, yielding results that are simple numeric types, or they are relations and Boolean expressions resulting in TRUE or FALSE.

The following symbol strings are not Oberon expressions:

b b − 4 a c	multiplication operator missing, should read b∗b − 4∗a∗c
a + −b	adjacent operators, should read a + (−b)
a < b & c = 5	parentheses missing, should read (a < b) & (c = 5)

4.2.2 Type rules

Let us look at a second set of syntactically well-formed expressions:

"a"+ 3.14159
(a = b) − sqrt("144")

It is not clear how these expressions should be evaluated. What sense does it make to add a character constant to a number? Can a truth value be used as a number? There are various schools of thought with respect to these questions. Some languages (e.g. PL/I) define elaborate type conversion rules or treat truth values as the numerical constants 0 and 1 (e.g. APL). We believe that what such languages teach us is the *way not to do it*. In essence, Oberon requests the type of operands to be identical and allows mixing of types in only a few well-understood cases, for example when the type of one operand includes the type of the other one. For a given operator, the types of operands that are *expression compatible* are listed in Table 4.1. More details about the basic types follow in subsequent sections; the types ARRAY, POINTER and RECORD await later chapters.

Table 4.1 Expression compatibility.

Operator	Valid operand types (or operands)	Result type
+ − *	numeric types	largest numeric type of the operands
/	numeric types	smallest real type that includes both operands
+ − * /	SET	SET
DIV MOD	integer types	largest integer type of the operands
OR & ~	BOOLEAN	BOOLEAN
= # < <= > >=	numeric types, CHAR, ARRAY OF CHAR, string constant	BOOLEAN
= #	BOOLEAN, SET, POINTER, procedure variable	BOOLEAN
IN	*left*: integer type *right*: SET	BOOLEAN
IS	*left*: POINTER, RECORD[1] *right*: type identifier	BOOLEAN

4.2.3 Relations

Relations are expressions of syntax

> expression = SimpleExpr relation SimpleExpr.
> relation = "=" | "#" | "<" | "<=" | ">=" | ">" | "IN" | "IS".

They yield a result of type BOOLEAN. The type compatibility rules are stated in Table 4.1. The *relational operators* are

=	equal	>	greater
#	not equal	>=	greater or equal
<	less	IN	set membership
<=	less or equal	IS	type test

[1] Must be a variable parameter.

The meaning of comparison operators is straightforward. A relation *i* IN *S* holds if integer *i* is member of set *S*. More on the type test will be found in Section 11.2.2.

Examples of relations include

"a" < "b"	TRUE ORD("a") = 97, ORD("b") = 98)
"abc" >= "xyz"	FALSE, collating sequence
e < pi	TRUE
2 IN {1, 3..7, 11}	FALSE
"a" < "ab"	illegal, argument types not compatible

For the precise definition of relations involving strings and character arrays of different length, we refer to Section 8.2.6.

4.2.4 Arithmetic expressions

Arithmetic expressions are composed of numeric constants, variables of numeric types, functions whose evaluation results in a number, and the (dyadic) operators:

+	addition		/	real division
−	subtraction		DIV	integer division
*	multiplication		MOD	modulus

Integer division DIV and modulus MOD admit integer arguments only and are defined by the algebraic identity

$$x \equiv (x \text{ DIV } y)*y + (x \text{ MOD } y) \qquad (1)$$
$$0 \leq (x \text{ MOD } y) < y \quad \text{or} \quad y < (x \text{ MOD } y) \leq 0 \qquad (2)$$

Thus the integer division yields the largest value not greater than the quotient x/y and the modulus is the remainder of the integer division. Parentheses are used to control the order of evaluation. The *monadic minus sign* is used to express negative numbers and to negate terms, for example −3 or −*a*.

Type rules

The numeric types may be mixed in arithmetic expressions. At the application of each operator, the smaller type, *T1*, is first converted to the larger one, *T2* say. The result of the operation is then also of type *T2* (see Table 4.1).

Let us illustrate the type rule with a few examples. Assume s: SHORTINT; i: INTEGER; l: LONGINT; r: REAL; lr: LONGREAL. Then

l MOD s	LONGINT	i ∗ r	REAL
1.0 / s	REAL	r DIV i	illegal
i − lr	LONGREAL	1 / lr	LONGREAL

Type conversion functions

In arithmetic expressions, most type conversions are handled automatically. There are, however, cases where explicit type conversions are required. The example r DIV i is such a case. For this purpose, Oberon affords the following type conversion functions:

Table 4.2 Type conversion functions.

Name	Argument type	Result type	Function
ENTIER(a)	real type	LONGINT	$\lfloor a \rfloor$ [1]
SHORT(x)	x: LONGINT x: INTEGER x: LONGREAL	INTEGER SHORTINT REAL	identity (truncation is possible)
LONG(x)	x: SHORTINT x: INTEGER x: REAL	INTEGER LONGINT LONGREAL	identity

Using explicit type conversions, the erroneous expression r DIV i may be corrected; that is, ENTIER(r) DIV i.

4.2.5 Boolean expressions

The constituents of a Boolean expression are the truth values denoted by the standard identifiers TRUE and FALSE, variables of type BOOLEAN, relational expressions and the operators

    OR   logical disjunction   ~ logical negation
    &   logical conjunction

The precedence relation is "~" → "&" → "OR". Therefore

    p OR q & s OR t = p OR (q & s) OR t

---

[1] Largest integer not greater than a.

Oberon defines the Boolean connectives as *conditional evaluations*; that is,

$$p \text{ OR } q \Rightarrow \text{if } p \text{ then TRUE else } q$$
$$p \ \& \ q \Rightarrow \text{if } p \text{ then } q \text{ else FALSE}$$
$$\sim p \Rightarrow \text{if } p \text{ then FALSE else TRUE}$$

where *p* and *q* are variables or expressions of type BOOLEAN. This definition is different from the mathematical one using truth tables. It implies that the *second argument is not evaluated* if the result is already known from the first argument. The notable property of this definition is that the result may be well defined even if the second argument is not. As a consequence, the order of the operands may be significant – *they are not commutative*.

De Morgan's law Boolean expressions may often be simplified using *De Morgan's law* stating the equivalences

$$(\sim p) \ \& \ (\sim q) \equiv \sim(p \text{ OR } q) \tag{1}$$
$$(\sim p) \text{ OR } (\sim q) \equiv \sim(p \ \& \ q) \tag{2}$$

Relation as factor Relations result in the type BOOLEAN and thus may appear as factors in Boolean expressions. For example,

$$(i < N) \ \& \sim \text{eof}$$

If relations appear in Boolean expressions, they must always be enclosed in parentheses. Thus a construct such as $i < N \ \& \sim eof$ is illegal because it would be parsed as $i < (N \ \& \sim eof)$, which violates type rules.

4.2.6 Set expressions

Sets are factors defined syntactically as

> set = "{" [element {"," element}] "}".
> element = expression [".." expression].

The expressions must evaluate to numerical results of integer type. The notation *E1..E2* is a shorthand for *E1, E1+1, E1+2, ... E2–1, E2*.

Examples include

{ }	the empty set
{1, 4..8, 20}	the set {1, 4, 5, 6, 7, 8, 20}
{1, n+1 .. 2 * k}	the set {1, n+1, n+2, ... 2k–1, 2k}

Set expressions comprise sets, set variables and the operators

+	set union	/	symmetric set difference
–	set difference	*	set intersection

The *monadic minus sign* denotes the complement, that is –*U* represents the set of integers between 0 and MAX(SET) that are not elements of *U*. The operators "*" and "/" are multiplicative operators and hence take precedence over "+" and "–".

As an exercise, let us express the definition of the set operators in Oberon notation, using the membership relation IN:

i IN (–U)	⇒	(i IN {0..MAX(SET)}) & ~(i IN U)
i IN (U + V)	⇒	(i IN U) OR (i IN V)
i IN (U – V)	⇒	(i IN U) & ~(i IN V)
i IN (U * V)	⇒	(i IN U) & (i IN V)
i IN (U/V)	⇒	((i IN U) # (i IN V))

where *i* is an integer and *U* and *V* are sets.

4.2.7 Predeclared functions

Oberon provides a set of predeclared functions for

- some frequently occurring computations ;
- access type-specific information.

An example of the first kind is ABS(*x*) that computes the absolute value of a variable *x* of integer type. The functions MAX(*T*) or MIN(*T*) that we encountered earlier are typical for the second kind. A complete list of the predeclared functions is given in Appendix A, Tables A.1 and A.2, page 302.

4.3 The assignment statement

The assignment statement serves to evaluate an expression and assign its value to a variable. Its syntax is:

| assignment = designator ":=" expression.

The action of the assignment statement consists of three parts:

(1) evaluate the designator resulting in a variable;
(2) evaluate the expression yielding a value;
(3) replace the current value of the variable identified in 1 by the value obtained in 2.

In the simple case that we consider here, evaluating a designator means accessing the memory location that holds its value. When discussing the array data structure, we will encounter designators such as $a[i + 1]$ whose evaluation involves integer computations.

4.3.1 Type rules

The *type of the designator must be compatible with the type of the expression*. In general, this means that the two types must be identical, or in the case of numerical types the designator may be of a larger type that includes the type of the expression.

For reference purposes, Table 4.3 lists the full set of rules for *assignment compatibility* of an expression with a given designator. Rows 3–7 relate to concepts that will be introduced in later chapters.

Table 4.3 Assignment compatibility of $v := e$.

Type or value of expression e	Type of designator v
Both types are equal (but not an open array)	
numeric type	numeric type, includes type of expression
record type	record type, type is a base type of expression[1]
pointer type	pointer type, type is a base type of expression
value NIL	pointer or procedure type
string of length l	ARRAY n OF CHAR $(n > l)$
name of a procedure	procedure type with matching parameter list

[1] Condition is met if the type of the designator is equal to the type of the expression.

4.3.2 Formal definition, pre-condition and post-condition

A formal way to reason about the effects of an assignment is to record explicitly the states holding before and after its execution. We characterize a set of states by a *predicate* over the involved variables (see references at end of Chapter 5). Then all states satisfying the predicate belong to the considered set.

Pre-condition, result condition

Let R denote a predicate that defines the set of states after the execution of the assignment statement. It is natural to view these states as the *result* of the assignment, and hence R is referred to as the *result condition* (the term *post-condition* is sometimes used synonymously). The predicate P holding before execution is called the *pre-condition*. It is often useful to add the pre-condition and the result condition as comments to the left and to the right of our statement S:

$$(* P *) \; S \; (* R *) \tag{4}$$

This formalism is useful since, given the goal R, it is possible to infer the precondition P. We state the main result in the following axiom.

Axiom of assignment

Consider the assignment
$$(* P *) \; v := e \; (* R *)$$
where v is a variable and e an expression.

The weakest precondition P is derived from R by substituting every (free) occurrence of v in R by e.

Examples

Let us proceed with the simplest example. The goal R is $i = 1$ and the assignment $i := 1$. We substitute 1 for i in the relation $i = 1$ and obtain the pre-condition $1 = 1$ or TRUE; in other words,

$$(* \text{TRUE} *) \; i := 1 \; (* i = 1 *).$$

Thus, whatever the state prior to executing the assignment $i := 1$, the assertion $i = 1$ holds afterwards.

In a second example, we strive for the result condition $i = N$ after the assignment $i := i + 1$. Substitution of $i + 1$ for i in the relation $i = N$ yields $i + 1 = N$ or $i = N - 1$; hence

$$(* i = N - 1 *) \; i := i + 1 \; (* i = N *).$$

The following table lists a number of further examples:

P	S	R
c = a * b	x := a * b	x = c
x < y + 2	x := x − 2	x < y
i < N	i := i + 1	i ≤ N

4.3.3 Statement sequence

A computation is a sequence of actions that transforms an initial state into a final one that, it is hoped, satisfies the stated result condition. In Oberon, the statement is the basic unit of action. Thus the sequence of actions is expressed in a *statement sequence*

$$S_1; S_2; S_3; ... S_i; ... S_n$$

The semicolon is a *statement separator* that indicates that the action specified by a given statement, S_i say, is to be *succeeded* by the one textually following the separator.

It is straightforward to express the syntax of the statement sequence in EBNF notation:

| StatementSequence = statement {";" statement}.

The assignment discussed here is just one of a number of statements that will be treated in later chapters:

```
statement = [ assignment | ProcedureCall
            | IfStatement | CaseStatement
            | WhileStatement | RepeatStatement
            | LoopStatement | WithStatement
            | ExitStatement | ReturnStatement ].
```

The syntax of statements implies that a statement may consist of no symbols at all. In this case, the statement is said to be empty, and evidently denotes the null action. This curiosity among statements has a reason: it allows semicolons to be inserted at places where they are actually superfluous, such as at the end of a statement sequence.

HALT   A statement sequence is terminated, and the enclosing program brought to an abnormal halt if the predeclared procedure

HALT(e)

is called (call statement: see Section 6.1). The argument e is an integer expression whose value identifies the termination. Typically, that value is displayed by the operating system.

Return statement A statement sequence is also terminated if a return statement is executed (see Section 6.4.2).

Formal definition Given the result condition R, the pre-condition of the statement sequence may be computed by stepwise application of the substitution rule, starting with S_n and ending with S_1:

$$(* P *)\ S_1;\ S_2;\ S_3;\ \ldots\ S_i;\ \ldots\ S_n\ (* R *).$$

Consider the task of determining P in the following example:

$$(* P *)\ \ i := i + 1;\ j := 2*i\ \ (* j = n *).$$

We introduce intermediary predicates:

$$(* P *) \equiv (* P_1 *)$$
$$(* P_1 *)\ \ i := i + 1;\ \ (* R_1 *) \equiv (* P_2 *)$$
$$(* P_2 *)\ \ j := 2*i\ \ (* R_2 *) \equiv (* R *)$$
$$(* R *)$$

We know R_2, namely $j = n$, and S_2, the assignment $j := 2*i$. Using the substitution rule, we find for P_2 the predicate $n = 2*i$. Now we equate $R_1 = P_2$ and derive $P_1 \equiv n = 2*(i + 1)$:

$$(* 2*(i + 1) = n *)\ \ i := i + 1;\ j := 2*i\ \ (* j = n *).$$

Next we invert the order of evaluation; that is, our sample statement sequence is $j := 2*i;\ i := i + 1$. Similar formal manipulations yield

$$(* 2*i = n *)\ \ j := 2*i;\ i := i + 1;\ \ (* j = n *).$$

It is evident that the two pre-conditions specify different states. For example, if $n = 4$ then the preconditions are $i = 1$ for the first case and $i = 2$ for the second one. From this simple example, we conclude that the *order in which the statements are executed matters*.

4.3.4 Special assignment statements as predeclared procedures

For some frequently occurring assignment statements, Oberon provides an alternative notation. For example, to increment an integer variable i, the assignment $i := i + 1$ may be replaced by INC(i). Similarly, DEC(i) is equivalent to $i := i - 1$.

Syntactically, INC(i) and DEC(i) are procedure calls (see Chapter 6). All predeclared procedures that abbreviate assignments are listed in Appendix A, Table A.3, page 303. The rationale behind these procedures is the possibility of producing efficient code, using special machine instructions. The programmer is thus advised to use the procedures whenever applicable.

4.4 Summary

In Oberon, all identifiers must be declared. In this chapter, we have introduced the *constant* and the *variable declarations*. A constant declaration associates an identifier with a constant. As the name implies, the variable declaration defines a variable that is represented by an identifier. The variable declaration associates a type with the variable. This association is constant and valid throughout the existence of the variable. The type defines the set of values that the variable may assume and the operations in which it can participate.

A fundamental construct of procedural languages, such as Oberon, is the assignment statement

$$v := e$$

Expression e is evaluated and the result replaces the old value of the variable v.

Expressions differ by the operator and the type of the operands. For example, we introduced relations, arithmetic expressions, Boolean expression and set expressions.

Of particular importance is the requirement that the factors entering expressions and the constituents of the assignment must be *type-compatible*. Expression compatibility and assignment compatibility are summarized in Tables 4.1 and 4.3. This compatibility requirement, called *strong typing*, empowers the compiler to check whether expressions and assignments are meaningful, thereby diagnosing a large number of programming errors.

We have introduced a formal method for defining the semantics of the assignment. The set of desired states after the assignment is characterized with a predicate: *the result condition* or post-condition. The axiom of assignment is used to transform that predicate into a *pre-condition* defining the admissible set of states prior to the assignment.

A number of statements, separated by semicolons, is called a *statement sequence*. It represents a sequential computation. The statements are executed from left to right.

4.5 Exercises

4.1 Identify well-formed identifiers:
next_item   nextItem   1stStreet   FirstStreet   LONGINT
WHILE   0FFFH

4.2 Identify well-formed numbers:
a4.4.3   15,13222↑10   .2213   1.33333E354777   3FFX   3FFH
1.44E–88   7FFH E–18

4.3 Identify the predeclared identifiers:
ARRAY   TRUE   ABS   DIV   MOD   COPY   DEC
INTEGER   OR   RETURN   Max   MAX   FFFFH

4.4 Identify legal declarations. Some are legal but nonsensical: why?
CONST a = 11;   CONST a := 234;
CONST TRUE = FLSE;   CONST DO = TRUE;
CONST i = ORD("a");   INF = MAX(real);   inf = MAX(REAL);
CONST random = RandomNumbers.Uniform();
VAR REAL: INTEGER;   VAR DO: REAL;   VAR do: REAL;
VAR Real: INTEGER;   VAR Real := INTEGER;
VAR a; b; c: REAL;   VAR i, j, k: INTEGER;

4.5 Determine the value and the type of the following constants (assuming extremal values of Appendix B):
CONST
i = 3;   j = 10000;   k = 300000;   l = 7FFAH;   s = {1,2,3};   pi = 3.14159;
inf = MAX(INTEGER);   p = ENTIER(pi);   l = i∗pi;   ich = ORD(44X);

4.6 Assume the declaration
CONST z = 0;
VAR si: SHORTINT; i: INTEGER; li: LONGINT; ch: CHAR;
s: SET; r: REAL; lr: LONGREAL; b: BOOLEAN;
Evaluate the following assignments. Some of them are illegal: which?
si := ORD(CHR(71)); i := ORD("G"); li := ORD(CHR(72));
i := 1 + ENTIER(r); si := SHORT(ENTIER(3.14));
b := 3 < MAX(REAL) OR li > i + 4; ch := 44X; b := 44X > "a";
ch := "this is true"; b := ("abc" > "this") & (MAX(REAL) > 1/z);
b := (CAP(6DX) = "M") & (li = 1/z);
i := 4 + CHR("a");

4.7 Determine the pre-condition P of the following assignments, for which result conditions R are known:

Assignments	Result condition R
j := i DIV 2	j = 0
d := a*a − 4*a*c	d ≥ 0
r := r − Y; q := q + 1	qY + r = X
x := x*n	x = n!

4.8 Write a statement sequence that interchanges the values of two variables a and b. Prove the result using the axiom of assignment.

5 Control structures

The prime characteristic of a computation is a sequence of actions to be executed sequentially. If this sequence were a fixed one, the computer would not have developed in its present form. Individual actions can be selected, repeated or performed conditionally, depending on previously computed results. Hence the temporal sequence of actions is normally not identical to the textual sequence of statements. It is this dynamic sequencing of actions, also known as *control structure*, that is the foundation of the phenomenal success of software.

The sequence of actions is determined by *control statements* indicating conditional execution, selection, or repetition of statements or whole statement sequences. Since a control statement governs other statements, it is said to be a *structured statement*. Languages with structured statements are known as *structured languages*. Years of experience prove that proper control structures go hand in hand with purpose tuned development of a program text – thereby making it readable and ultimately trustworthy. This goal, however, is only achieved if the structure is made visible – the use of one line per statement (or statement sequence) and proper indentation are indispensable tools. For example, recall from the introduction

```
IF  gamma > 0  THEN
   z := gamma
ELSE
   z := gamma + m
END;
```

Syntactically, structured statements are expressed recursively, having *StatementSequence* and hence *statement* as constituents. As in the case of the assignment statement, we will formally define the control structures by means of predicates and their transformation rules (Gries, 1981; Cohen, 1990).

5.1 Conditional statements

5.1.1 The if statement

Selecting a statement sequence among a set of sequences under the control of Boolean expressions is one of the main constituents of programs. As an introductory example, consider the the signum function $y = \text{sign}(x) = (1 \text{ if } x > 0, 0 \text{ if } x = 0, -1 \text{ otherwise})$ which in Oberon notation is expressed as follows, with obvious meaning:

```
IF  x < 0  THEN  y := -1
ELSIF  x > 0  THEN  y := 1
ELSE  y := 0
END;
```

The conditional statement, also called the *if statement*, observes the syntax

> IfStatement = "IF" expression "THEN" StatementSequence
> {"ELSIF" expression "THEN" StatementSequence}
> ["ELSE" StatementSequence]
> "END".

The expressions must be of type BOOLEAN, which means they yield, after evaluation, one of the truth values TRUE or FALSE. Note that the if statement is always terminated with an END, even in the simplest form IF B THEN S END, where S is a single statement.

To explain the operation of the if statement, we express its general form as follows:

```
IF B₁ THEN S₁
ELSIF B₂ THEN S₂
...
ELSIF Bₙ THEN Sₙ
ELSE S
END
```

Here $B_1...B_n$ denote Boolean expressions and $S, S_1...S_n$ denote statement sequences (a single statement is also a statement sequence). The else clause ELSE S is an abbreviation for ELSIF $\sim B_1$ & $\sim B_2$ & ... & $\sim B_n$ THEN S.

B_1 is evaluated. If it yields FALSE then B_2 is evaluated, and so forth, until the *first Boolean expression that is satisfied* is encountered: B_i, say.

The statement sequence S_i associated with B_i is executed and the if statement terminated. Note that at most one of the statement sequences executes; if the ELSE clause is present, exactly one is carried out.

The Boolean expression B_i ($i = 1, 2...n$) is also termed the *guard* of its statement sequence S_i.

5.1.2 Formal definition of the if statement

As in the case of the assignment, we wish to be able to state

(∗ P ∗) If B THEN S END (∗ R ∗).

What are the necessary and sufficient properties of the component statements (or statement sequences) that let us make the above conclusion? They are specified in the axiom of alternatives, which serves as a formal specification of the semantics of the if statement. It demonstrates the essence of a structured language: *it is possible to derive properties of a composite statement from those of its components and, vice-versa.*

Before stating the axiom of alternatives, let us consider a simple example: the computation of the absolute value of an expression; that is, $y := ABS(x)$. It can be expressed by an if statement:

```
IF x < 0 THEN y := -x
ELSE y := x
END.
(* y = ABS(x) *)
```

As before, we have added the result condition $R \equiv y = ABS(x)$ as a comment at the end of the if statement. The condition R can be expressed as follows

$$R \equiv (x < 0) \,\&\, (y = -x) \text{ OR } (x \geq 0) \,\&\, (y = x).$$

If, prior to the if statement, precondition P is satisfied, then $(x < 0) \,\&\, P$ holds before the assignment $y = -x$. Similarly, the predicate $(x \geq 0) \,\&\, P$ is the precondition of the assignment $y = x$. Therefore

```
(* P *)
IF x < 0 THEN (* (x < 0) & P *)  y := -x  (* R *)
ELSE  (* (x ≥ 0) & P *)  y := x  (* R *)
END;
```

Thus we seek a pre-condition P such that

$$(*\ (x < 0)\ \&\ P\ *)\quad y := -x \quad (*\ R\ *) \text{ and}$$
$$(*\ (x \geq 0)\ \&\ P\ *)\quad y := x \quad (*\ R\ *)$$

can be established. For our simple example, this is not a difficult task. Direct application of the axiom of assignment yields for the first statement $y := -x\ (*\ R\ *)$:

$$(x < 0)\ \&\ (-x = -x)\ \text{OR}\ (x \geq 0)\ \&\ (-x = x) \equiv x \leq 0$$

Similarly, $y := x\ (*\ R\ *)$ leads to

$$(x < 0)\ \&\ (x = -x)\ \text{OR}\ (x \geq 0)\ \&\ (x = x) \equiv x \geq 0$$

from which we conclude $P \equiv \text{TRUE}$, establishing unconditional validity of the computation of the absolute value.

These preliminaries motivate the following axiom:

Axiom of alternatives

$(*\ P\ *)$
  IF B_1 THEN S_1
  ELSIF B_2 THEN S_2
  ...
  ELSIF B_n THEN S_n
  ELSE S
  END
$(*\ R\ *)$

holds if there exist conditions P_i such that

$(*\ P_i\ *)\ S_i\ (*\ R\ *)$ for all $i = 1, 2,\ldots n$	(1)
$P\ \&\ {\sim}B_1\ \&\ {\sim}B_2\ \&\ \ldots\ \&\ {\sim}B_{i-1}\ \&\ B_i \Rightarrow P_i$	(2)
$P\ \&\ {\sim}B_1\ \&\ {\sim}B_2\ \&\ \ldots\ \&\ {\sim}B_n \Rightarrow R$ (else clause is missing)	(3a)
$(*\ P\ \&\ {\sim}B_1\ \&\ {\sim}B_2\ \&\ \ldots\ \&\ {\sim}B_n\ *)\ S\ (*\ R\ *)$ (with else clause)	(3b)

$A \Rightarrow B$ means A implies B in the sense of predicate calculus (that is, ${\sim}A\ \text{OR}\ B$).

The following example illustrates the use of the axiom of alternatives. The task is to compute $y := \text{sign}(x)$, which can be expressed by the if statement S:

5.1 Conditional statements

```
IF x < 0 THEN y := -1
ELSIF x > 0 THEN y := 1
ELSE y := 0
END;
```

We have $B_1 \equiv x < 0$ and $B_2 \equiv x > 0$. Our goal is to establish

$$(* \text{ TRUE } *) \; S \; (* \; y = \text{sign}(x) \; *).$$

The result condition $R \equiv y = \text{sign}(x)$ can be written as

$$R \equiv (x < 0) \; \& \; (y = -1) \; \text{OR} \; (x > 0) \; \& \; (y = 1) \; \text{OR} \; (x = 0) \; \& \; (y = 0).$$

The axiom of assignment applied to $y := -1$, $y := 0$ and $y := 1$ (in that order) yields

$$(x < 0) \; \& \; (-1 = -1) \; \text{OR} \; (x > 0) \; \& \; (-1 = 1) \; \text{OR} \; (x = 0) \; \& \; (-1 = 0) \equiv x < 0$$
$$(x < 0) \; \& \; (1 = -1) \; \text{OR} \; (x > 0) \; \& \; (1 = 1) \; \text{OR} \; (x = 0) \; \& \; (1 = 0) \quad \equiv x > 0$$
$$(x < 0) \; \& \; (0 = -1) \; \text{OR} \; (x > 0) \; \& \; (0 = 1) \; \text{OR} \; (x = 0) \; \& \; (0 = 0) \quad \equiv x = 0$$

Therefore

$$P_1 \equiv x < 0: \quad (* \; x < 0 \; *) \; x := -1 \quad (* \; R \; *)$$
$$P_2 \equiv x > 0: \quad (* \; x > 0 \; *) \; x := 1 \quad (* \; R \; *)$$
$$ (* \; x = 0 \; *) \; x := 0 \quad (* \; R \; *)$$

The assertion $(* \text{ TRUE } *) \; S \; (* \; P \; *)$ can be established according to the axiom of alternatives if

TRUE & $B_1 \Rightarrow P_1$	using (2)
TRUE & $\sim B_1$ & $B_2 \Rightarrow P_2$	using (2)
$(* \text{ TRUE } \& \sim B_1 \& \sim B_2 \; *) \; S \; (* \; R \; *)$	using (3a)

Substituting $B_1 \equiv x < 0$ and $B_2 \equiv x > 0$ into the above predicates, we find

$$\text{TRUE} \; \& \; B_1 \equiv \; x < 0$$
$$\text{TRUE} \; \& \; \sim B_1 \; \& \; B_2 \equiv \; x > 0$$
$$\text{TRUE} \; \& \; \sim B_1 \; \& \; \sim B_2 \equiv \; x = 0$$

In all three cases, the above conditions are satisfied, and the correct computation of sign(x) is thus formally established.

5.1.3 The case statement

An if statement with a number of ELSIF clauses allows the selection of a statement sequence under the control of several conditions – one for each sequence. In practice, one often finds a series of comparisons of a *common expression with a set of constants*.

Let us illustrate this situation. Assume that we have renamed a file. The appropriate system routine yields a so-called result code, an integer variable *res* that reports various termination conditions. An appropriate message is generated by the if statement:

```
IF res = 0 THEN Out.String("renamed")
ELSIF res = 1 THEN Out.String("name existed already")
ELSIF res = 2 THEN Out.String("name does not exist")
ELSIF res = 3 THEN Out.String("system error")
END;
```

The following case statement is equivalent:

```
CASE res OF
    0: Out.String("renamed")
  | 1: Out.String("name existed already")
  | 2: Out.String("name does not exist")
  | 3: Out.String("system error")
END;
```

Besides notational convenience, the case statement allows the compiler to generate very efficient code if the compared values are constants and more or less contiguous.

The formal EBNF specification of the case statement reads

```
CaseStatement = "CASE" expression OF
                   case {"|" case}
                   ["ELSE" StatementSequence]
                "END".
case = [CaseLabelList ":" StatementSequence].
CaseLabelList = CaseLabels {"," CaseLabels}.
CaseLabels = ConstExpression [".." ConstExpression].
```

The expression and all the case labels must be of the same type, which is either an integer type or CHAR. Case labels are constants or constant expressions, and *no value must appear more than once*. The following rules determine the execution of the case statement:

(1) The expression is evaluated.
(2) The first statement sequence whose case label list contains the value obtained from step 1 is executed and the case statement terminates.
(3) If no match exists, the statement sequence following ELSE is selected. If it is omitted then lack of a match is considered an error.

As in set notation, $E1..E2$ is shorthand for the filled-in series $E1, E1+1, ... E2-1, E2$.

5.1.4 Formal definition of the case statement

Once again, we wish to find the assertions about the component statements that must hold in order to establish $(*\ P\ *)$ CASE k OF $k_1: S_1$ | $k_2: S_2$ | ... | $k_n: S_n$ END $(*\ R\ *)$. These assertions follow easily from the axiom of alternatives, and they are as follows:

$(*\ P\ *)$ CASE k OF
         $k_1: S_1$ | $k_2: S_2$ | ... | $k_n: S_n$
         END $(*\ R\ *)$

holds, if there exist conditions P_i such that for all $i = 1, 2, ... n$

$(*\ P_i\ *)\ S_i\ (*\ R\ *)$
$P\ \&\ (k = k_i) \Rightarrow P_i$

5.2 Repetitive statements

The repetition of a statement or a statement sequence under the control of a condition is a frequent constituent of programs. Oberon features three kinds of repetitive statements: the *while statement*, the *repeat statement* and the *loop statement*. The three statements are, in essence, equivalent but cater for different programming situations.

5.2.1 The while statement

Assume that a statement, or a statement sequence, should execute exactly *n* times; a requirement that we specify as follows:

```
j := 0;
WHILE j < n DO
    ... ; j := j + 1
END;
```

Since variable *j*, the *control variable*, counts from 0 to *n* − 1, we call the preceding repetition a *counting loop*.

The syntax of the while statement reads

> WhileStatement = "WHILE" expression "DO"
>   StatementSequence
>   "END".

The expression must be of type BOOLEAN. The action of the while statement is described by the rules:

(1) Evaluate the expression, which results in a truth value.
(2) If the value is TRUE, execute the statement sequence and then repeat with step 1; if the value is FALSE, terminate.

If the condition is not satisfied initially (that is, the expression yields FALSE), then the statement is vacuous; that is, no action takes place.

The while statement introduces for the first time the danger of a nonterminating program, a frustrating experience every programmer, novice or expert, is familiar with. Evidently, loops must be considered with care. Consider, for example,

```
WHILE j # 0 DO j := j − 2 END;
```

It is easy to realize that this loop terminates only under the pre-condition (*j* >= 0) & (*j* DIV 2 = 0). The program must enforce that pre-condition, otherwise it will be in error about half of the time it is run.

5.2.2 Formal definition of the while statement

Verification of the claim that a repeated statement establishes a specified result characterized by the condition *R* rests on the notion of a condition *Q* that holds invariably, no matter how many times a statement (or statement sequence) has already been executed. Q is therefore called a *loop invariant*, or simply *invariant*.

Let us explain this concept with a simple example. We wish to compute $z := X*Y$ (for $x \geq 0$) using repeated addition. The obvious solution is

```
x := X; z := 0;
WHILE x > 0 DO z := z + Y; x := x – 1 END;
(* z = XY *)
```

The relevant invariant (that is, the condition holding before each execution of the repeated statement sequence) is

$$Q \equiv (z + xY = XY) \ \& \ (x \geq 0).$$

It holds at the beginning, because $0 + XY = XY$. It remains unchanged during the repetition because each time 1 is subtracted from x, Y is added to z, leaving the sum intact. Most importantly, this invariant yields the desired result, if the condition $x > 0$ no longer holds and repetition terminates:

$$\sim(x > 0) \ \& \ (z + xY = XY) \ \& \ (x \geq 0) \equiv$$
$$(x = 0) \ \& \ (z + xY = XY) \equiv (z = XY) \equiv R$$

The verification condition of the while statement is summarized in the axiom of repetition:

Axiom of repetition

(* P *) WHILE B DO S END (* R *)

holds if an invariant Q exists such that

$P \Rightarrow Q$
(* Q & B *) S (* Q *)
$Q \ \& \sim B \Rightarrow R$

If a while statement satisfies the axiom of repetition, it is said to be *partially correct*. It establishes the result condition R whenever it manages to falsify B. However, it may never do that, and repetition never terminates.

Loop variant

In order to demonstrate full correctness, we also have to show that the *repetition terminates*. In order to do so, we have to establish that at each iteration, the loop makes some progress towards a goal. This is the case if we can find an expression involving variables participating in the condition B, that is strictly decreasing at each turn, and whose falling below a fixed threshold, for example 0, implies ~B – that is, termination of the loop. Such a function is termed a *loop variant*, or again simply a *variant*.

In our example of multiplication, x is that variant. It is decremented by the repeated statement sequence, and $x \leq 0$ implies ~$(x > 0)$, and hence termination.

In order to exemplify these ideas, we present a more sophisticated version of a multiplication algorithm, which happens also to be much more efficient:

```
x := X;  y := Y;  z := 0;  (* x >= 0 *)
WHILE x > 0 DO
    IF ODD(x) THEN  z := z + y;  x := x – 1  END;
    y := 2*y;  x := x DIV 2
END;
```

The invariant Q remains the same, and so does the variant x. We must demonstrate that the statement sequence leaves Q invariant and decreases x. We leave this exercise to the reader, but point out an important detail.

In order that Q not be invalidated by the statement sequence

```
y := 2*y;  x := x DIV 2
```

x must be even; otherwise the DIV operation loses the remainder 1. However, this condition is established – if it does not already hold – by the preceding $x := x - 1$, which is executed (or guarded) by the condition ODD(x).

A second example concerns the division of positive integers $q := X$ DIV Y. The algorithm proceeds by repeatedly subtracting the divisor Y from the dividend X; that is,

```
r := X;  q := 0;
WHILE r >= Y DO
    r := r – Y; q := q + 1
END;
```

The invariant is

$Q \equiv (qY + r = X)\ \&\ (r \geq 0)$.

Q is established by the initial statements. It is maintained by the statement pair $r := r - Y; q := q + 1$, because it leaves the sum $qY + r$ unchanged. The condition (guard) $r > 0$ guarantees that r does not become negative. And finally, Q & $\sim B$ or Q & $(r < Y)$ yields the desired result

$$R \equiv (qY + r = X) \& (0 \leq r < Y)$$

which, as we recall, is the definition of the division

$$X \text{ DIV } Y = q, \quad X \text{ MOD } Y = r.$$

The expression $r - Y$ is a variant function. At each repetition of the loop, Y is subtracted from r; hence $r - Y$ is strictly decreasing. In addition, $r - Y \leq 0$ implies $r \leq Y$ and hence $\sim B$, the terminating condition of the loop. Thus correctness of the integer division is guaranteed.

5.2.3 The repeat statement

The second repetitive statement is syntactically defined as

> RepeatStatement = "REPEAT"
> StatementSequence
> "UNTIL" expression.

Again, the expression is of type BOOLEAN. The essential difference from the while statement is that the termination condition is checked each time *after* (instead of before) execution of the statement sequence. As a consequence, the sequence is *executed at least once*. The advantage is that the condition may involve variables that are undefined when the repetition is started.

For example, a counting loop may also be expressed as

```
j := 0;
REPEAT
   ... ; j := j + 1
UNTIL j = n;
```

In this version of the counting loop, it must be guaranteed that $j = 0$ is a valid pre-condition for the statement sequence.

The 'danger' of using the repeat statement lies in the fact, that the statement sequence is not guarded by an explicit condition. As a consequence, it is easier to overlook the proper termination condition. For example, the calculation of the harmonic series:

i := 0; s := 0;
REPEAT s := s + 1/i; INC(i) UNTIL i = n;

does not terminate for $n \leq 0$. In general it is *wise to use the while statement* whenever repeat does not offer a clear advantage.

5.2.4 Formal definition of the repeat statement

The loop invariant and variant play the same role as in the case of the while statement. We will be brief and state the appropriate axiom without further examples:

(∗ P ∗) REPEAT S UNTIL B (∗ R ∗)

holds, if there exists an invariant Q such that

(∗ P ∗) S (∗ Q ∗)
(∗ Q & ~B ∗) S (∗ Q ∗)
Q & B ⇒ R

5.2.5 The loop statement

The third repetitive statement is the loop statement, which specifies the unconditional repeated execution of a statement sequence. It is terminated by the execution of an exit statement within the statement sequence. Syntactically, the loop statement looks as follows:

LoopStatement = "LOOP" StatementSequence "END".
ExitStatement = "EXIT".

The execution of an *exit statement* in the statement sequence causes termination of the loop. Program execution will continue with the statement immediately following the END of the loop. Thus exit statements are contextually – although not syntactically – bound to their loop statement.

Evidently, the loop statement is more general than either the while statement or repeat statements. The latter two can easily be expressed in terms of a loop statement with a single exit. However, we recommend the use of the loop statement only for cases with more than one exit point (or with an exit point that must lie in the middle of the statement sequence).

The composition of a loop statement typically looks like

> LOOP
>   ...;
>   IF B_1 THEN EXIT;
>   ...
>   IF B_2 THEN EXIT;
>   ...
> END;

where B_1 and B_2 denote expressions of type BOOLEAN.

5.3 Summary

Control statements allow conditional execution of a statement sequence under the control of a Boolean expression. They are *structured statements*; that is, their definition is recursive.

The most basic control statement is the *if statement* that puts a statement sequence under a *guard* – which means the statement sequence is only executed if a Boolean expression holds. The *case statement* specifies the *selection* of a statement sequence – a case – according to the value of an integer expression or character variable.

Two repetitive statements control the iterated execution of a statement sequence under the control of a Boolean expression: the *while statement* and the *repeat statement*. A third repetitive statement, the *loop statement*, allows several exit points within the statement sequence indicated by *exit statements*.

Like the assignment, the control statements are defined formally by axioms that state how a post-condition is transformed into a pre-condition that must hold in order that the specified result be obtained. The axiom of alternatives covers the if statement. In the case of repetition, we have introduced the important concept of a *loop invariant*, a condition that holds prior to every execution of the loop's statement sequence. In addition, a *variant function* is used to assure termination of the repetition.

We have given several simple examples, and have used the axioms to prove their correctness. A more ambitious example is given in Section 8.2.5, where we prove the binary search algorithm.

5.4 Exercises

5.1 Which of the following control statements are well-formed?
CONST c = 3; VAR i, j, k: INTEGER;

(a) REPEAT j := j – 1 UNTIL j = 0;
(b) WHILE j # 0 DO INC(j); IF ODD(j) THEN EXIT END;
(c) IF j>10 THEN j := 10;
(d) CASE i OF 1: j := i | k: j := k END;
(e) CASE i OF 1: j := i | c: j := k END;
(f) LOOP j := j + c UNTIL j > k;
(g) REPEAT j := j + c UNTIL j > k;

5.2 Which of the following loop statements terminate?
VAR i, j, k: INTEGER; VAR y: REAL;

(a) j := 5; REPEAT j := j – 1 UNTIL j = 0;
(b) j := 5; REPEAT j := j – 2 UNTIL j = 0;
(c) j := 5; REPEAT j := j – 2 UNTIL j < 0;
(d) j := –5; REPEAT j := j DIV 2 UNTIL j = 0;
(e) i := 1 j := 1; WHILE i # 100 DO k := i; i := j + i; j := k END;
(f) i := 1 j := 1; WHILE i < 100 DO k := i; i := j + i; j := k END;
(g) i := 1 j := 1; WHILE i < 100 DO j := j + i END;
(h) j := 5; LOOP j := j – 1 END;

5.3 [Min] Write an if statement that assigns the minimum of three integers x, y and z to *min*. Prove correctness, using the axiom of alternatives and the axiom of assignment.

5.4 [Fast multiplication] The following statement sequence computes the product $X*Y$ slightly faster than the sophisticated version of the multiplication given in Section 5.2.2:

```
x := X, y := Y; z := 0;
WHILE x > 0 DO
    IF ODD(x) THEN z := z + y END;
    y := 2*y; x := x DIV 2
END;
```

Why is it permissible to omit the statement $x := x - 1$ that followed $z := z + y$ in the original version?

5.5 [Power] Use repeated multiplication to compute the power x^n, where x is a real and n a positive integer. Formulate invariant and variant functions.

5.6 [Logarithm base 2] The following statement sequence computes the logarithm to the base 2 for real values $1 \leq x < 2$:

```
VAR x, a, b, s: REAL;
a := x;  b := 1;  s := 0;
WHILE b > 0 DO
    a := a*a;  b := b/2;
    IF a >= 2 THEN  s := s + b;  a := a/2  END
END;
```

Establish the invariant $\log_2(x) = s + b*\log_2(a)$. Can you find a variant? Why does the loop terminate? How many iterations are needed to complete?

5.7 [Greatest common divisor] Write a program fragment that computes the *greatest common divisor* of two integers x and y, denoted by $\gcd(x, y)$, by repeated subtraction. Formulate an invariant.

Hint: use the identities (1) $\gcd(x, x) = x$, (2) $\gcd(x, y) = \gcd(y, x)$ and (3) if $x > y$ then $\gcd(x, y) = \gcd(x - y, y)$.

5.8 [Euclid's algorithm] The following method to compute $\gcd(x, y)$ is known as *Euclid's algorithm*:

```
WHILE y > 0 DO
    r := x MOD y;  x := y;  y := r
END;
```

State pre-condition, invariant and variant functions. How can the computation be generalized to include negative integers x and y?

5.9 Work out a few examples of gcd computation using both methods. Which is faster? (See Knuth, 1971).

5.10 [Bisection] Let $f(x)$ denote an expression that computes a real value for a given argument x (how to actually specify user-programmed functions in Oberon is the subject of Chapter 6).

We are interested in finding the root of $f(x)$. A simple and robust method is *bisection*. The procedure starts with an interval $(x1, x2)$ such that $f(x1) > 0$ and $f(x2) < 0$ (or vice versa). The intervals are then successively halved and either $x1$ or $x2$ is set to the midpoint, depending on the sign of $f(x)$ there.

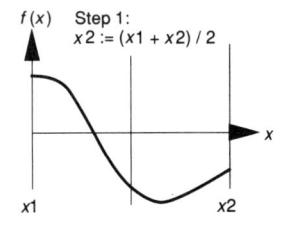

The method of bisection is expressed by the following while loop (assume that $f(x)$ stands for an expression of type REAL):

```
VAR x1, x2, y: REAL;
...
(* (f(x1) > 0) & (f(x2) < 0) & (x1 < x2) *)
x := (x1 + x2)/2;
WHILE (x1 < x) & (x < x2) DO  y := f(x);
    IF y > 0 THEN  x1 := x  ELSE  x2 := x  END;
    x := (x1 + x2)/2
END;
```

Questions:

(a) Work out an example by hand.

(b) Determine the invariant of the loop.

(c) Determine a variant function.

(d) Does the loop terminate for all $x1 \leq x \leq x2$? If yes, how accurate is the computation of the root?

(e) Is the following statement sequence equivalent?

```
WHILE x1 < x2 DO
    x := (x1 + x2)/2;
    y := f(x);
    IF y > 0 THEN x1 := x ELSE x2 := x END
END;
```

References

Cohen E. (1990). *Programming in the 1990s: An Introduction to the Calculus of Programs*. New York: Springer-Verlag.

Gries D. (1981). *The Science of Programming*. New York: Springer-Verlag.

Knuth D.E. (1971). *The Art of Computer Programming* Vol II: *Seminumerical Algorithms*, pp. 293–338. Reading, MA: Addison-Wesley.

6 Procedures and modules

Thus far, we have introduced two broad notions:

(1) *declarations* that bind an identifier to a type or a value;
(2) *statement sequences including control statements* that express algorithms.

This chapter connects the two concepts by establishing *textual scopes*, namely *procedures* and *modules*.

In its simplest form, the procedure can be visualized as a *named statement sequence*. In essence, a module is a textual scope comprising constant and variable declarations and a number of procedures.[1] The module is the *unit that is accepted by the compiler*. Translated modules, termed object modules, can be stored in the computer's library, and are units that are loaded into the memory for execution.

Operating systems afford controls that allow the user to execute code stored in the computer's object library. In Oberon, the unit that can be executed is the procedure. This contrasts with the traditional notion of a main program being the basic executable unit.[2]

A procedure, however, goes far beyond the simple notion of a named statement sequence. In particular, it encompasses:

- the concept of *local variables*;
- the concept of a *result*: a procedure with a result can be used as a factor in expressions, like the predeclared functions such as ABS(x);
- the concept of *parameters* that are passed to the procedure like the arguments of a mathematical function.

In the way that a procedure is more than a named statement sequence, a module goes beyond a mere compilation unit. It may have

---

[1] Later we will also introduce type declarations.
[2] For example, in PL/I it is the procedure with the option main, in Modula-2 the main module.

63

an optional statement sequence and – more importantly – controls the visibility of declared identifiers beyond its scope. For example, if a procedure is intended to be invoked by the computer operator, it must be marked for visibility outside the module.

Box 6.1
A fractal fern

Fractals are fascinating objects of mathematics. The observation by Mandelbrot of the existence of a 'fractal geometry of nature' has led to a new way of thinking about many natural phenomena such as the length of coastlines or the edges of clouds (Mandelbrot, 1977).

A simple algorithm – known as the *iterated function system* (IFS) – produces the fractal fern shown on the left (Barnsley, 1988). The fern is drawn by a pen that moves over the drawing area and paints a dot at a computed sequence of consecutive points. If the pen is at a point (x, y) then the next point is computed by applying a simple transformation of its coordinates:

$$x_{new} = ax + by + e \qquad (1)$$
$$y_{new} = cx + dy + f \qquad (2)$$

Equations (1) and (2) are called an affine transformation. The art of producing an interesting picture such as a natural scene is to find a sequence of such transformations that are *applied at random* to determine the position of the moving pen. The fern is produced by the following four transformations:

a	b	c	d	e	f	p	Action
0	0	0	0.16	0	0	0.01	Stem
0.85	0.04	–0.04	0.85	0	1.6	0.85	Turn of leave
0.2	–0.26	0.23	0.22	0	1.6	0.07	Right sub-leaves
–0.15	0.28	0.26	0.24	0	0.44	0.07	Left sub-leaves

The column labelled p contains the probability with which the respective transformation is applied. The table contains all the information about the fern. While storing the pixels of the fern's image may require hundreds of thousands or even millions of bits, the table can be stored in about 1000 bits – a tremendous compression. However, finding the set of transformations characterizing an arbitrary scene remains a difficult task.

Both procedures and modules play important roles in the *structuring of complex programs*. An explanation of these roles, however, has to wait until Chapter 10. In this chapter, we will deal with the syntax and semantics of procedures and modules. We will do this by means of an example – drawing a fractal fern, see Boxes 6.1 and 6.2.

Box 6.2
Iterated function system: Oberon formulation

The algorithm for drawing a fractal fern relies on a random selection of a particular transformation. Assuming that rn is a uniform random variable between 0 and 1, a random selection with given probabilities $p1, p2, p3$ and $p4$ is achieved as follows:

```
IF rn < p1 THEN ...              (* first selection *)
ELSIF rn < (p1 + p2) THEN ...    (* second selection *)
ELSIF rn < (p1 + p2 + p3) THEN ...(* third selection *)
ELSE ...                          (* fourth selection *)
END;
```

It is now easy to write the statement sequence of an algorithm to draw the fractal fern:

```
"open a viewer representing a drawing plane";
X := 0;  Y := 0;  (* initial position of pen *)
REPEAT
    "Generate a real random number rn (0 < rn <=1)";
    IF rn < p1 THEN
        x := a1*X + b1*Y + e1;    y := c1*X + d1*Y + f1
    ELSIF rn < (p1 + p2) THEN
        x := a2*X + b2*Y + e2;    y := c2*X + d2*Y + f2
    ELSIF rn < (p1 + p2 + p3) THEN
        x := a3*X + b3*Y + e3;    y := c3*X + d3*Y + f3
    ELSE
        x := a4*X + b4*Y + e4;    y := c4*X + d4*Y + f4
    END;
    X := x;  Y := y;
    "Paint dot at position (X, Y)"
UNTIL "User terminates loop ";
```

This sequence of statements is merely a fragment of an Oberon program. The actions to open a viewer, compute a random number, paint a dot, and provide a user-enacted termination stimulus are not yet formally specified. We also know that all variables must be declared. We will fill in the missing part in the remainder of this chapter and in Chapter 7.

6.1 The procedure: a statement sequence with a name

Like all objects of the Oberon language, a procedure needs to be declared. The procedure declaration consists of a procedure heading and a procedure body. The heading specifies the procedure identifier and possibly parameters and a result type. The body is composed of a declaration sequence and a statement sequence. The procedure declaration is terminated with the symbol "END" followed by a repetition of the identifier. Formally, the syntax is given by

> ProcedureDeclaration =
>   ProcedureHeading ";" ProcedureBody ident.
> ProcedureHeading =
>   "PROCEDURE" ident ["*"] [FormalParameters].
> ProcedureBody = DeclarationSequence
>   ["BEGIN" StatementSequence]
>   "END".

The declaration sequence, the export mark (asterisk "*") and the formal parameters will be described in subsequent sections.

In its simplest form, the procedure is composed of a heading with a mere identifier and a body that consists of a statement sequence only. This is the named statement sequence mentioned before. We are now able to complete the example of Box 6.2 by casting the statement sequence that draws a fractal fern into a procedure called *Draw*:

    PROCEDURE Draw;
    BEGIN
        ... (* Statement sequence of Box 6.2 *)
    END Draw;

Note that it is assumed that all variables that occur in the statement sequence are declared in a larger context (the module) in which the procedure is embedded.

Procedure call

To exercise the statement sequence of a procedure, *it has to be called* or *invoked*. Such a call can originate from another procedure or from a human operator of the computing system.

For the simple (parameter-less) procedure, the call statement consists simply of the procedure identifier, for example

    ... Draw; ...

When the call statement is executed, control passes to the first statement in the statement sequence of the procedure. After the procedure is finished, processing resumes with the statement that follows the call.

Processing of a procedure terminates with the execution of the last statement in its statement sequence or explicitly with a return statement (see Section 6.4.2).

The procedure concept would be useful, even if restricted to the simple form discussed so far. Two additional features, however, forge it into an essential programming tool: the locality of identifiers and the notion of parameters.

6.2 The concept of locality

Procedure *Draw* operates on two groups of variables:

(1) X, Y, x, y and rn;
(2) $a1...a4, b1...b4, c1...c4, d1...d4, e1...e4, f1...f4$ and $p1...p4$.

The first group comprises variables defining pen position and random numbers. They are strictly local to the procedure; hence they are termed *local variables*. In contrast, the variables of the second group have global significance.

All objects – in particular, variables – must be declared. *The declaration sequence in the procedure body is used to define local objects* such as the variables of the first group. The syntax of the declaration sequence is given by the EBNF production

> DeclarationSequence =
>   { "CONST" {ConstDeclaration ";"}
> | "TYPE" {TypeDeclaration ";"}[1]
> | "VAR" {VarDeclaration ";"}}
> | {ProcedureDeclaration ";"}.

The declaration sequence lists constant declarations, variable declarations and type declarations in any order, followed by the procedure declarations. Since the declarations in the body of a procedure are strictly local to that procedure, export marks are not meaningful.

To give an example, we refine procedure *Draw* by making the first group of variables local:

---

[1] Type declarations are the subject of Section 8.1.

```
PROCEDURE Draw;
VAR
    X, Y: REAL;  (* local variables for pen position *)
    x, y: REAL;  (* local variables for new position *)
    rn: REAL;    (* local variable for random number *)

BEGIN
    ... (* Statement sequence of Box 6.2 *)
END Draw;
```

6.2.1 Scope

The section of program text in which an identifier is defined is called its *scope*. The object represented by such an identifier can only be used within its scope. The scope of declarations appearing in the body of a procedure is the remainder of that body. Applied to variables, the locality concept asserts that they exist only within their scope. Therefore the value of a local variable is not defined when the procedure is called, and, similarly, its value is lost upon termination. Hence, if a variable should retain its value between successive calls of a procedure, it must be declared outside of the procedure. As a consequence, *local variables consume memory resources only during the execution of the statement sequence of their procedure*. As soon as control reverts to the statement following the call, the memory of the local variables is released.

In our example, the scope of the variables X, Y, x, y and rn is the procedure *Draw* – specifically the text from their declaration to the terminating symbol "END". Suppose that the identifier rn also designates an object outside of *Draw*, a procedure, say. The local declaration of rn excludes this procedure from the scope of the text representing the procedure *Draw*. The programmer is thus free to *reuse identifiers*. In fact, local identifiers can be used without the need to know all globally defined objects. This decoupling of knowledge about different program parts is particularly useful – even vital – in the design of large programs created by a team of programmers.

6.2.2 Nesting of scopes

What is noteworthy about the syntax of the declaration sequence is that the procedure declaration is recursive. In other words, the declaration sequence of a procedure may contain nested procedure declarations. In analogy to local variables, the procedures thus defined are local objects within the scope of their enclosing procedure.

Scope rules Since procedure declarations can be nested, their scopes follow this nesting pattern. The scope rules are best remembered by the method used to search the declaration of an identifier, i say. First, search the declarations of the procedure P in which i is used. If the declaration of i is not among them, continue the search in the procedure or module (see Section 6.3) surrounding P; then repeat this rule until the declaration is encountered. If an identifier is not declared, the text is not a valid Oberon program unless it is one of the predeclared identifiers. These standard identifiers are considered to be declared in an *imaginary global scope enveloping all modules*.

6.2.3 Advantage of locality

It is good programming practice to declare objects locally. This confines their existence to the procedure in which they have meaning. In summary, the use of local variables has the following significant advantages:

- The declaration is textually close to the use of the object, aiding in the readability of the program text.
- The inadvertent use of a global object locally is eliminated. There is no need to know all global objects.
- Memory requirements can be minimized because local variables are released upon termination of the procedure to which they belong.

6.3 Modules

The module is another construct that defines a scope. In the previous section, we have referred to a 'larger context' in which variables were assumed to be declared. For procedures that are not local to other procedures, such as *Draw*, this context is the *module*. Oberon modules observe the syntax

```
module = "MODULE" ident ";"
         [ ImportList ]
         DeclarationSequence
         ["BEGIN" StatementSequence ]
         "END" ident ".".
```

The two identifiers must match. The import list and the statement sequence are optional.

Let us cast the IFS example into a module:

Declaration sequence

```
MODULE IFS;
VAR
    a1, b1, c1, d1, e1, f1, p1: REAL;   (* 1st affine transformation *)
    a2, b2, c2, d2, e2, f2, p2: REAL;   (* 2nd affine transformation *)
    a3, b3, c3, d3, e3, f3, p3: REAL;   (* 3rd affine transformation *)
    a4, b4, c4, d4, e4, f4, p4: REAL;   (* 4th affine transformation *)

PROCEDURE Draw*;
    ... (* Procedure body *)
END Draw;
```

Statement sequence

```
BEGIN
    a1 := 0.0;     a2 := 0.85;    a3 := 0.2;     a4 := –0.15;
    b1 := 0.0;     b2 := 0.04;    b3 := –0.26;   b4 := 0.28;
    c1 := 0.0;     c2 := –0.04;   c3 := 0.23;    c4 := 0.26;
    d1 := 0.16;    d2 := 0.85;    d3 := 0.22;    d4 := 0.24;
    e1 := 0.0;     e2 := 0.0;     e3 := 0.0;     e4 := 0.0;
    f1 := 0.0;     f3 := 1.6;     f3 := 1.6;     f4 := 0.44;
    p1 := 0.01;    p3 := 0.07;    p3 := 0.07;    p4 := 0.07
END IFS.
```

Our sample module contains a declaration sequence specifying the variables $a1 \ldots p4$, the procedure *Draw* and a statement sequence that assigns values to the global variables.

6.3.1 The scope defined by a module; declaration of global variables

Like the procedure, the module defines a scope for the identifier declared in its declaration sequence. The scope extends from the point where the identifier is declared to the final "END" of the module. Procedures declared within the module open a nested scope, and the rules for nested scopes apply.

Static scope, Global variables

Each time the procedure is executed, its scope is newly opened – the local variables are newly defined. In contrast, the *scope of the module is static*. The module is in existence for the whole computation or the whole user session. This means that variables declared in a module also exist – and consume storage – throughout the duration of the module's activation. We call these variables *global variables*. In contrast to procedures, modules cannot be nested.

The module as compilation unit

In order for Oberon texts to be executable on a machine, they require a translation into machine code by a compiler. In Oberon, the syntactical unit accepted by the compiler is the module. Translated modules are called *object modules*. They are part of libraries residing on disk storage, and may be loaded into the machine's memory for execution.

6.3.2 The statement sequence of a module

The statement sequence of a module is executed when the module is first activated and thus loaded into memory. The statement sequence in our example is quite typical – it is used to *initialize global variables*. Thus, when module *IFS* is first loaded into memory, the assignments are carried out and the global variables receive their initial values.

6.3.3 Export and import of declarations

Declared objects such as variables and procedures are visible only within their scope that is opaque if viewed from the outside. This scope rule also applies to the module – its only external property is the module name. Clearly, a mechanism is needed to make objects of the module accessible from the outside. The procedure *Draw* from module *IFS* is an example: it should be made known to the operating system, to be invoked from the computer's controls. Procedure *Uniform* from module *RandomNumbers*, which we encountered in Chapter 2, is another example. We would like to be able to call it in procedures declared in other modules – for example in *IFS*, where random numbers are needed. The *export mark* and the *import list* are the constructs that Oberon provides to make the module scopes partially transparent.

Export mark

Any identifier being declared in a module may be marked for export. Exported variables or procedures are visible outside the scope of the module. *The export mark is an asterisk following the identifier being declared.* For example, in the declaration sequence

```
VAR height*, width*, i, j: INTEGER;
PROCEDURE Draw*;
   ... (* declaration and statement sequence *)
END Proc;
```

the variables *height* and *width* and the procedure *Draw* are marked for export.

Import list

The library of a given computer may contain a large number of modules. Clearly, it is not beneficial if all objects exported by them are simultaneously visible within each module. One of the important benefits of the module concept is that programs may be written by different programmers, who do not need to know the declarations and conventions made in other modules except, of course, those that they intend to use. The *import list* and the *qualified identifier* provide the mechanism to avoid naming conflicts.

Those modules whose exported declarations should become visible in a given module have to be imported explicitly. The imported modules appear in the import list, which immediately follows the module heading and has syntax

```
importList = "IMPORT" import {"," import} ";".
import = ident [":=" ident].
```

For example,

```
MODULE IFS;
IMPORT RN := RandomNumbers, XYplane;
... (* declaration and statement sequence *)
END IFS.
```

Within the scope of module *IFS*, the declarations of the exported objects of modules *RandomNumbers* and *XYplane* are visible. In the form *M1* := *M*, the imported module is known under the *alias* M1 in the scope of the importing module. Thus, in the example, *RandomNumbers* is known as *RN*.

Qualified identifier

Imported objects are always referred to by a *qualified identifier* consisting of a prefix – the exporting module's name or alias – followed by the name of the object. For example, assume that *V* is an exported variable of a module *M*. Then it is referred to in a module that imports *M* as

M.V

A qualified identifier is used as a designator in expressions and assignments in the same way as a simple identifier. In EBNF notation,

> qualident = [ident "."] ident.
> designator = qualident.[1]

A qualified identifier is composed of two juxtaposed identifiers separated by a period. Oberon considers the qualified identifier *M.V* to be different from the simple identifier *V*. Therefore *V* may be simultaneously declared in module *M* as well as in the client of *M*.

In the previous example of module *IFS*, the procedure *Uniform* from module *RandomNumbers* is called as *RN.Uniform*. Assuming that module *XYplane* exports a variable *W*, that variable is referenced by *XYplane.W*.

Commands

In an Oberon system, the main computations are performed by the statement sequences of procedures that are exported by modules.[2] Such procedures are also called *commands*. *Draw* in sample module *IFS* is such a command.

The system running Oberon provides facilities allowing the operator to activate commands from the system controls. An example of such a system was provided in Chapter 2.

6.4 Function procedures and parameters

The function is an important concept in mathematics. The formula

$$r = f(x, y) \tag{1}$$

states that *r* is the result of the computation *f* applied to the arguments *x* and *y*. While the notation (1) makes the value of the arguments explicit, mathematicians often use another notation – that of the *mapping*. If we assume that *f* is integer-valued and operates on integer arguments *x* and *y*, the mapping *f* is expressed formally as

$$f: \mathfrak{J} \times \mathfrak{J} \to \mathfrak{J} \tag{2}$$

---

[1] More general designators will be introduced later.
[2] To be precise, parameter-less procedures (parameters will be discussed in subsequent sections).

In (2), $\mathfrak{I}$ denotes the set of integer numbers and $\mathfrak{I} \times \mathfrak{I}$ their Cartesian product. Equation (2) reads 'f maps each pair of integers into an integer.' In contrast to (1), the range of values admissible as arguments and produced by the mapping are clearly indicated.

Oberon supports the notion of the mathematical function. In Chapter 4 we have already come across a number of predeclared functions such as ABS(*x*), ASH(*i, n*) and ODD(*i*) that perform a computation on their arguments and return a result. Such functions may be factors in expressions, for example

$$x := y + ABS(z).$$

The function introduces two new concepts:

(1) The function identifier stands for a statement sequence (a computation) as well as for a *result*.
(2) The function has arguments, called *parameters*, which pass input values to the computation.

Oberon allows programmers to define their own functions by declaring *function procedures*. Let us start with a simple illustration:

```
PROCEDURE Min(x, y: INTEGER): INTEGER;
BEGIN
    IF x <= y THEN RETURN x ELSE RETURN y END
END Min;
```

The procedure heading defines the identifier *Min* to be a function procedure. It specifies *formal parameters* (*x* and *y*) and their type as well as a *result type* (after the colon). The return statement terminates the statement sequence and returns the result to the point of invocation.

6.4.1 The function procedure heading

The function procedure heading *must have formal parameters*. The formal parameter list is enclosed in parentheses and follows the function identifier. It consists of formal parameter sections, which look like variable declarations. The formal parameter sections define name and type of the parameters that serve as arguments of the function. The type of the result is shown following the right parenthesis, from which it is separated by a colon. The EBNF definition of the function procedure is

ProcedureHeading =
    "PROCEDURE" ident ["*"] FormalParameters.
FormalParameters =
    "(" [FPSection {";" FPSection}] ")" ":"qualident.
FPSection = ["VAR"] ident {"," ident} ":" FormalType.
FormalType = qualident.[1]

The qualident that terminates *FormalParameters* denotes the type of the result. It must be a *simple type*; that is, array and record structures cannot be the result of function procedures (see Chapter 8). The option VAR preceding the identifier list will be explained in Section 6.5.2.

A few examples of function procedure headings may be instructive:

    PROCEDURE gcd(x, y: INTEGER): INTEGER;
    PROCEDURE power(x: REAL; i: INTEGER): REAL;
    PROCEDURE XYinRect(x, y, X, Y, W, H: REAL): BOOLEAN;
    PROCEDURE New* (text: Texts.Text; pos: LONGINT): Frame;[2]
    PROCEDURE InitText*(f: Files.File; p: LONGINT): Texts.Text;
    PROCEDURE Uniform(): REAL;

The last example is a procedure heading without parameters, such as our random number generator of the introduction. The empty parentheses are mandatory.

In a sense, the Oberon procedure heading combines the characteristics of the two mathematical notations: it introduces names for the parameters as in (1) and defines the ranges of parameter and function values as in (2).

6.4.2 Formal parameters and the return statement

Within the statement sequence of the procedure, *the formal parameters may be used exactly like local variables*. The fact that they are declared in the procedure heading rather than in the body's declaration sequence ensures that they have a *defined initial value*, namely the one specified by their corresponding actual parameters at the time of the call (see Section 6.4.3). As is the case with local variables, memory for formal parameters is only tied up when the function's scope is active.

---

[1] A more general *FormalType* will be introduced in Chapter 8.
[2] This is an example involving declared types. The type *Frame* is declared in the same module whereas *Text* is a type exported by module *Texts*. See Chapter 8.

The function declaration is characterized by the indication of the result's type behind the parenthesized list of formal parameters. In the function's body, the return statement ends the computation and passes the result to the point of invocation. It consists of the symbol "RETURN" followed by an expression yielding a result:

| ReturnStatement = RETURN [expression].

The expression must be assignment-compatible with the result type specified in the procedure heading (Table 4.3); at least one return statement is mandatory.

6.4.3 Actual parameters, the function call

The function call is a factor in an expression. We recapitulate its syntax:

| FunctionCall = designator "(" [ActualParameters] ")".
| ActualParameters = expression {"," expression}.

For the time being, a designator is simply a qualident that denotes a function procedure. We will encounter more complex designators later.

Each expression is an actual parameter that is used to initialize a corresponding formal parameter. Evidently, the number of expressions must match the number of formal parameters. Actual parameters are paired with formal parameters according to their respective position in the list. At the time of the function call, the expression is evaluated and *its value assigned to the formal parameter*. Therefore the expression must be assignment-compatible with the type of the formal parameter (see Table 4.3).

For example, consider the procedure *Min* listed earlier. A possible function call to *Min* is

$$Min(3*i + j, 17)$$

At the time of the call, the expression $3*i + j$ is evaluated and assigned to formal parameter x. Subsequently, the constant 17, syntactically also an expression, is assigned to y. Then control passes to the first statement of procedure *Min*. The result is returned to the point of call after the first return statement executed.

6.5 Proper procedures

Earlier, we portrayed the procedure as a named statement sequence that can be called from another point in a program text or that can be executed as a command. To distinguish it from the function procedure, we also speak of a *proper procedure*.

Parameters can also be associated with proper procedures. The benefits are twofold:

(1) When the procedure represents a general computation, such as determining the roots of a polynomial, it can be applied to various sets of variables without changing its text.

(2) Identifiers used within the procedure are decoupled from the names adopted elsewhere in the program.

Such a decoupling is essential if a large programming task should be attempted by a team of programmers. For this purpose, however, the parameter mechanism needs to be generalized to encompass the *concept of substitution*. Before we will turn to this generalization, we state the syntax of the proper procedure and of the call statement.

6.5.1 Syntax, the call statement

The proper procedure is identified through its heading with EBNF syntax:

> ProcedureHeading = "PROCEDURE" ident ["*"] [FormalParameters].
> FormalParameters = "(" [FPSection {";" FPSection}] ")".
> FPSection = ["VAR"] ident {"," ident} ":" FormalType.
> FormalType = qualident.[1]

Proper procedure headings are, for example,

> PROCEDURE Draw*;
> PROCEDURE ComputeRoots(a, b, c: REAL; VAR r1, r2, i1, i2: REAL);

Return statement The return statement may also appear in a proper procedure. In this case, it is optional and consists of the solitary keyword "RETURN". When executing a return statement, processing of the procedure's

---

[1] A more general *FormalType* will be introduced in Chapter 8.

statement sequence is terminated and control returns to the statement immediately following the call.

Call statement The call of a proper procedure is a statement with syntax:

> ProcedureCall = designator ["(" ActualParameters ")"].
> ActualParameters = expression {"," expression}.

As in the case of the function procedure, the actual parameters are paired with the formal ones.

6.5.2 Value and variable parameters

From previous examples, we are familiar with the fact that a (proper) procedure may *interact with the state of the computation through global variables*. The benefit that one expects from the concept of parameters is a *decoupling of the procedure text from global variables*.

Value parameters The formal parameters introduced so far are like local variables. In order to refer to this type of parameter, we speak of a *value parameter* – the value of the expression that represents the actual parameter is assigned to the formal parameter prior to execution of the procedure's statement sequence.

Variable parameters Evidently, value parameters serve only to pass information *to* the procedure. We seek a parameter scheme that empowers the proper procedure to change the global state of the computation. This is possible through the notion of *substitution*.

Such a scheme passes an actual variable and not merely its value to the procedure. We therefore speak of a *variable parameter*. Variable parameters are specified with the keyword "VAR" in front of the formal parameter section. For example,

> PROCEDURE ComputeRoots(a, b, c: REAL; VAR r1, r2, i1, i2: REAL);

has two sets of parameters: *a, b* and *c* are value parameters, and *r1, r2, i1* and *i2* are variable parameters, used to return results.

As the name implies, the actual parameter corresponding to a variable parameter *must be a variable*. If the formal variable parameter changes its value within the procedure, for example by means of an assignment, the corresponding actual parameter is changed accordingly. Thus the formal *variable parameter substitutes a different local name for the corresponding actual parameter*. This achieves the desired decoupling from the global environment and represents a flexible substitution mechanism of variable names.

Syntactically, actual parameters are expressions. An actual parameter corresponding to a formal variable parameter *must be an expression composed of a single designator*. At this point, the only such expression is a solitary qualident. Designators corresponding to structured types may be a little more complex, such as an array element (a[i+j]) or the field of a record (r.f). Structured types are introduced in Chapter 8. No memory is consumed in the procedure to account for variable parameters and no assignment takes place.

Type rule

The substitution mechanism of the variable parameter requires that the types of the actual parameter and the corresponding formal parameter must be identical.[1]

Let us proceed with an example – the evaluation of the roots of the quadratic equation

$$ax^2 + bx + c = 0.$$

There are two solutions, which may be complex numbers. Their respective real and imaginary parts are denoted by $r1$, $r2$, $i1$ and $i2$. The multitude of output variables precludes the use of a function procedure, which would be natural for such computations as the square root.

We therefore opt for a proper procedure that returns the result by means of variable parameters:

```
PROCEDURE ComputeRoots(a, b, c: REAL; VAR r1, r2, i1, i2: REAL);
VAR det: REAL;
BEGIN
  b := b/2; det := b*b – a*c;
  IF det >= 0 THEN (* real roots *)
    r1 := (ABS(b) + sqrt(det))/a;
    IF b >= 0 THEN r1 := –r1 END;
    r2 := c/(a*r1);² i1 := 0; i2 := 0
```

---

[1] This is somewhat generalized in the case of record types and their extension; see Chapter 11.
[2] The second real root is computed using the theorem of Vieta to avoid possible loss of accuracy when one of the roots is close to zero.

ELSE (* complex roots *)
    r1 := –b/a; r2 := r1; i1 := sqrt(–det); i2 := –i1
  END
END ComputeRoots;
```

The first three formal parameters are value parameters and pass the coefficients *a*, *b* and *c* to the procedure.

The remaining four parameters are variable parameters used to report the real and imaginary parts of the roots. A possible call of the procedure *ComputeRoots* is

    ComputeRoots(2.0, x*y, q, r1, r2, i1, i2);

## 6.6 More on function procedures

### 6.6.1 Side-effects

Pursuing a tutorial development, we have introduced the concepts of the function procedure and value parameters together. However, function procedures are by no means restricted to that mechanism – in addition to the result returned to the point of call, they may change the state of the computation through global variables and through variable parameters. Such a change is termed a *side-effect* of the function.

Our very first example, the procedure *Uniform*, is a function procedure with a side-effect. We recapitulate:

    PROCEDURE Uniform(): REAL;
    CONST a = 16807; m = 2147483647; q = m DIV a; r = m MOD a;
    VAR g: LONGINT;
    BEGIN
      g := a*(z MOD q) – r*(z DIV q);
      IF g > 0 THEN z := g ELSE z := g + m END;
      RETURN z*1.0 / m
    END Uniform;

The side-effect of a call to *Uniform* is the change of the global variable *z*. This is, of course, the essence of the intended recurrence relation that produces our random numbers. However, consider the following two statement sequences:

    z := 1; x := z + Uniform();
```

and

> z := 1; x := Uniform() + z;

In the first case, the value of x is 1.0000080E+00; in the second case, we find 1.6807000E+04 – seemingly defying the commutative law of addition. The programmer should always be fully aware of the capability of side-effects to produce unexpected results when the function is used inappropriately.

We emphasize that changes of global variables through side-effects of functions is considered neither desirable practice nor good programming style. Nevertheless, it is sometimes justified, as in the case of Uniform. In any case, *side-effects should be restricted to variables that do not occur in the call's parameter list.*

6.6.2 Recursion

Of course, the statement sequence of a procedure may contain calls to other procedures. Since any procedure that is visible can be called, a procedure may call itself. This self-reactivation is called *recursion*. Its use is natural when either the algorithm or the data structure is defined recursively.

One of the simplest examples is furnished by the factorial, which is defined by:

$$\text{fact}(0) = 1 \qquad (1)$$
$$\text{fact}(n) = n \, \text{fact}(n-1) \quad \text{for } n = 1, 2, \ldots \qquad (2)$$

which translates into

```
PROCEDURE fact(n: INTEGER): LONGINT;
BEGIN
  IF n = 0 THEN RETURN 1
  ELSE RETURN n*fact(n – 1)
END fact;
```

It is important that the recursion terminate. The test for $n = 0$ ensures termination in the case of *fact*. Besides loop statements, recursive procedures are another source of nonterminating programs.

Of course, we recognize that the factorial can be almost as easily computed using iteration:

```
PROCEDURE fact(n: INTEGER): LONGINT;
VAR fact: LONGINT;
BEGIN  fact := 1;
    WHILE n > 0 DO  fact := fact*n;  DEC(n) END;  RETURN fact
END fact;
```

Since every procedure call causes some overhead for bookkeeping, the second version should be expected to run more efficiently. A repetitive formulation is always possible, in principle, but it may obscure the algorithm to such a degree that the gain in execution time is not worth the effort.

We will introduce more interesting examples of recursive procedures in Section 9.3 when discussing trees.

6.7 Compiler hints

The goals of the designer of a language and the implementer of its compiler are sometimes at odds – the former wishing to adopt constructs of maximal convenience to the user, the latter advocating compromises in the syntax leading to a simple compiler. One such compromise is the *one-pass compiler* that promises to be especially fast. Since such a compiler cannot look ahead, it requires a *forward declaration* when a procedure call occurs textually before the respective procedure declaration. The forward declaration has syntax:

```
DeclarationSequence =
    { "CONST" {ConstDeclaration ";"}
    | "TYPE" {TypeDeclaration ";"}
    | "VAR" {VarDeclaration ";"}}
    | {ProcedureDeclaration ";" | ForwardDeclaration ";" }.
ForwardDeclaration = "PROCEDURE" "↑"[1]
                ident ["*"] [ FormalParameters ].
```

The actual declaration following the forward declaration – which specifies the body of the procedure – must have exactly the same name and formal parameter list. The symbol "↑" decrees the forward declaration.

---

[1] In the standard ASCII character set "↑" is represented by the caret "^" with ORD("^") = 94.

Some Oberon compilers require that procedures intended to be assigned to procedure variables or used as parameters are marked with an asterisk following "PROCEDURE", viz.

> ProcedureHeading =
> "PROCEDURE" ["*"] indent ["*"] [FormalParameters].

Note that only one of the asterisks is required, in other words, the export mark (after *indent*) implies the first mark.

6.8 Summary

In this chapter, we have introduced a wealth of concepts and constructs that can be summarized in a cursory fashion only.

(1) Modules and procedures define a *scope* – that is, a stretch of program text in which declarations are valid. The *concept of locality* states that declarations are local to their scope.

(2) The *module* establishes a global scope – its declarations define *global objects*, constants, types (see Chapter 8), variables, and procedures that are valid throughout the computation. The module is also the compilation unit. Declarations may be made visible outside of the module's scope by means of *export marks*, and exported identifiers of other modules can be imported.

The module may have an optional *statement sequence* that executes at the time the module is loaded into memory. This statement sequence is typically used to initialize global variables.

(3) The *procedure* is a named statement sequence and a parameter mechanism. Procedures are either *function procedures* or *proper procedures*. The statement sequence of the procedure can be executed from any point in the program through a call statement or a function call. Procedures can be *recursive*.

(4) *Parameters* are used to pass values to and from the procedure. The *formal parameters* appear in the procedure heading, *actual parameters* in the call statement. Parameters come in two varieties: value parameters and variable parameters.

A *value parameter* acts like a local variable that is initialized by the results of evaluating their corresponding actual parameters. An assignment takes place. Memory is allocated for the formal parameter during the time the procedure is active.

A *variable parameter* ("VAR") implements the notion of substitution. The actual parameter is substituted for the formal one. Assignments made to the formal parameter are assignments to the actual parameter. Variable parameters are used to return results.

(5) The *return statement* terminates the execution of a procedure. In the case of a function procedure, it returns the result to the point of call.

(6) If a function procedure changes the state of the computation through assignments made to global variables or variable parameters, a *side-effect* is said to have occurred.

We have used a common example to derive the main concepts: drawing a fractal fern. This chapter is about the basics: how to apply procedures and modules properly will remain a major theme throughout the rest of the book. The example of the fractal fern will be completed in Chapter 7, after the introduction of appropriate input and output operations.

6.9 Exercises

6.1 Which of the following procedure headings are legal?

(a) PROCEDURE f(x: REAL): ARRAY OF CHAR;
(b) PROCEDURE f(x: REAL): REAL;
(c) PROCEDURE g(i: INTEGER): VAR x: REAL;
(d) PROCEDURE P(x: REAL, y: CHAR);
(e) PROCEDURE P(x: REAL), (y: CHAR);
(f) PROCEDURE Q(a, b, c: REAL; VAR r1, r2, i1, i2: REAL);

6.2 Assume

CONST x1 = 1; x2 = 2; x3 = 3; x4 = 4; x = 3.14159;
VAR a, b, c, aR, bR, aI, bI: REAL; i: INTEGER;
    xR, yR, xI, yI: LONGREAL;
PROCEDURE Root(a, b, c: REAL; VAR x1, x2, y1, y2: REAL);
PROCEDURE Sin(x: REAL): REAL;
PROCEDURE Min(x, y: INTEGER): INTEGER;

Which of the following statements containing procedure calls are correct?

Root(a, b, c, aR, bR, aI, bI);   Root(1, 3, 4, x1, x2, x3, x4);
Sin(3.14159);   a := Sin(x1);   i := Min(x, x1);   i := Min(x1, x2);
Root(a, b, c, 3, 4, 5, 6);   Root(a, 3*b, c + 1, xR, yR, xI, yI);

6.9 Exercises

6.3 Is the following an Oberon module? If not, which are the errors?

```
MODULE M;
CONST a = 10;  IMPORT Math;
PROCEDURE P(x: INTEGER): INTEGER;
    RETURN x*x
END P;
VAR y: REAL;
BEGIN  y := P(a)
END M;
```

6.4 [**Scope rules**] Identify the scopes of all identifiers in the following module. Find one error. What is the value of the global variables after module M is loaded into memory (given that the error is corrected)?

```
MODULE M;
VAR i, j: INTEGER;
PROCEDURE A*;
VAR i: INTEGER;
PROCEDURE B*(VAR i, j: INTEGER);
VAR k: INTEGER;
BEGIN k := i;  i := j;  j := k  END B;
BEGIN  i := 2; B(i, j)
END A;
PROCEDURE C;
BEGIN  A; i := 2*j  END C;
BEGIN  C
END M.
```

6.5 What is wrong with the following procedure?

```
PROCEDURE Square(x: REAL): REAL;
VAR y: REAL;
BEGIN  y := x*x
END Square;
```

6.6 [**Fibonacci numbers**] The Fibonacci numbers are defined by the recurrence relation

$$f_0 = 1, \ f_1 = 1, \ f_n = f_{n-1} + f_{n-2} \quad \text{for } n = 2, 3, \ldots$$

Using recursion and iteration, write two versions of a procedure with heading

PROCEDURE Fibonacci(n: INTEGER): INTEGER;

that computes f_n.

How many recursive invocations of *Fibonacci* result from a call to *Fibonacci(n)*? Similarly, how many iterative steps are needed? Why is the iterative solution so much faster (independent of the bookkeeping of recursive function calls)? *Hint*: consider whether the work to compute f_{n-1} is independent of f_{n-2}.

6.7 Determine the number of function calls of the recursive version of *Fibonacci* empirically. *Hint*: use a side-effect. Is this a legitimate use of a side-effect?

6.8 What mathematical function does F compute?

```
PROCEDURE F(n: INTEGER): INTEGER;
VAR i, j: INTEGER;
BEGIN  i := 1; j := 1;
    WHILE n > 1 DO i := i + j; j := i - j; DEC(n) END
END F;
```

6.9 [**Exponential random numbers**] An exponential random number rn_{exp} can be obtained from a uniform random number rn_{uni} (see Box 10.1). Augment module *RandomNumbers* from Chapter 2 with

PROCEDURE Exp(mu: REAL): REAL

which produces exponentially distributed random numbers. Assume that a module *Math* is available that exports the logarithm *ln*(x: REAL): REAL.

References

Barnsley M. (1988). *Fractals Everywhere*. New York: Academic Press.
Mandelbrot B. B. (1977). *The Fractal Geometry of Nature*. San Francisco: W. H. Freeman.

7 Input and output

One of the foundations of the success of high-level programming languages is the *principle of abstraction*. The essence of abstraction is the hiding of details pertaining to the specific computer that is used to execute a program. Different languages and systems differ in the abstractions that are advocated. Since abstraction means hiding of details, it invariably also precludes the use of some facilities – presumably existing to perform a certain task directly and efficiently. Simplification and generalization by suppression of details is then in direct conflict with the desire for transparency for efficient use.

While a consensus seems to emerge as far as basic types and control structures are concerned, a great diversity is observed in the area of *input and output operations*, especially when considering the graphics subsystems of modern workstations.

Recognizing this intrinsic dilemma, Oberon does not incorporate input and output abstractions in its language definition. This approach is made possible by two facts:

(1) *Abstractions are not only delivered through the language, but also through the module concept.* The module allows hiding of details – only those data and procedures consciously marked for export will be visible in client modules. We will say more about this role of the module in Chapter 10 and Part III.

(2) It is assumed that the system that runs Oberon offers *input and output operations packaged in Oberon modules*. Such modules, already compiled and ready for use, comprise part of the computer's library. Suitable modules can be imported by the user's program, and yield access to the input and output devices. Typically, there is not only one such module, but a whole hierarchy, where each layer advances the level of abstraction – that is, hides more details.

7.1 Sequential input and output, modules *In* and *Out*

One of the most successful abstractions in the domain of input and output is that of the *stream*. A stream is a sequence of data elements. The number of data elements is not known a priori – the stream is therefore a simple case of a dynamic data structure. The number of elements is called the stream's *length*. Only one element is visible at a given time, namely the element at the stream's current *position*. That element can be read – the read operation implicitly increments the position. Writing (normally) occurs at the end of the stream.

Historically, the vast majority of input and output devices have been sequential: paper tape, punched cards and then magnetic tapes. For these devices, the abstraction of the stream is quite close to the actual device operation. Today, the importance of sequential devices is waning – they are supplanted by disk storage capable of random access and by graphical output devices that are inherently non-sequential. The stream abstraction, however, has not lost its usefulness, since many operations are still sequential on the logical level.

In the examples of this book, we assume the existence of two modules, *In* and *Out*, that implement an input stream and an output stream, respectively.[1] To document a module, we *list its exported constants, variables* and *procedure headings*.

Module *In*

For module *In*, such a definition reads as follows:

```
DEFINITION In;
    VAR Done: BOOLEAN;
    PROCEDURE Open;
    PROCEDURE Char(VAR ch: CHAR);
    PROCEDURE Int(VAR i: INTEGER);
    PROCEDURE LongInt(VAR l: LONGINT);
    PROCEDURE Real(VAR x: REAL);
    PROCEDURE Name(VAR nme: ARRAY OF CHAR);[1]
    PROCEDURE String(VAR str: ARRAY OF CHAR);
END In.
```

The meaning, or semantics of the variable and the procedures exported by module *In* are as follows:

---

[1] The source text of a particular implementation is listed in Appendix C.
[2] A variable of type ARRAY OF CHAR may have a string as value, see Section 8.2.6.

- The variable *Done* holds as long as read operations terminate properly. The first abnormal termination falsifies *Done*, which will remain FALSE until the next call to *Open*. This variable should be tested before using the variable parameter that returns the result of the input operation.
- *Open* initializes the input stream. The position is set to the origin and *Done* = TRUE.
- *Char*: If *Done* holds, returns the character found at the position of the input stream and increments that position. If an attempt is made to read beyond the end of the stream, *Done* is falsified.
- *Int, LongInt, Real, Name*: If *Done* holds, these procedures scan the input stream for a token of appropriate type, starting at the current position. The syntax is that of the basic Oberon tokens (a *name* is a sequence of identifiers, juxtaposed with periods). Leading blanks, tabs or carriage return characters are skipped. If a token is found, it is translated into internal representation and returned in the variable parameter. The position is advanced to the character immediately following the token. If no token of appropriate type is encountered, *Done* = FALSE.
- *String*: If *Done* holds, the input stream is scanned for the first non-blank character. All consecutive characters whose value is at least a blank are returned in *s*. *Done* is falsified if the end of the stream was encountered.

If a sequence of input operations is performed, *Done* = TRUE after the last call indicates that all operations were successful.

Module *Out* In the same style, the exported procedures of module *Out* are summarized in the definition

```
DEFINITION Out;
   PROCEDURE Open;
   PROCEDURE Char(ch: CHAR);
   PROCEDURE Ln;
   PROCEDURE Int(i, n: LONGINT);
   PROCEDURE Real(x: REAL; n: INTEGER);
   PROCEDURE String(s: ARRAY OF CHAR);
END Out.
```

The meanings of the procedures of module *Out* are as follows:
- *Open* initializes the output stream.
- *Char* writes character *ch* at the end of the stream.

- *Ln* appends a carriage return control character to the end of the stream. On a printer or on a display device, a new line will be started.
- *Int* and *Real*: translates the internal representation of the actual parameter to a textual representation composed of *n* characters, and appends it to the end of the stream.
- *String* appends the characters of the string passed as parameter to the end of the stream.

The noteworthy fact is that neither the input nor the output data stream appears explicitly in the definition of module *In* or *Out*. Their data structure, which is quite complex is completely hidden. This hiding is the essence of the abstraction termed stream.

Browser In Modula-2 the text between "DEFINITION" and the keyword "END" is termed a *definition module*. It lists all exported declarations – hence it is also known as the *public view* of the module. Such a definition module is accepted by the compiler. Its function is the identification of exported objects – it substitutes for Oberon's export marks.

The advantage of the definition module is its textual compactness. Oberon systems therefore typically offer a tool called the *browser* that accepts the module text and constructs the public view in the form of the definition module.

7.2 Graphics output

As we have indicated, finding generally agreed upon abstractions for programming the display of a graphics-based workstation is still a challenge. Here we merely wish to introduce a high-level module providing graphics output for animated simulations, such as drawing the fractal fern.

The model is that of a Cartesian plane with origin in the lower left corner of the screen. Graphics output devices provide a raster of points, called *pixels*. The pixel is the smallest unit that can be turned black or white – or be assigned a color. It is therefore sensible to choose the pixel size as unit and measure the coordinates in multiples of that unit; that is, to use integers to represent x and y (Figure 7.1).

The visible area of the Cartesian plane (window provided by viewer) has its lower left corner at coordinates (X, Y), is of width W and height H.

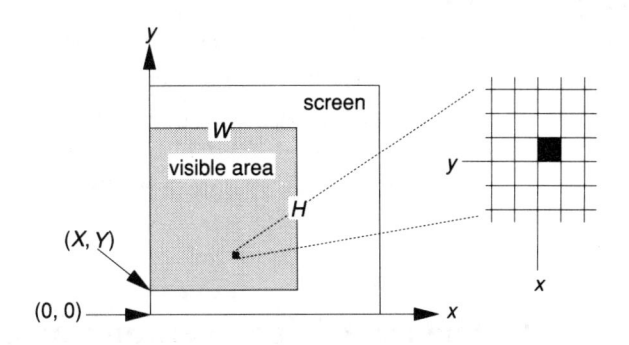

Figure 7.1 Raster display.

Catering to the special task of animation is a provision to read the keyboard while the simulation is running. This allows the definition of 'command keys' useful to interrupt the action and control the course of events.

We introduce the definition of module *XYplane*[1] in the same style adopted for modules *In* or *Out*:

```
DEFINITION XYplane;
    CONST erase = 0; draw = 1;
    VAR X, Y, W, H: INTEGER;
    PROCEDURE Open;
    PROCEDURE Dot(x, y, mode: INTEGER);
    PROCEDURE IsDot(x, y: INTEGER): BOOLEAN;
    PROCEDURE ReadKey(): CHAR;
    PROCEDURE Clear;
END XYplane.
```

The actions of the procedures can be easily guessed; the following is a short description:

- Constants *erase* and *draw* are the values for the formal parameter *mode* in procedures *Dot* and *Line*.
- Variables X, Y, W and H report location and size of the visible drawing area. They are defined after a call of procedure *Open*.
- *Open* initializes a drawing area.

---

[1] The source text of a particular implementation of module *XYplane* is found in Appendix C.

- *Dot* draws (erases) a dot at coordinates *x, y* controlled by *mode*.
- *IsDot* tests whether a dot is drawn at coordinates *x, y*.
- *ReadKey* reads the keyboard. If a key was pressed prior to invocation, it is returned; else 0X results.
- *Clear* erases all dots in the drawing area.

7.3 The fractal fern, completion of the example

We have now all the required knowledge to complete the initial example of drawing fractals. Procedure *Draw* is capable of painting an infinite variety of fractals. The fern is just one of them. We are therefore interested in reading the parameters of the iterated function system from the input stream. This has the distinct advantage that the user does not have to change the program text and recompile module *IFS* for each change in the parameters. We assume that the modules *RandomNumbers, XYplane, In* and *Out* are in the computer's library.

The coordinates in module *IFS* are reals, whereas the display coordinates of *XYplane* are integers. The two sets of coordinates are related by the transformation

$$\xi = x_0 + \text{ENTIER}(X * e), \quad \eta = y_0 + \text{ENTIER}(Y * e)$$

where x_0 and y_0 are the pixel coordinates of the origin of the plane and e measures the unit interval (in pixels).

With these preliminaries, we can restate our module *IFS*:

```
MODULE IFS;
IMPORT RandomNumbers, In, Out, XYplane;

VAR
    a1, b1, c1, d1, e1, f1, p1: REAL;    (* IFS parameters *)
    a2, b2, c2, d2, e2, f2, p2: REAL;    (* IFS parameters *)
    a3, b3, c3, d3, e3, f3, p3: REAL;    (* IFS parameters *)
    a4, b4, c4, d4, e4, f4, p4: REAL;    (* IFS parameters *)
    X, Y: REAL;      (* the position of the pen *)
    x0: INTEGER;     (* Distance of origin from left edge[pixels] *)
    y0: INTEGER;     (* Distance of origin from bottom edge[pixels] *)
```

7.3 The fractal fern, completion of the example

```
        e: INTEGER;      (* Size of unit interval [pixels] *)
        initialized: BOOLEAN;  (* Are parameters initialized? *)


        PROCEDURE Draw*;    (* command marked for export *)
        VAR
           x, y: REAL;          (* new position *)
           xi, eta: INTEGER;    (* pixel coordinates of pen *)
           rn: REAL;            (* temp. variable for random number *)
        BEGIN
(1) →   IF initialized THEN
           REPEAT
              rn := RandomNumbers.Uniform();
              IF  rn < p1 THEN
                 x := a1*X + b1 *Y + e1;   y := c1*X + d1*Y + f1
              ELSIF  rn < (p1 + p2) THEN
                 x := a2*X + b2 *Y + e2;   y := c2*X + d2*Y + f2
              ELSIF  rn < (p1 + p2 + p3) THEN
                 x := a3*X + b3 *Y + e3;   y := c3*X + d3*Y + f3
              ELSE
                 x := a4*X + b4 *Y + e4;   y := c4*X + d4*Y + f4
              END;
(2) →         X := x;  xi := x0 + SHORT(ENTIER(X*e));
              Y := y;  eta := y0 + SHORT(ENTIER(Y*e));
              XYplane.Dot(xi, eta, XYplane.draw)
(3) →      UNTIL "s" = XYplane.Key()
        END
        END Draw;


        PROCEDURE Init*;   (* command marked for export *)
        BEGIN
           X := 0;  Y := 0;   (* Initial position of pen *)
           initialized := FALSE;    In.Open;
           In.Int(x0);    In.Int(y0);    In.Int(e);
           In.Real(a1);   In.Real(a2);   In.Real(a3);   In.Real(a4);
           In.Real(b1);   In.Real(b2);   In.Real(b3);   In.Real(b4);
           In.Real(c1);   In.Real(c2);   In.Real(c3);   In.Real(c4);
           In.Real(d1);   In.Real(d2);   In.Real(d3);   In.Real(d4);
           In.Real(e1);   In.Real(e2);   In.Real(e3);   In.Real(e4);
           In.Real(f1);   In.Real(f2);   In.Real(f3);   In.Real(f4);
           In.Real(p1);   In.Real(p2);   In.Real(p3);   In.Real(p4);
```

```
            IF In.Done THEN XYplane.Open; initialized := TRUE
            ELSE Out.String("Parameter error"); Out.Ln
            END
         END Init;

(4) →    BEGIN initialized := FALSE
         END IFS.
```

Notes

(1) *initialized* is a Boolean variable that prevents execution of *Draw* unless the parameters are properly *initialized*.

(2) Note the type transfer function SHORT.

(3) The keyboard is read and the computation ended if the "s" key is hit.

(4) *initialized* is set to FALSE when the module is loaded.

The procedures *Draw* and *Init* are exported. They are *commands,* since they have no formal parameters. Why are we dividing the work into two procedures? The initialization performed by the statement sequence of *Init* could just as well be prefixed to the statement sequence of *Draw*.

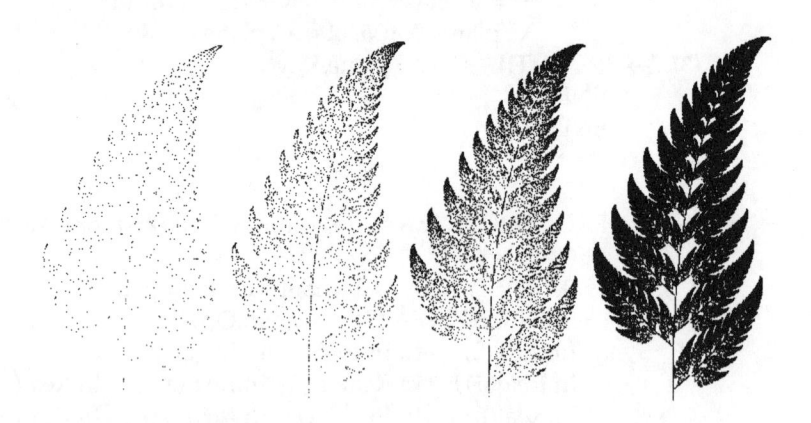

Figure 7.2 Four stages in the computation of the fractal fern.

The reason lies in the nature of the method for drawing a fractal. After the parameters have been initialized, executing *Draw* will start drawing a fern. First, there are only a few points. The fern becomes visible after a short while. Now press the "s" key – the computation stops. If a continuation is desired, one may invoke *Draw* again – the drawing continues and the fern gets darker and darker. Four stages towards convergence are shown in Figure 7.2, the last the result of about 30 minutes of computation.[1]

7.4 The Oberon system: a short digression

As a language, Oberon does not impose any particular requirement on the system on which programs will execute. However, it was conceived as a tool for developing an extensible operating system for a graphics-based workstation. As suggested earlier in this chapter, the Oberon system is composed of a hierarchy of modules, each providing an abstraction on a suitable level (see Figure 1.1).

The Oberon system departs from the 'bandwagon trail' in many important ways. An adequate treatment is the object of several journal papers and two other books (see Reiser, 1991; Wirth and Gutknecht, 1989, 1992). In this section, we will restrict the discussion to two key concepts:

- *Execution of commands* – instead of programs.
- A new and unifying role played by the *notion of a text*.

7.4.1 Execution of commands

Running a program on a conventional computer system entails the following steps:

(1) All the parts of the program (for example its modules) are translated, and in a separate step[2] coalesced into a single executable unit[3] that is stored on disk.

(2) The operating system affords controls that enable the user to start programs. The program is loaded into memory, and control passed to the first instruction.

(3) Upon termination, memory and possibly other resources, such as files, are released.

---

[1] On a 15.6672 MHz Motorola MC68030 processor with MC68882 math co-processor.
[2] Usually performed by a program called the linkage editor.
[3] Also termed the object program.

Program loading is known to be a slow process, and, since memory is released upon termination, a sequence of programs can only communicate through files. It is therefore not attractive to compose an interactive application as a set of programs that are called from the operation system's command interpreter.

The command activation mechanism of the Oberon system is meant to support efficiently the design of extensible interactive programs. This goal requires an architecture that has the following characteristics:

- The smallest unit of program text that can be executed from the computer's controls is reduced: it is the *exported procedure* without formal parameters – also termed the *command* in Oberon terminology.
- To avoid the overhead of swapping programs in and out of memory, the modules are loaded only once, when one of their resources[1] is referenced first. After a module has been *dynamically loaded*, it remains memory-resident for the rest of the session (or until it is explicitly unloaded). At the time of the first loading, the statement sequence of the module is executed.
- Oberon allows the user to execute commands using the computer's controls, in particular the mouse. *Once a command gains control, it runs to completion.* It does not require (or allow) any further interactions with the user.[2]

The result is that the Oberon command mechanism is highly efficient. An important additional benefit of memory-resident modules is the fact that *commands may communicate through data structures in memory*. This makes the notion of abstract data types particularly relevant. They are explored in Chapter 10 and Part III.

7.4.2 The role of texts

One of the first surprises of the novice gaining acquaintance with a computer is the discovery that text displayed on the monitor is *modal*. Some text is merely meant to be looked at. It is a volatile entity on the screen, written by the system. Other text, written in a special place, will be interpreted as commands, instructing the system what to do. The special place is known as the *command line*. Still a third kind – close to

---

[1] Procedures or global data.
[2] With the exception of the CTRL-SHIFT-DEL key combination, which (on Ceres) aborts the execution of a (long-running) command.

what a naive user would expect as normal – is text ready to be edited, changed, stored or printed.

In Oberon, there is only one kind of text: it is editable, storable, printable, and can be interpreted as commands. Texts exist in windows called *text viewers*. In every text viewer, a simple editor is available. *The text modes are abolished.*

The layout of a text viewer is depicted in Figure 7.3. The perimeter of the viewer is marked with a thin line. On top is a *title bar*, rendered in reverse video. A scroll bar with a position mark is placed at left. The title bar contains the viewer name separated by a vertical bar "|" from the commands *System.Close*, *System.Copy*, *System.Grow*, *Edit.Locate* and *Edit.Store*. These commands can be executed with the mouse and perform operations on the viewer or on the text contained in the viewer.

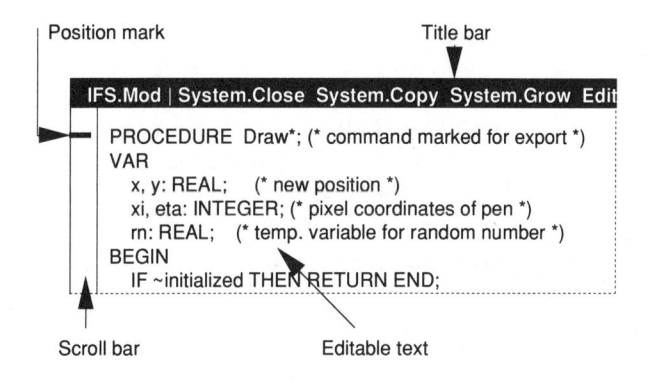

```
IFS.Mod | System.Close  System.Copy  System.Grow  Edit
PROCEDURE  Draw*; (* command marked for export *)
VAR
    x, y: REAL;    (* new position *)
    xi, eta: INTEGER; (* pixel coordinates of pen *)
    rn: REAL;   (* temp. variable for random number *)
BEGIN
    IF ~initialized THEN RETURN END;
```

Position mark · Title bar · Scroll bar · Editable text

Figure 7.3 Layout and elements of an Oberon text viewer.

Command activation

Commands are identified through a qualified identifier of the form *Mod.Proc*, where *Proc* is the name of the command and *Mod* denotes the module in which *Proc* is declared. Oberon provides the facility to execute any command by simply pointing at its name – typed anywhere in a text – and pressing the execute key of the mouse.

Tool texts

The fact that commands are activated out of text viewers allows the user to create a highly efficient working environment. One simply types the group of commands that comprise the current work into a text viewer and stores the text on disk. Such a text is appropriately termed a *tool*. Figure 7.4 portrays such a tool, written to execute the commands from our sample module *IFS*. Three commands are prepared: *IFS.Init*,

IFS.Draw and *Paint.Print*, the last will print the file *XYplane.Pict* that can be created from a *XYplane* viewer. The mouse pointer (arrow) is over *IFS.Init*, which appears underlined. That means the user is pressing the execute key. Upon release of that key, *IFS.Init* will execute.

Note that tool texts in text viewers are *like menus* of conventional user interface designs – except that they offer a lot more flexibility.

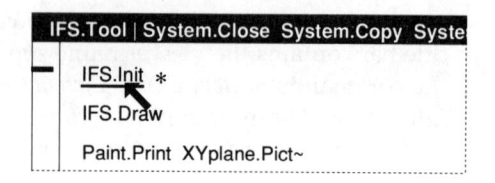

Figure 7.4 A tool viewer; the command *IFS.Init* is about to be executed.

Text output

If commands produce output, a new text viewer is opened and the output text displayed within its perimeter. Again, the text can be modified, printed and stored. Module *Out* can be used to create such text output.

7.4.3 Modules *In* and *Out*

The abstractions of modules *In* and *Out* are general enough to be implementable on any computer. Such implementations differ in the way the input and output streams are defined. The input stream may be the keyboard or a file – the output stream a display device or again a file. In the Oberon system *both streams are texts that are displayed in viewers*.

The output stream

Invocation of *Out.Open* opens an empty text viewer with title *Out.Text*. The text displayed in that viewer represents the output stream. Each time a write procedure is called, the textual addition becomes visible in the viewer. The important thing to remember is that, even though viewer *Out.Text* is home of the output stream, it is also a normal text viewer. That means that the displayed text can be edited, stored or printed at any time the system admits input from mouse and keyboard. Such modifications do not interfere with the fact that further calls of write procedures add output at the end of the text.

The input stream

The input stream is also embedded in a text displayed in a text viewer. There are three possibilities, depending on the character that follows

7.4 The Oberon system: a short digression

the command name whose execution led to a call of *In.Open*:

(1) If that character is an asterisk, "*", then the text displayed in the marked viewer represents the input stream that begins at the first character of that text. A viewer may be marked by pointing at it and pressing a special mark key. An asterisk identifies the marked viewer.

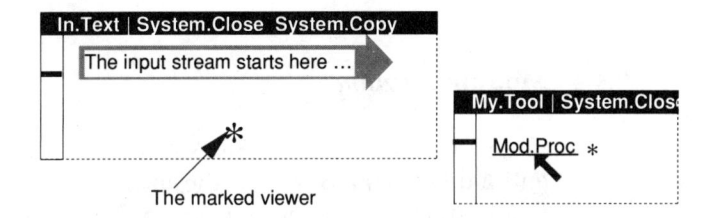

Figure 7.5 The input stream is in the marked viewer.

(2) If that character is the upward-pointing arrow, "↑",[1] then the text that contains the most recent selection contains the input stream. The first selected character is also the first character of the stream.

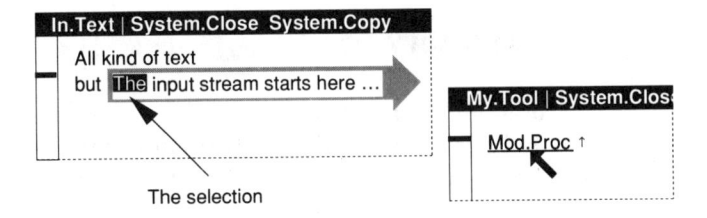

Figure 7.6 The input stream starts at the first selected character.

(3) If neither case 1 or case 2 applies, the text from which the command was executed contains the input stream. The stream starts with the character that follows the blank after the command name.

---

[1] In the standard ASCII character set, "↑" is represented by the caret "^", with ORD("^") = 94.

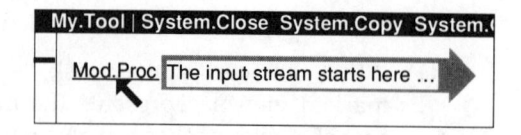

Figure 7.7 The input stream starts after the command name.

7.4.4 Module *XYplane*

If a command results in the execution of *XYplane.Open* then a viewer entitled *XYplane* opens in the user track. The viewer consumes the whole track. However, it is created as an overlay; hence, when the command *System.Close* is executed, the previous screen is restored. After a plane is opened, draw procedures are used to create a graphic. The graphic may be stored to disk using the command *XYplane.Store* from the title bar.

Figure 7.8 shows an *XYplane* viewer that was opened as a consequence of executing the command *IFS.Init*. A fractal fern is in the process of being painted. The inset enlarges the tool from which the command *IFS.Draw* was executed.

7.5 Summary

It is debatable whether a programming language should define input and output operations. Our point of view is that appropriate abstractions should be provided through modules that extend the operating system.

In this chapter, we have provided the definition of two modules, *In* and *Out*, that are based on the abstraction of the *input and output stream* and will be used in the examples in this book. We have introduced a useful notation called the *definition module* for documentation purposes.

Abstractions for graphics output are even less established than textual input and output. A module *XYplane* is presented that allows writing to individual pixels of the display and reading the keyboard.

Using those input and output modules, we have completed the example of the fractal fern that was begun in Chapter 6. An important notion is that of the *command* – a parameter-less procedure exported by a module. The command is the unit accepted for execution by the Oberon operating environment.

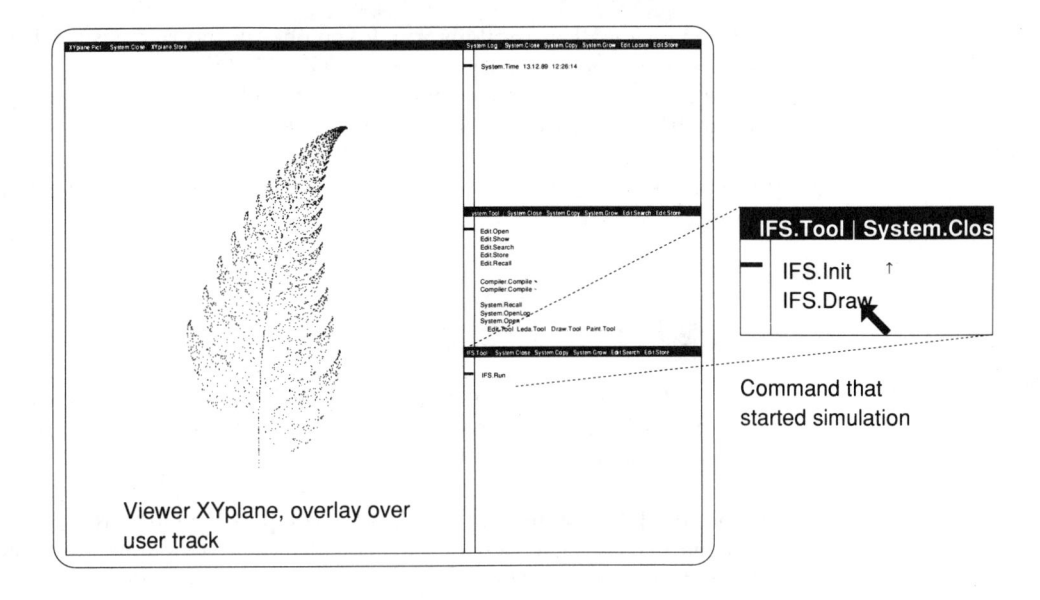

Figure 7.8 An *XYplane* viewer, opened after execution of *IFS.Init*.

We have concluded this chapter with a digression: a short introduction to the basic user interface of the Oberon system based on *viewers* and *non-volatile texts*. A particular implementation of modules *In*, *Out* and *XY plane* is portrayed in this context.

7.6 Exercises

7.1 [**Summation of infinite series**] Write procedures to compute sin (*x*) for *x*: REAL according to the series:

$$\sin(x) = x - \frac{x^3}{3!} + \frac{x^5}{5!} - \frac{x^7}{7!} + \cdots$$

Find an appropriate condition for terminating the addition. Count the number of required terms to obtain the desired accuracy. Evaluate sin (x) for various arguments and compare the results with a function table (or the result produced by a mathematical library). If you observe incorrect results, explain. Does the use of double precision (type LONGREAL) help?

Note: Efficient and accurate computation of mathematical function requires mathematical sophistication. *We recommend the use of standard libraries.*

7.2 [**Harmonic function**] Write a procedure to compute the harmonic function $H(n)$ for integer arguments n:

$$H(n) = 1 + \frac{1}{2} + \frac{1}{3} + \cdots + \frac{1}{n}$$

Compute this function in two ways: once by beginning the summation with the first term (1), once by beginning with the last ($1/n$). Compare the results for large n and explain any difference.

7.3 [**Square root**] Write a function procedure to compute the square root y of a real argument x according to Newton's method; that is, by computing a sequence of y_i until two consecutive values differ by less than a specified small value:

$$y_{i+1} = \frac{1}{2}\left(y_i + \frac{x}{y_i}\right)$$

Formulate an invariant first. Is $y_{i+1} = y_i$ a correct stopping condition? How accurate is the result?

7.4 [**Input of integer**] Using only procedure *Char* of module *In* implement the procedure *Int* of the same module. *Hint*: ORD("0") = 48, ORD("1") = 49, ...

7.5 [**Calculator**] Implement a calculator that uses RPN notation (reversed Polish notation). The number format is that of reals. Four registers X, Y, Z and T form a stack. Command *Enter* pushes new numbers onto the stack according to the statement sequence $T := Z; Z := Y; Y := X; X := newNumber$. Commands *Add* results in $X := X + Y; Y := Z; Z := T$. Commands *Subt, Mult* and *Div* are defined analogously.

Provide visual feedback as shown on the right. Numbers entered are prefixed with a ">" sign. The results show an explanative sign such as a "+".

```
> 3.14159
> 2.71828
+ 5.85987
```

Insure that only syntactically correct numbers can be entered. Display an error message in the case of a violation. When the module is first loaded, the registers are initialized to 0. *Hint*: study the operation of a calculator from Hewlett-Packard Company.

7.6 [**IFS**] Implement module *IFS*. Prepare the text shown in Figure 7.9 in an Oberon text viewer with title *IFS.Text*. The second parameter set will produce a fractal that looks like a maple leaf.

```
IFS.Text | System.Close  System.Copy  System.Grow  Edit.Search
─ Fractal fern
  320    0       64
  0.0    0.85    0.2    −0.15   0.0    0.04    −0.26   0.28
  0.0    −0.04   0.23    0.26   0.16   0.85     0.22   0.24
  0.0    0.0     0.0     0.0    0.0    1.6      1.6    0.44
  0.01   0.85    0.07    0.07
  Fractal maple leaf
  90     0       450
  0.65   0.65    0.32   −0.32   −0.013 −0.026  −0.32   0.32
  0.013  0.026   0.32    0.32    0.65   0.65    0.32   0.32
  0.175  0.175   0.2     0.8     0.0    0.35    0.0    0.0
  0.3    0.3     0.2     0.2
```

Figure 7.9 Sample input viewer for module *IFS*.

7.7 **[Module Shapes]** Using procedure *Dot* from module *XYplane*, implement module *Shapes* with definition

> DEFINITION Shapes;
> IMPORT XYplane;
> PROCEDURE Hline(x, y, l, mode: INTEGER);
> PROCEDURE Vline(x, y, l, mode: INTEGER);
> PROCEDURE FilledRect(x, y, w, h, mode: INTEGER);
> PROCEDURE Rect(x, y, w, h, mode: INTEGER);
> END Shapes;

Formal parameter *mode* takes the values *XYplane.erase* and *XYplane.draw*. *Hline* and *Vline* draw horizontal or vertical lines of length *l* starting at (*x*, *y*). *FilledRect* draws a filled rectangle with a corner at coordinates *x* and *y*, width *w* and height *h*. *Rect* produces a 'wire frame' rectangle. It is assumed that *XYplane.Open* is issued prior to the use of the procedures exported by *Shapes*.

Remark: For real applications, module *Display*, which is part of the Oberon system, affords a far more efficient solution to drawing a filled rectangle (see next exercise).

7.8 The standard Oberon library has a module *Display* for basic output to the screen. Among its export is

> PROCEDURE ReplConst(col, x, y, w, h, mode: INTEGER)

which draws a rectangle, filled with color *col*, with lower left corner at position *x*, *y*, width *w* and height *h*. Use *Display.ReplConst* to implement module *Shapes*.

Procedure *ReplConst* does not limit output to the drawing area of *XYplane* (as *XYplane.Dot* does). Make sure that drawing is limited to the visible area of the viewer. *Hint*: use the variables *XYplane.X*, *XYplane.Y*, *XYplane.W* and *XYplane.H* for clipping.

Display.white and *Display.black* are the color values, *Display.replace* is used in place of *mode*. Note that *Display.white* and *Display.black* are defined relative to a black background.

Compare the speed of the two implementations of *Shapes*. If one is faster, discuss the reason why.

7.9 **[Drawing a line]** *Bresenham's algorithm for lines* is used to draw a straight line between the coordinate origin and the endpoints a, b where $a \leq b$ by marking dots in the discrete raster using *XYplane.Dot*. In order to make the computation of the dot coordinates fast, integer arithmetic is used exclusively.

The principle of Bresenham's algorithm is the following: proceed from $x = 0$ towards $x = a$, in each step incrementing x by 1 and y by 0 or 1. *Hint*: use a variable $h = (bx - ay + b - a/2)$, and increment y if $h > 0$.

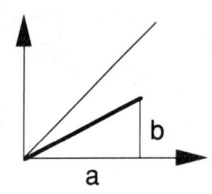

7.10 Add a procedure with heading

   PROCEDURE Line(x1, y1, x2, y2, mode: INTEGER)

to module *Shapes* that draws a line between the points with coordinates $x1, y1$ and $x2, y2$. Use appropriate coordinate transformations such that Bresenham's algorithm becomes applicable for all $x1, y1, x2$ and $y2$ values. *Hint*: distinguish between the eight octants of the plane.

7.11 **[Turtle Graphics]** Implement module *Turtle* with definition

   DEFINITION Turtle;
   IMPORT Shapes;
   PROCEDURE SetPen(x, y: INTEGER);
   PROCEDURE Move(l: INTEGER);
   PROCEDURE TurnLeft;
   PROCEDURE TurnRight;
   END Turtle.

A pen draws curves composed of vertical and horizontal lines. *Turtle* has a global state comprised of the *pen position* and a *direction* that is restricted to north, west, south and east. *SetPen* sets the pen position to x and y. *Move* draws a line segment of length l emanating at the current position. After *Move*, the pen position is at the end of the new line segment. *TurnLeft* and *TurnRight* turn the direction relative to the current direction by a right angle.

Discuss the implication of *Turtle* relative to the abstraction of the stream.

7.12 **[Mandelbrot set]** Write a module *Mandelbrot* that displays the Mandelbrot set *M*. *M* is composed of those points c of the complex plane for which z_i remains bounded as i tends to infinity, where the values z_i are computed according to

$$z_0 = 0, \quad z_i = z_{i-1}^2 + c, \quad i = 1, 2, \ldots$$

Select a square of N by N pixels in the *XYplane* viewer. Map the raster defined by the pixels onto an area of the complex plane. Each complex point so defined is one of the c values for which the sequence $\{z_i\}$ is computed. Select a maximal value, I_{max} say, for the index i. If for any $i < I_{max}$: $|z_i| > 2$, then color the pixel white. If the maximal value is reached, color the pixel black—the corresponding c value is in the Mandelbrot set (or close to it).

The number of pixels N, the maximum value of iteration I_{max} and the location of the square in the complex plane are parameters to be read from the input stream. A good first choice is

$$-2.1 \leq \text{Re}(c) \leq 0.7, \quad -1.4 \leq \text{Im}(c) \leq 1.4.$$

Zoom into various areas for example, try the values

-0.66	$\leq \text{Re}(c) \leq$	$-0.41,$	0.49	$\leq \text{Im}(c) \leq$	0.74
-0.5373	$\leq \text{Re}(c) \leq$	$-0.5195,$	0.6597	$\leq \text{Im}(c) \leq$	0.6775
-1.8293	$\leq \text{Re}(c) \leq$	$-1.7173,$	-0.056	$\leq \text{Im}(c) \leq$	0.056
-0.793	$\leq \text{Re}(c) \leq$	$-0.7,$	0.0466	$\leq \text{Im}(c) \leq$	0.14

7.13 If you have a color monitor, color the pixels according to the index i for which $|z_i| \geq 2$ for the first time. Experiment with various color assignments. If you have a monochrome monitor, divide the range $0 \leq i \leq I_{max}$ into black and white bands.

7.14 The points

$$z_1 = c, \quad z_i = z_{i-1}^2 + c, \quad i = 2, 3, \ldots$$

are said to form an *orbit*. Add two commands *StartOrbit* and *StepOrbit* to the module *Mandelbrot*. *StartOrbit* selects a c value, *StepOrbit* steps through the orbit, point by point. Make the points of the orbit visible. If an orbit point is inside the Mandelbrot set, show it in white; if it is outside, draw it black. Use a mark that is bigger than just a pixel so that the orbit point clearly stands out.

7.15 [Deterministic IFS] Write a deterministic IFS module. Divide the drawing area of *XYplane* into two square areas. In each area, a coordinate system with origin at the lower left corner is assumed. In the first square, draw an initial shape, for example a filled rectangle. Then apply each one of the four transformations to every point that is black (use *XYplane.IsDot*). Draw the transformed points in the second square. Erase the point that is thus processed. Once all points in the first square are processed, switch the role of the two squares. Iterate until the stop key is pressed. The first four iterations together with iteration 100 are depicted in Figure 7.10.

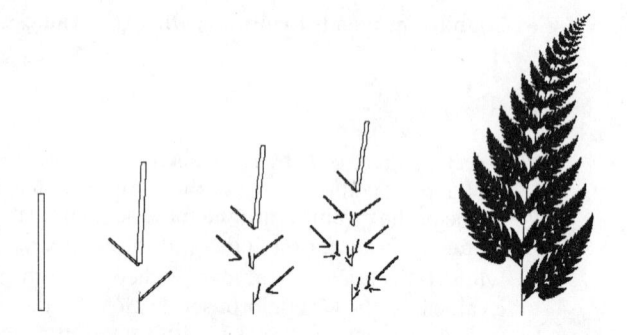

Figure 7.10 The 1st, 2nd, 3rd, 4th and 100th iterate of the deterministic IFS algorithm.

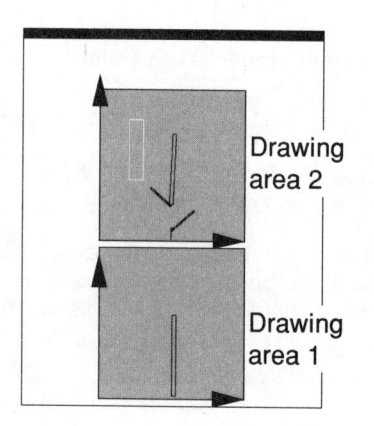

Even more instructive is a version, where four sweeps are made over the pixels of the source area. In each sweep, one of the transformations is applied. The pixel in the source area is cleared in the fourth sweep.

A study of the evolution of the deterministic algorithm should take away the mystery – probably prevailing after first observing the probabilistic drawing algorithm.

References

Reiser M. (1991). *The Oberon System: User Guide and Programmer's Manual*. Wokingham: Addison-Wesley.

Wirth N. and Gutknecht J. (1989). The Oberon system. *Software–Practice and Experience*, **19**, 857–93.

Wirth N. and Gutknecht J. (1992). *Project Oberon: The Design of an Operating System and Compiler*. Wokingham: Addison-Wesley.

Part II

Arrays
Records
Pointers
Dynamic data
Stepwise refinement
Data abstraction

Synopsis

Part I contains all the necessary knowledge needed to write complete Oberon programs. However, if the language were restricted to that scope, a solution to most real problems would be tedious at best – but more likely downright impractical.

The reason is that each variable is identified with a single name. In Part II, we will introduce two structured types – the *array* and the *record* – each comprising elements of basic types.

Records and arrays are static structures. There are situations where the volume of data and the relationship of data elements changes dynamically. The pointer, in conjunction with records, allows the construction of such *dynamical data* structures as lists, trees or graphs.

Using these tools, we will develop a realistic sample program: simulation of a queue. We will write the program in a structured way known as *stepwise refinement*. In this context, we will discover the virtue of *hiding details* in modules – a technique called *data abstraction*.

8 Type declarations, array and record types

So far, we have given each variable an individual name. This may be tedious – if not downright impractical – in the case of a large number of variables of the same type. In other situations, it is desirable to refer to a collection of variables, possibly of different types, with a common name. In this section, we will encounter two such structured types that are familiar in programming languages: the *array* and the *record*.

The model for the array data structure is the indexed variable of mathematics:

$$a_i \quad \leftrightarrow \quad a[i]$$
$$a_{i,j} \quad \leftrightarrow \quad a[i,j]$$

The array carries a name for the whole set of variables. Individual array elements are selected with a computable index. Obviously, arrays play a major role in numerical programs. But they also model tables and sequences of characters.

Records have their origin in commercial data processing. They represent collections of variables that are typically of different types. A personnel record with fields for name, address, date of birth and salary furnishes an often used example. Records are also of great utility in system programming, where they are known as control blocks. Finally – in conjunction with the pointer type – records provide the basis to construct dynamic data structures such as lists and trees.

A declaration is a specification of an identifier. Through the declaration, the given identifier represents an object of the Oberon language such as a variable or a procedure. Oberon treats the type also as an object that may be declared. Such *type declarations* go beyond a mere convenience – together with the module concept, they are the basis for abstract data types – a topic that will be introduced in Chapter 10 and expanded in Part III.

8.1 Type declaration

The declaration binds an identifier to properties of the object that it represents. In Oberon, the declared properties are constant and valid within the scope of the identifier. While the value of a variable may change, its declared properties remain the same throughout the time of its existence.

The concept of type is important because it divides the variables into *disjoint classes*. Each type defines the *set of values* that a variable may assume. Inadvertent assignments among members of incompatible classes can therefore be detected by mere inspection of a program's text without executing the program. Similarly, factors in an expression and the pairing of actual to formal parameters can be *checked for compatibility*.

In Chapter 3, we have encountered the primitive types that reflect properties of the underlying computing machine. The primitive types are SHORTINT, INTEGER, LONGINT, REAL, LONGREAL, BOOLEAN, SET and CHAR. That the standard types are named with predeclared identifiers rather than with reserved keywords suggests that the user may declare identifiers to introduce additional types.

Such a type declaration in fact exists, for example

```
TYPE
    Time* = REAL;
    Vector = ARRAY 3 OF REAL;
    Person = RECORD first, given: Name END;
```

The general syntax of a type declaration is expressed by:

```
TypeDeclaration = ident ["*"] "=" type.
type = qualident | ArrayType | RecordType |
    PointerType | ProcedureType.
```

The asterisk is the familiar export mark that renders the identifier visible in importing modules. The qualident represents a type – either one of the predeclared types or one declared by the programmer. Array and record types are covered in subsequent sections, pointer types are covered in Chapter 9 and procedure types await Chapter 11.

Type compatibility

Recall that the operands of operators must be *expression-compatible* (see Table 4.1). Similarly, the type of the designator in an assignment (left-hand side) must be *assignment compatible* with the type of the expression of that assignment (Table 4.3).

Generally, for a type *T2* to be (assignment-) compatible with another type *T1*, we require that

(1) *T2* be *included* in *T1*, that is,
LONGREAL ⊇ REAL ⊇ LONGINT ⊇ INTEGER ⊇ SHORTINT
(2) *T2* be *declared equal* to *T1*.

For example in the type definition,

TYPE T1 = REAL; T2 = T1; T3 = INTEGER;

T2 is compatible with *T1* (equal), and *T3* is compatible with *T1* and *T2* (included).

However, in the type declaration

TYPE
  A1 = ARRAY 10 OF INTEGER;
  A2 = ARRAY 10 OF INTEGER;
  A3 = A1;

only *A1* and *A3* are compatible. *A1* and *A2* are incompatible, even though the specifications on the right-hand side of the equal sign are the same. Technically, rule (2) is known as a *name equivalence* – as opposed to the *structural equivalence* of *A1* with *A2*.

Variable declaration

A variable, *t* say, may be declared to be of a certain type in either of two ways:

TYPE T = someType; VAR t: T;

or simply

VAR t: someType;

In both cases, *t* is of the same type – only, in the second case, the type remains anonymous (unless, of course, *someType* is an identifier). For example, in the declaration

VAR a: A1; b: ARRAY 10 OF INTEGER;

the type of *b* is an anonymous array type. Furthermore, because of the name equivalence rule, variable *b* is not type-compatible with *a*.

8.2 Arrays

8.2.1 The array type and the array declaration

An array is a data type that represents a set of elements that are all of the same type – the *element type*. The number of elements is fixed and is called the array's *length*. The name of an array variable refers to all elements. An individual member is identified with a number – the so-called *index*. Indices are integers between 0 and the length minus one.

The array is said to be a *structured data type*. It is a homogeneous structure, because all elements are of the same type. The structure is defined mathematically by the mapping of the set of integers {0...*length* – 1} onto the set of values defined by the element type (Figure 8.1).

a: ARRAY N OF elementType

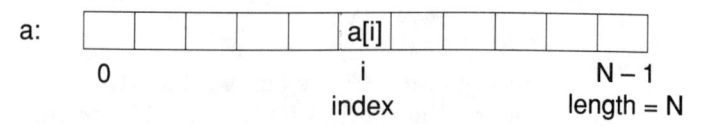

a: [| | | | a[i] | | | |]
    0   i   N – 1
                index   length = N

Figure 8.1 An array.

In the following example of an array declaration, the variable v consists of 3 elements, each of type REAL:

VAR v: ARRAY 3 OF REAL;

If we wish to make the array type explicit, we may give it a name, for example *Vector*:

TYPE Vector = ARRAY 3 OF REAL; VAR v: Vector;

The array type declaration has the syntax

ArrayType = "ARRAY" length {"," length} "OF" type.
length = ConstExpression.

We see that the array length may be expressed by a constant expression. For example, we could declare type *Vector* as follows:

8.2 Arrays

```
CONST n = 3;
TYPE Vector = ARRAY n OF REAL;
```

Multidimensional array The elements of an array are all of the same type. The element type, however, is not restricted to the basic or unstructured types. In particular, the array elements may themselves be arrays. An array of arrays is called a *multidimensional array*, because each index may be considered as spanning a dimension in a Cartesian space. For example a three-dimensional array type, *ThreeD*, with element type T is declared as follows:

```
TYPE ThreeD = ARRAY k1 OF
                 ARRAY k2 OF
                    ARRAY k3 OF T;
```

The total number of elements of type T is $k1 \times k2 \times k3$. For such a multidimensional array declaration, Oberon admits the shorthand notation

```
TYPE ThreeD = ARRAY k1, k2, k3 OF T;
```

The outermost nesting level is said to be *dimension zero*. In the example, this is the index that ranges over $\{0...k1-1\}$. The next nesting level corresponds to dimension one, and so on.

Predeclared function LEN The predeclared function

LEN(a, n)

produces the length of dimension n of an array a. For example, if a is of the type *ThreeD*, then $LEN(a, 0) = k1$, $LEN(a, 1) = k2$ and $LEN(a, 3) = k3$. $LEN(a)$ is a shorthand notation for $LEN(a, 0)$.

8.2.2 The array designator, assignment and expressions

An element in an array is a variable that is designated by the array's identifier followed by a selecting index that is set in square brackets. For the example, *v: Vector* has the elements $v[0]$, $v[1]$ and $v[2]$.

Syntactically, $v[i]$ is an array *designator* and $[i]$ is the *selector*. Selectors are integer expressions in square brackets. Thus, a *selector may be computed* – a fact on which the prominent role of arrays in programming is founded. The array designator has the syntax:

114 Type declarations, array and record types

```
designator = qualident { "[ " ExpList "]" }.
ExpList = expression {"," expression}.
```

The expressions must be of integer type, and the number of entries in the expression list must not exceed the dimension of the array declaration.

Rules

The semantics of an array designator a[expr] observe the straightforward rules:

(1) The expression *expr* is evaluated and results in the integer *j*, say.

(2) [*j*] is the selector of the designated array element a[*j*], *which results in a variable*. This variable may enter as a factor in an expression, serve as actual parameter or appear on the left-hand side of an assignment statement.

(3) If the designator has two selectors, a[*expr1*][*expr2*], then *expr1* is evaluated and applied to *a*. The resulting variable must again be of array type. Next, *expr2* is evaluated and applied to that variable.

The generalization of rule (3) to more than 2 selectors is self-evident. It is obvious that the value of *expr* must be within the range $0 \leq expr < LEN(a)$. What happens if this condition is violated depends on the computing system used. Normally, Oberon programs will come to an abnormal halt.[1]

Abbreviated index notation

The syntax of designators allows for a similar abbreviation as used in the corresponding declarations, namely A[i, j] is equivalent to A[i] [j] etc. For example consider the declaration

```
TYPE
    Vector = ARRAY n OF REAL;
    Matrix = ARRAY m OF Vector;
    Tensor = ARRAY k OF Matrix;
VAR x, y: Vector;  A: Matrix; T: Tensor; i, j: INTEGER;
```

Then we have

x[i]	*i*th element of array *x* (type REAL)
A[i]	sub-array of *A* (type *Vector*)
A[i][j] or A[i, j]	*j*th element of *i*th sub-array (type REAL)

[1] Since checking array bounds consumes computing cycles, some compilers afford options to switch range checking on and off.

T[i]   *i*th sub-array of *T* (type *Matrix*)
T[i][j] or T[i, j]   *j*th sub-array of *i*th sub-array of *T* (Type *Vector*)
T[i][j][k] or T[i, j, k]   element of type REAL

Of course, more complicated expressions, such as A[$i*j + k$] may substitute for i, j and k.

Array assignments and expressions

An array variable may be the recipient of an assignment. The only array expression, however, is a solitary array designator or a string. Array variables *cannot be compared* with the exception of the type ARRAY *n* OF CHAR (see Section 8.2.6).

For example, considering the above declarations, the following are valid array assignments:

  y := x;   y := A[i + 1];   A[j] := T[i, j];

After an assignment $y := x$, y is equal to x, element by element.

8.2.3 Parameters of array type

Arrays can be parameters of procedures. The array type appears explicitly in the formal parameter section. For example,

  TYPE: Vect = ARRAY n OF REAL;

  ...
  PROCEDURE Norm(v: Vect): REAL;
  VAR s: REAL; j: INTEGER;
  BEGIN
   j := 0; s := 0;
   WHILE j < LEN(v) DO s := s + v[j]*v[j]; INC(j) END;
   RETURN s
  END Norm;

A declaration of formal parameters that leaves the array type anonymous, is illegal; an example is the heading

  PROCEDURE Norm(v: ARRAY n OF REAL): REAL;

Oberon provides a relaxation of the need to give array parameters explicit types: the *open array parameter*, to be discused in the next section.

If the formal parameter is of array type, the actual parameter is always *a solitary array designator* or a *string*. We distinguish between value and variable parameters – the same rules as in the scalar case apply. Recall the following:

- A formal *value parameter* is a local variable of the procedure that is initialized at the time of the call. When the procedure's scope is activated, memory is allocated for the formal array parameter. The corresponding actual parameter is assigned to the formal parameter.
- A formal *variable parameter* (keyword "VAR") represents the actual parameter, and assignments made to the formal parameter within the scope of the procedure are reflected in the actual parameter. No memory is tied up and no assignment takes place.

We emphasize that an array assignment can be an expensive operation. *Value parameters for arrays should therefore be used only if truly justified*. The lack of an array constant (an exception is a string; see Section 8.2.6) should make such justification a rare case. Observing this recommendation, our previous example, procedure Norm, should really have the heading

PROCEDURE Norm(VAR v: Vector): REAL;

even though parameter *v* remains unchanged.

Array designator as actual parameter

Of course, an array designator may serve as an actual parameter. If it is paired with a value parameter, the designator is simply evaluated and the result assigned to the formal parameter. What happens in the case of a variable parameter is more interesting:

(1) In executing the call statement, the selector is evaluated and applied to the array, resulting in a variable.
(2) That variable is substituted for the formal parameter.

This substitution is sometimes referred to as *call by reference*. Note that there exists a more general substitution mechanism where the unevaluated designator is substituted for the formal parameter. This is known as call by name, but is not present in Oberon.

Consider another example, procedure *SetZero*, which initializes an array passed as parameter:

```
PROCEDURE SetZero(VAR v: Vector);
VAR j: INTEGER;
BEGIN
    j := 0;
    WHILE j < LEN(v) DO  v[j] := 0; INC(j) END
END SetZero;
```

Assuming the earlier declarations (that is, x: *Vector*; A: *Matrix*), we may call *SetZero* as follows:

    SetZero(x);
    i := 2; SetZero(A[i + 1]);

The second call statement illustrates the rule governing array designators as actual parameters. The selector [i + 1] is evaluated, resulting in [3]. Then variable A[3] is passed to the procedure. it is of compatible type *Vector*. After completion of the call, all elements of the 3rd subarray of A are zero. The other elements of A remain unaffected.

Loops over arrays The two preceding examples, simple as they are, exhibit a typical feature of array processing: the loop ranging over all elements. The while loop is recommended for that purpose. The integer that is incremented in the loop is called the *control variable*. The predeclared function LEN is convenient to refer to the array length. Upon termination, the control variable has the definite value LEN(v).

8.2.4 The open array parameter

To appreciate the rationale for the introduction of the open array parameter, consider the following example. A module *LinAlg* is being created by a group of numerical analysts. It should offer a collection of matrix methods using one- and two-dimensional array types, for example

    DEFINITION LinAlg;
    CONST n = 100;
    TYPE
       Vector = ARRAY n OF REAL;
       Matrix = ARRAY n, n OF REAL;
       ... (* Further declarations, including procedures *)
    END LinAlg.

But the designers face a dilemma: what array bound n should they choose? If the bound is high, considerable storage is consumed and quite likely wasted in most cases. If the bound is chosen low, important users will probably be frustrated.

For the user, there is a dilemma too. Suppose an existing program should be converted to be a client of *LinAlg*. This requires the owner to convert all array types to *LinAlg.Matrix* and *LinAlg.Vector*, a task which

118 Type declarations, array and record types

is tedious and error prone. The solution is provided by the open array parameter.

The open array parameter is a formal type *that is compatible with any actual array parameter with the same dimension and the same element type*. Its syntax is

| FormalType = {"ARRAY" "OF"} qualident.

The previous example *SetZero* can benefit from making its parameter an open array:

```
PROCEDURE SetZero(VAR v: ARRAY OF REAL);
VAR j: INTEGER;
BEGIN
   j := 0;
   WHILE j < LEN(v) DO v[j] := 0; INC(j) END
END SetZero;
```

Formal parameter v is an open array. Any actual (one dimensional) array parameter with element type REAL is compatible with v. The array bound of v is left open – hence the name open array parameter.

Open array parameters may be multidimensional too. For example,

ARRAY OF ARRAY OF REAL

is compatible with all two-dimensional arrays with element type REAL.

Matrix multiplication

A general procedure for matrix multiplication is usually given as an example for array processing. Let

    A: left operand (m by l matrix)
    B: right operand (l by n matrix)
    C = **A** × **B**:   product (m by n matrix).

The matrices are stored in two-dimensional arrays of appropriate lengths. The procedure for multiplication reads

```
PROCEDURE Mult(VAR A, B, C: ARRAY OF ARRAY OF REAL;
                                    m, n, l: INTEGER);
VAR i, j, k: INTEGER; s: REAL;
BEGIN  i := 0;
   WHILE i < m DO  j := 0;
      WHILE j < n DO  k := 0; s := 0;
```

```
          WHILE k < 1 DO  s := s + A[i, k]*B[k, j]; INC(k)  END;
          C[i, j] := s;  INC(j)
        END;
        INC(i)
      END
    END Mult;
```

Formal parameter C yields the result and must be a VAR parameter. A and B may be value parameters. However, as stated earlier, a VAR parameter is recommended for efficiency reasons.

8.2.5 The array as a table

The common characteristics of the examples we have given so far is the fact that the loops always range over *all elements* of the arrays.

One of the typical applications of the array structure is a *table* that may be updated, sorted and searched for entries. In this case, loops often run only until an appropriate element is found.

To give a simple illustration, we wish to find the index j that corresponds to a given entry x in a table t:

```
TYPE Table = ARRAY n OF INTEGER;
VAR t: Table; j, x: INTEGER;
...
j := 0;
WHILE  (j < n) & (t[j] # x)  DO  INC(j)  END;
```

From the negation of the continuation condition, applying De Morgan's law, we infer that upon termination of the while statement, the condition $(i = n)$ OR $(t[j] = x)$ holds. If the first term is FALSE, the desired element is found and j is its index; if $j = n$, no $t[j]$ equals x.

The number of inspections needed to find x grows, on average, linearly with the size of the table. Hence this algorithm is also known as *linear search*.

Let us briefly consider a slightly changed version of the above program, namely

```
WHILE  (t[j] # x) & (j < n)  DO  INC(j)  END;
```

The interchange of the two Boolean factors appears quite legitimate at first sight. But if we consider the case where all elements differ from x, we find that at the very end the relation $t[n] \# x$ would be tested,

120 Type declarations, array and record types

implying access to an undeclared element. Hence this version is *wrong*. We now recall that the Boolean connectives $p \,\&\, q$ and $p \text{ OR } q$ have been defined in the form of a conditional evaluation of the second operand. As a consequence, they are *not commutative*. This conditional evaluation avoids, in the first and correct version, evaluation of $t[j] \# x$ when $j = n$.

Binary search

A more challenging problem is the search for a desired element, x say, in an array that is ordered; that is, $t[i] \leq t[j]$ for all i and j: $0 \leq i < j < n$ where n denotes the size of the table.

The best technique in this case is the so-called *binary search*: inspect the middle element, then apply the same method to either the left or the right half of the array:

```
PROCEDURE Search(VAR t: Table; x: INTEGER; VAR i: INTEGER);
VAR j, m: INTEGER;
BEGIN
  i := -1;  j := LEN(t);
  WHILE j # i + 1  DO  (* t[i] <= x < t[j] *)
    m := (i + j) DIV 2;
    IF t[m] <= x THEN  i := m ELSE  j := m  END
  END
  (* (t[i] <= x < t[j]) & (j = i + 1) *)
END Search;
```

Formal parameter i reports the position of x; hence it has to be a variable parameter. This is not the case for x, for which we choose a value parameter. A value parameter is also admissible for t, the table. However, for the stated reasons of efficiency, a variable parameter is advisable. Another good possibility is to make t an open array parameter.

We take this opportunity to use the formalism introduced in Chapters 4 and 5 to give a proof of this elegant piece of program. A clever trick avoids the need to consider special cases: the table t is augmented with two virtual elements $t[-1] = -\infty$ and $t[n] = \infty$. The virtual elements enter only into the predicates – they are not accessed in the statements.

Loop invariant

The loop invariant is the assertion

$$t[i] \leq x < t[j].$$

Formal parameter *i* and local variable *j* initially satisfy $i = -1$ and $j = n$. Using the value of our virtual elements, the invariant is easily established.

If the left branch of the if statement is taken, the value of *i* changes. We know, however, from the guard that $t[i] \leq x$. Since *j* remains unchanged, the invariant still holds.

If the right branch is activated, it follows that $\sim(t[j] \leq x)$, which is equivalent to $x < t[j]$. Again, since in this case *i* remains unchanged, the invariant remains valid.

Variant function In order to prove the program correct, we have to find a variant function that decreases monotonically with each iteration. In our case,

$$j - i$$

is this function.

At the start of each iteration, $i + 1 < j$. It follows that $i < m < j$ after the assignment to *m* is executed. Hence both assignments, $i := m$ and $j := m$, decrease the value $j - i$.

The binary search is therefore guaranteed to stop and to yield two indices *i* and *j* such that $j = i + 1$ and *x* is in the interval $t[i] \leq x < t[j]$. Test element *x* is found if $0 \leq i < n$ and $t[i] = x$. If, on the other hand,

- $i = -1$ then $x < t[0]$;
- $i = n - 1$ then $x > t[n - 1]$.

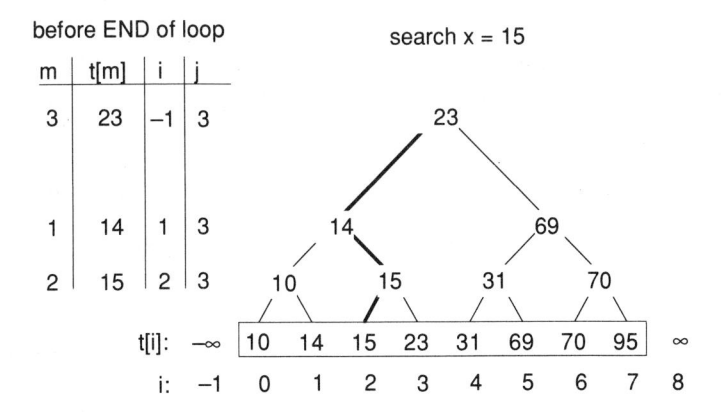

Figure 8.2 Analysis of the binary search algorithm.

Figure 8.2 portrays the binary search algorithm at work. The tree displays of all possible sequences $t[m]$ that may occur for any argument x. The interpretation as a tree reveals that the number of inspections is given by $\log_2(n)$ – a substantial saving over the linear count.

8.2.6 Strings and the type ARRAY n OF CHAR

Besides matrices and tables, *texts* are a third major application of arrays. A natural model of a text is an ordered sequence of characters. The character array (that is, an instance of the type ARRAY n OF CHAR) represents this notion in Oberon terms. Some sample declarations are

```
CONST n = 4048; m = 32;
TYPE
   Text = ARRAY n OF CHAR;
   Pattern = ARRAY m OF CHAR;
   NameList = ARRAY n OF ARRAY m OF CHAR;
VAR
   txt: Text; pat: Pattern; nl: NameList; str: ARRAY 5 OF CHAR;
```

Oberon affords facilities to assist in the manipulation of character arrays:

(1) String constants may be assigned to a character array.
(2) Character arrays can be compared; that is, they may form relations <, <=, >, >=, = and #. Variables and string constants can be mixed in such comparisons.

String termination

A string is represented as an ARRAY n OF CHAR with n greater than the length of the string (in characters). The string is terminated with the special character 0X. Similarly, if s denotes a character array, its textual value is represented by the array elements up to the first occurrence 0X. The *length* of a string s is the index of the terminator 0X. It should not be confused with LEN(s), the number of array elements of s.

The effect of the assignment s := "this" is depicted in Figure 8.3.

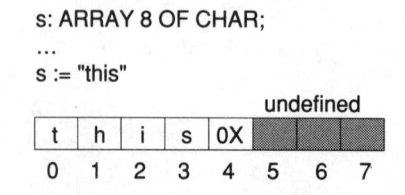

s: ARRAY 8 OF CHAR;
...
s := "this"

					undefined		
t	h	i	s	0X			
0	1	2	3	4	5	6	7

Figure 8.3 String termination and assignment.

To render the discussion of length more precise and to provide a first example, consider the function *Len*:

```
PROCEDURE Len(x: ARRAY OF CHAR): INTEGER;
VAR j: INTEGER;
BEGIN  (* there exists a k: 0 <= k < LEN(x): x[k] = 0X *)
    j := 0;
    WHILE x[j] > 0X DO INC(j) END;
    RETURN j
END Len;
```

Note that the open array parameter is essential. Also, since *x* is a value parameter, the function may be called with a string as actual parameter, for example *Len*("abc") = 3. The type ARRAY OF CHAR is one of the (few) good justifications for using a value parameter of array type.

COPY(s, x)

At first sight, the predeclared function COPY seems identical to the array assignment $x := s$. However, in COPY, only those elements of *x* participate in the copy operation that have indices smaller or equal to the length of *s*; that is, to that of the first 0X character. It follows that a precondition for COPY is LEN(*x*) > *Len*(*s*). COPY can be expressed as

```
PROCEDURE COPY(s: ARRAY OF CHAR; VAR x: ARRAY OF CHAR);
VAR j: INTEGER;
BEGIN  (* Len(x) > Len(s) *)
    j := 0;
    WHILE s[j] # 0X DO x[j] := s[j]; INC(j) END;
    x[j] := 0X
END COPY;
```

x := "*string*"

Note that since *s* is a value parameter, COPY may be called with a string as actual parameter. Such a call COPY("*string*", x) is identical to the assignment $x := $ "*string*". Obviously, LEN(*x*) must be bigger than the string length. In *x*, only those array elements with indices less than *Len*("*string*") are affected.

Relations

Character arrays and strings may be compared. The type rules are relaxed, the operands may be strings, variables of type ARRAY *n* OF CHAR or open array parameters. Using the declarations of our earlier example, the following comparisons are legal:

$$txt = pat \quad str = nl[3] \quad pat <= \text{"really?"}$$

Let $L_x = Len(x)$ and $L_y = Len(y)$. Then the definitions of the comparison operations are

$$x = y \equiv (L_x = L_y) \;\&\; (\forall k: 0 \leq k < L_x: x[k] = y[k]) \qquad (1)$$
$$x < y \equiv (L_x < L_y) \text{ OR } (\exists k: 0 \leq k < L_x: x[k] < y[k] \;\&\;$$
$$(\forall j: 0 \leq j < k: x[j] = y[j])) \qquad (2)$$

The inequality # follows from (1), and the comparisons <=, > and >= are defined analogously to (2).

It may be easier to remember the definitions of string comparison by the following rule: the shorter of the operands is padded with 0X to match the longer operand. The two are then compared using the ASCII collating sequence. Note, however, that this definition is algorithmic in nature, whereas Equations (1) and (2) are not.

A few examples should elucidate these concepts. Let s: ARRAY 8 OF CHAR and s := "this". Then the following hold:

s = "this"   s # "this."   s > "that"   s < "Xenon".

With these definitions, we have laid the groundwork for a few programming examples.

Search for a string in a table

Let the first task be to search a table *nl* of type *NameList* for a given character array *x*.

```
PROCEDURE Search(VAR nl: NameList; x: ARRAY OF CHAR;
                                            VAR j: INTEGER);
BEGIN
  j := 0;
  WHILE (j < LEN(nl)) & (nl[j] # x) DO INC(j) END
END Search;  (* x found if j < LEN(nl) *)
```

We observe that, thanks to the convenience afforded by the Oberon definition of comparing strings and character arrays, the search procedure is almost identical to the simple search for an integer in an integer array. If the name list *nl* is sorted, the efficient binary search can be easily adopted.

Search for a pattern in a text

A more exacting problem is the search for a pattern *x* in a text *txt*. Both the text and the pattern are assumed to be character arrays, properly closed with the string terminator 0X.

```
PROCEDURE Locate(VAR txt: ARRAY OF CHAR;
                        x: ARRAY OF CHAR; VAR pos: INTEGER);
  VAR j, Lx, Lt: INTEGER;
  BEGIN Lx := Len(x); Lt := Len(txt):  pos := -1
    REPEAT  j := 0;
      INC(pos);
      WHILE (x[j] = txt[pos + j]) & (j < Lx) DO  INC(j)  END
    UNTIL (j = Lx) OR ((pos + Lx) > Lt);
    IF  j < Lx THEN  pos := -1 (* pattern not found *)  END
  END Locate;
```

Insertion of a pattern into a text

Text search is often paired with a deletion, a replacement or an insertion of a pattern. We illustrate the insert operation of a pattern *x* into the text *txt* after the character with index *pos*. We assume that $0 \leq pos < Len(t)$.

```
PROCEDURE Insert(VAR txt: ARRAY OF CHAR;
                        x: ARRAY OF CHAR; pos: INTEGER);
  VAR j, Lt, Lx: INTEGER;
  BEGIN
    Lt := Len(txt);  Lx := Len(x);
    IF (Lx + Lt < LEN(txt)) & (pos >= 0) & (pos <= Lt) THEN
      (* make room *) j := Lt;
      WHILE j >= pos DO  txt[j + Lx] := txt[j];  DEC(j)  END;
      (* copy pattern x after character txt[pos] *)
      j := 0;
      WHILE j < Lx DO  txt[pos + j] := x[j]; INC(j)  END
    END
  END Insert;
```

This example illustrates two typical disadvantages of arrays if used as data structures for tables or texts:

(1) We have to make sure that there is room for an insertion within the size of the table or of the character array and deal properly with the overflow exception.

(2) Prior to inserting an entry or string, we have to make room by shifting part of the table or of the character array.

Both problems may be circumvented using dynamic data structures. However, such an approach has also its price in either a more complex program and/or less efficient usage of storage resources.

8.3 Records

8.3.1 The record type and the record declaration

In an array all elements are of the same type. Elements may be accessed through a computed index. In contrast, the record structure offers the possibility to declare a collection of elements as a unit, even if the elements are of different types. The record is therefore called a *heterogeneous structure*.

The origin of this data structure lies in commercial data processing.[1] Records model rows in a table drawn on paper. If matrix multiplication is inevitable in the introduction of arrays, the personnel record is a similar requirement in the case of records. An excerpt from such a list of employees appears in Figure 8.4.

Name	First Name	IdNo	Salary
Ando	Gabi	766051	40150
Dowe	Sally	341749	31500
Smith	Kimber	416490	35500
Roke	John	843847	22000

Figure 8.4 An excerpt of a personnel record in table form.

A row in the list is called a record. The description of an employee consists of the person's name, given name, identification number, the date of birth and salary. In Oberon, this is expressed in the following type declaration:

```
TYPE
    Name = ARRAY 32 OF CHAR;
    Employee = RECORD
                family, first: Name;
                id, salary: INTEGER
            END;
```

---

[1] Programming language COBOL.

The record type declaration observes the following syntax:

> RecordType = "RECORD" FieldListSequence "END".
> FieldListSequence = FieldList { ";" FieldList }.
> FieldList = [IdentList ":" type].
> IdentList = ident ["*"] { ident ["*"] }.

The record structure makes it possible to refer either to the entire collection of data or to individual elements. Elements of a record are also called *record fields*, and their names are the *field identifiers*. Each identifier of the *IdentList* defines a record field of the declared type.

The asterisk is the familiar export mark that applies selectively to the fields. Only exported fields are visible in client modules. They are called *public fields*. Unmarked fields are known as *private fields*: they are only visible within the module containing the record declaration. Selective export is an important programming tool – leading to the notion of data abstraction. We will say more about this in Chapter 10. Note that when fields in a record *r* are exported, *r* should be exported too.

Recursive type declarations are prohibited. The following is an example of such a recursive type declaration that is not ruled out by the formal syntax but is still illegal:

> R = RECORD x: R END;

Scope of fields   The fields are local objects of their record. The scope of the field identifier is the record definition itself (from keyword "RECORD" to keyword "END"). Outside this scope, they are visible, but in the form of field designators of the form *r.f*, where *r* is the record and *f* the field identifier (see the next section). This implies that outside of the record scope, the identifier *f* may be reused. For example, the following declaration sequence is valid:

> TYPE R = RECORD a: INTEGER; b: REAL END;
> VAR a: REAL;

A variable of type record is declared in the usual way, for example

> VAR worker, manager: Employee;

As with arrays, a variable of record type may be declared with the type left anonymous. Instances of records that are identically structured to the type *Employee* are generated by the following declaration:

```
VAR
    person: RECORD
            family, first: Name;
            id, salary: INTEGER
          END;
```

Applying the type compatibility rules set forth in the first section of this chapter, we conclude that the type of the variable *person* is not compatible with the type of the variables *worker* and *manager*. Thus an assignment *person := worker* is rejected by the compiler.

Nested records Similarly to arrays, where an array element could itself be of array type, a record field may be of record type. We may augment the definition of the type *Employee* with the date of birth:

```
TYPE
    Date = RECORD  mo, day, yr: INTEGER  END;
    Employee = RECORD
                    family, first: Name;
                    birth: Date;
                    id, salary: INTEGER
               END;
```

Mixed record and array types In the preceding sections we have introduced the array and record structures as separate entities. The alert reader may have noted, however, that both declarations are recursive on *type*, not on *ArrayType* or *RecordType*. Thus the elements of arrays may be records and the field of records arrays – or arrays of arrays – in any desired order and depth of nesting.

We saw that the array is the model of a table and the record of a row in such a table. Hence only the combination of the two structured types properly models a table such as the employee data sheet depicted in Figure 8.4. A sample declaration may read as follows:

```
VAR DataSheet: ARRAY n OF Employee;
```

Fields of records may be arrays. For example, the type *Name* is likely a character array; that is, *name* = ARRAY *n* OF CHAR.

8.3.2 The record designator, assignments and expressions

We denote the field *f* of record *r* by

```
r.f
```

The field designator is thus composed of the record identifier followed by the field's name, juxtaposed with a period in between. The general syntax of a record designator is:

> designator = qualident {"." selector }.
> selector = ident.

We note that the added generality of the record compared with the array, namely its possible heterogeneity, is compensated by a restriction: the identification of an element is limited to a *fixed* name, the field's identifier. This is in contrast to the array, where elements may be selected by a computable index.

In the case of nested record types (that is, records that contain sub-records), *selectors can be sequenced*. Assume that *worker* is a variable of type *Employee* declared at the end of the preceding section. Then:

worker.id	field of type INTEGER
worker.birth	sub-record, type *Date*
worker.birth.yr	field of type INTEGER

Assume now that the variable *manager* which is of type *Employee* is imported from a module *Personnel*. Then we can construct the designators

Personnel.manager.id	type INTEGER
Personnel.manager.birth	type *Date*
Personnel.manager.birth.mo	type INTEGER

Looking at these designators, we observe that the first period belongs to the qualident *Personnel.manager* and thus differs from the subsequent use of the period to delineate field selectors.

Record assignments and expressions

A variable of record type may appear on the left-hand side of an assignment. The only expression is a mere solitary designator. Record variables cannot be operands or be compared.

For example, the following are valid record assignments:

> worker := manager;   person.birth := manager.birth;

Parameters

The rules for parameters of record type are analogous to simple variables or arrays. The type must be explicit. In the case of a value parameter, storage is reserved and a copy operation takes place at the time of the call. This is avoided with VAR parameters, where the actual parameter substitutes as variable. No extra storage is required and no copying takes place. Therefore, as with arrays, we recommend the use of VAR parameters for efficiency reasons, even if they remain unchanged by the procedure.

8.3.3 Use of records

The use of variables of record type in commercial programming has been mentioned. Databases, from small to gigantic, are a main application in this business, and the elements they contain are typically records.

Another use also goes back to the earliest days of operating systems: the *control block*, a record variable defining a collection of parameters describing a resource or a request. Terms such as file control block or task control block are familiar to most system programmers. Facilities to create records were already part of the more sophisticated assemblers in existence 30 years ago.

The record is always indicated if a set of parameters define a single object. For example, take a rectangle to be drawn on a display device. The rectangle is defined by the coordinates x and y of one of the corners, a width w and a height h. To handle a number of such rectangles, the programmer might declare four arrays:

    VAR x, y, w, h ARRAY n OF INTEGER;

Experience shows, however, that the clarity of the program will often benefit substantially if a record type is used:

    TYPE Rect = RECORD
        x, y, w, h: INTEGER
    END;
    VAR r ARRAY n OF Rect;

It is now possible to refer to rectangles as entities, for example in procedures such as

    PROCEDURE XYinRect(x, y: INTEGER; r: Rect): BOOLEAN;

Finally the record is the building block of dynamic data structures – one of the most powerful programming constructs. In such dynamic data structures, a record is composed of data fields and pointer fields providing links to other records. Pointers and dynamic data structures will be the object of Chapter 9.

8.4 Summary

In this chapter, we have introduced the *type declaration* and two important structured data types: the *array* and the *record*.

The *type declaration* allows user-defined types. An identifier is bound to a type that may be a basic type such as INTEGER or REAL or – more importantly – a structured type such as an array or a record. The type declaration is an essential tool in the formulation of abstract data types, a topic explored in Chapter 10 and Part III.

The *array* is a variable of *array type*. The array type defines a structure composed of a number of elements of the same type. Elements are selected by means of a computable index. The number of elements is called the *length* of the array. An array designator is of the form a[i]. The expression *i* is evaluated and selects the *i*th element of the array *a*. The array type definition is recursive: it allows the declaration of arrays of arrays or *multidimensional arrays*.

As with any variable, an array may serve as a parameter of a procedure. Especially versatile is the *open array parameter*, which is compatible with any array of the same dimension and element type.

Programming would hardly be what it is today without the array. Examples have been presented from the fields of numerical procedures, processing of tables and text handling.

Of special interest is the representation of textual data by the type ARRAY n OF CHAR. Oberon relaxes type rules to allow *assignments of strings* to character arrays and comparisons of character arrays with character arrays and strings.

While the array is a structured type of like elements, the record type offers the possibility of declaring a collection of *fields* as a unit, even if the fields are of different type. A field *f* of a record *r* is designated by *r.f*. Records are used in commercial programming, and they are the building blocks of dynamic data structures and represent abstract data types, the topics of Chapters 9 and 10.

8.5 Exercises

8.1 [**Galton board**] A Galton board is an apparatus named after the pioneering Victorian statistician Sir Francis Galton (1822–1911).

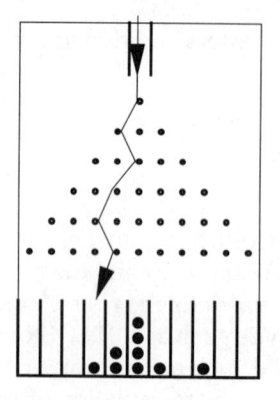

It is a triangular array of pegs in a slanted board. Marbles are released at the top and proceed to the bottom, where they are collected in an array of channels. Of interest to the experimenter is the resulting shape of the curve formed by the stacked marbles. Implement a module that simulates a Galton board.

Hint: there is no need to represent the configuration of pegs – all that matters is the *number of left and right bounces*.

Use an array to accumulate the balls in the channels. Run the simulation for 1000 balls and produce a print-out using procedures of module *Out*. Repeat the experiment with 1000, 10 000 and 100 000 balls. Draw the graph of the resulting curve.

8.2 **[Histogram]** Write a module *Histogram* that contains procedures and commands to compute and display histograms (see Box 10.1). The number of intervals, their width and the number of random samples are read from the input stream. Using module *XYplane*, provide graphical output of the histogram in the form of a bar chart like that in Box 10.1.

Experiment with uniform random numbers and with exponential random numbers. In the latter case, choose a variety of parameter values *mu*.

8.3 **[Backup file name]** An Oberon file name is composed of identifiers juxtaposed with periods, such as "Syntax.Scn.Fnt" or "IFS1.Mod". Write a procedure that takes a file name and appends the suffix "Bak", yielding for example "Syntax.Scn.Fnt.Bak" or "IFS1.Mod.Bak". Make sure that no index violation can occur.

8.4 **[Matrix output]** Write a procedure that displays a matrix (filled with random numbers) as a two-dimensional table of properly aligned rows and columns.

8.5 **[Extremal array elements]** Write a procedure that computes indices *min* and *max* such that $a[min]$ and $a[max]$ are the smallest and the largest elements of an array a: ARRAY n OF REAL. *Note*: a solution with $3n/2$ comparisons is possible. Can you find it?

8.6 **[Sorting]** Given an array a of n numbers, write a procedure to sort them by repeating the following process for $i = 1, 2,...,n - 1$:

  (1) Find the least number among $a[i]...a[n]$.
  (2) Interchange this number with $a[i]$, if appropriate.

Specify invariants for the repetition.

8.7 **[Phone directory]** Write a module *PhoneDir* that provides a phone directory based on the type declaration

```
TYPE Dir = ARRAY n OF RECORD
            name: ARRAY 32 OF CHAR;
            phone: ARRAY 16 OF CHAR
          END;
```

Provide commands to open the directory and add, delete and query entries. Guard against table overflow. Provide two versions: one based on a simple linear search, and another using a binary search.

8.8 **[Random walk]** Let a particle move on a discrete square lattice. From the current position, the next one is chosen at random from the four neighboring points.

Write a module that displays a random walk in a N by N square on the *XYplane* viewer. At any point in time, display the past k positions. Consider different strategies when the particle hits the boundary: (1) compute the position modulo N; (2) reflect the particle; (3) wait until the particle re-enters the area; or (4) the particle is lost.

8.9 **[Diffusion-limited growth]** Particles originating in random direction move according to a random walk. When a particle hits a growing aggregate, it sticks there. Diffusion-limited growth occurs in nature, for example in the accumulation of soot, the growth in electrolytic solutions and leaders in electrical discharge. The resulting figure is a fractal.

Work with a square lattice centered around the origin. Inscribe two circles. Random walks originate at an arbitrary position on the smaller circle. If a particle passes the extinction circle, it is lost and a new random walk is started. If a particle meets the aggregate, it sticks and a new random walks commences. When the process starts, the aggregate consists of a single square at the origin.

Working with *XYplane*, make the path of the random walk visible and draw the growing aggregate.

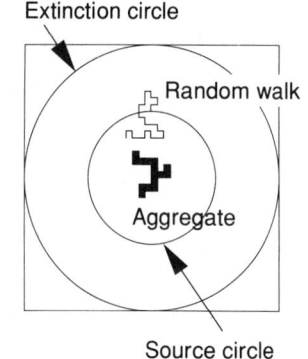

9 Dynamic data structures and pointer types

So far, we have introduced the eight basic types SHORTINT, INTEGER, LONGINT, REAL, LONGREAL, BOOLEAN, CHAR and SET. These basic types have a strong kinship with the hardware facility of the underlying computing machines.

The two structured types ARRAY and RECORD are built from elements of basic type. The array is an ordered assemblage of elements of identical type that can be selected by a computable index. The record is a named collection of fields, possibly of different types. Figure 9.1 depicts the array and record structures.

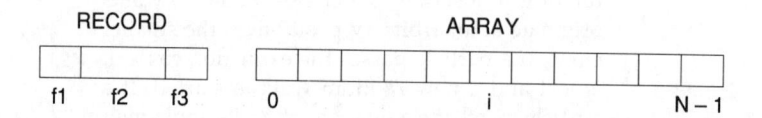

Figure 9.1 Mapping of a record and an array onto a linear address space.

Both the array type and the record type have the common trait that they are *static*. This implies that variables of such type maintain the same structure during the whole time of their existence. The array and the record also share the property that they can be easily mapped onto a linear address space – hence the compiler is able to generate efficient code for assignments and expressions.

Many applications process data that not only change their value – but also their *relationship and bulk*. Typical examples are lists (or chains) and trees that grow and shrink *dynamically*. Rather than adding further structured types to the language, Oberon offers the basic tool to construct arbitrary structures: the *pointer type*.

Every complex structure ultimately consists of elements whose structure is static. Pointers are used to establish relationships among those static elements – often called *nodes*. We say that a pointer *links* nodes or *points to* nodes.

What makes pointers such a powerful tool is the fact that they may point to records that themselves contain pointers. Consider the following declarations:

```
TYPE
    ListNode = POINTER TO ListNodeDesc;
    ListNodeDesc = RECORD
        key: Key;  next: Node
    END;
VAR first: ListNode;
```

The definition is obviously *recursive*. A schematic diagram of a list composed of instances of the type *ListNodeDesc* is shown in Figure 9.2.

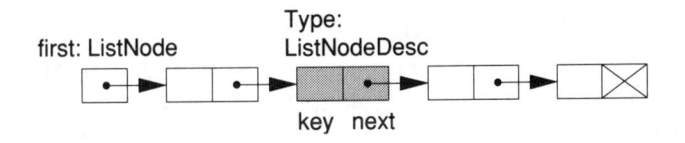

Figure 9.2 A linear list composed of records with pointer fields.

The variable *first*, which is a pointer of type *ListNode*, affords access to the first element of the list. Each node contains a pointer field that points to the next node in the list. Thus, from the first node, one can gain access to the second one, and so forth.

Evidently, different pointer variables may point to the same node, hence providing the possibility to construct arbitrarily complex structures. This apparent power of the pointer type is at the same time its nemesis – opening boundless possibilities for programming mistakes that are difficult to pinpoint. We end this introduction with a warning: *operating with pointers requires utmost care*.

There is a substantial body of knowledge concerning dynamic data structures and their algorithms. (Many textboks exist. Good introductions are Wirth (1976), Smith (1987) and Sedgewick (1988).) This chapter deals only with elementary examples of lists and trees. However, the list processing procedures will resurface in many subsequent examples and merit the reader's attention.

9.1 Pointers

9.1.1 The pointer type and pointer declarations

In Oberon, a pointer cannot point to arbitrary variables but only to an instance of a given array or record type. The pointer type is said to be *bound* to the referenced object's type, also termed the pointer's *base type*. The syntax of a pointer type declaration is

> PointerType = "POINTER" "TO" baseType.
> baseType = qualident | ArrayType | RecordType.

The qualident represents a type that is also either an array type or a record type.

The following are a few examples of pointer and pointer type declarations:

```
TYPE
    TreeNode = POINTER TO TreeNodeDesc;
    TreeNodeDesc = RECORD
                     key: Key;
                     left, right: TreeNode
                   END;

    FileCtlBlock = POINTER TO RECORD
                     length, date, pos, sectorTable: LONGINT;
                     name: ARRAY 32 OF CHAR
                   END;

    Vect = POINTER TO ARRAY n OF REAL;
```

Assignment and expressions Pointers may be assigned to pointer variables of compatible type. Pointers of compatible type can be compared for *equality* or *inequality* — the only expressions in which pointers enter as operands. At this stage, only pointer variables of equal type are compatible.

The value NIL A special pointer value is provided that points to no object and is *compatible with all pointer types*. The predeclared identifier NIL represents that constant. NIL may be assigned to or compared with every pointer. NIL is typically used to end referencing recursion.

9.1.2 Creation of variables referenced by pointers

Like the other variables that we have encountered so far, a pointer may be created in a VAR declaration. We say that the declaration creates an instance of the pointer type, P say. Storage for the pointer variable is allocated when the scope containing its declaration becomes active. If different from NIL, the value of such a pointer *designates a variable*. The type of that variable is the *base type* of P.

However, the declaration of the pointer does not produce the variable it points to. Such a variable must be *explicitly generated* invoking the predeclared procedure

   NEW(p)

where the actual parameter p is a pointer of type P. NEW(p) creates a variable that is an *instance of the base type of P*. The pointer p is initialized such that it points to that instance (Figure 9.3).

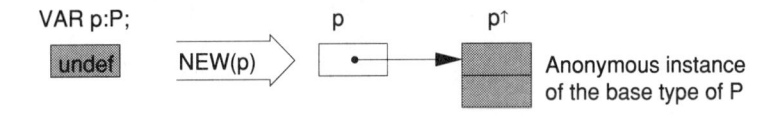

Figure 9.3 Creation of an instance of type P.

For example, assume *first*: ListNode and *root*: TreeNode. Then

   NEW(*first*) A variable of type ListNode is created, which is designated by pointer *first*.
   NEW(*root*)   A variable of type TreeNode is created, which is designated by pointer *root*.

9.1.3 Dereferencing a pointer

NEW(p) creates a variable that is an instance of the base type of P. This variable is dynamically created. It is therefore not designated by an identifier – we say the *variable is anonymous*. In order to reference an anonymous variable, the dereferencing operator ↑ is applied to the pointer, written as $p↑$.[1] Thus the designator $p↑$ denotes the variable

---

[1] In the standard ASCII character set "↑" is represented by the caret "^", with ORD("^") = 94.

pointed at by *p*. A pointer *cannot be dereferenced if its value is* NIL. Oversight of this rule results in abnormal program termination.

We are ready to generalize the syntax of the designator to include the dereferencing operator:

designator = qualident { ident | "[" ExpList "]" | "↑" }.

Implied dereferencing

In programs using pointers, dereferencing occurs quite frequently. As a convenience for the programmer and to enhance the readability of program texts, Oberon *implies dereferencing* in the case where a record field or array element is accessed through a pointer variable. For example, using our earlier sample declarations and the array pointer *vector*: *Vect*, we find that

first.next stands for first↑.next
root.key stands for root↑.key
vector[i] stands for vector↑[i]

Thus if a field or index selector is present we may use the pointer *as if it were a name of the variable pointed at*. We stress, however, that this abbreviation holds only for fields and array elements. The designator *first*, for example, denotes a pointer value, not an object of type *ListNode*. Such an object is referenced by *first*↑. To refine this point, let *node*: *ListNode* and consider the assignments:

node := first   illegal assignment, pointer to record
node := first↑   legal assignment, record to record.

Nested dereferencing

Dereferencing may be nested. To illustrate this concept consider the list shown in Figure 9.4, for which the following relations hold:

first↑.*key* = *first.key* = *k1*
first↑.*next*↑.*key* = *first.next.key* = *k2*
first↑ *next*↑.*next*↑.*key* = *first.next.next.key* = *k3*
first↑.*next*↑.*next*↑.*next* = *first.next.next.next* = NIL

first: ListNode

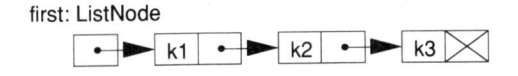

```
[•]→[k1] [•]→[k2] [•]→[k3][⊠]
```

Figure 9.4 Sample list composed of three nodes.

9.1.4 Memory management

Memory resources for a module's statement sequence, the statement sequences of its procedures, and for its *global variables* is allocated, at the latest, when an exported identifier is used. These memory resources are *statically allocated*. They exist as long as the module remains loaded.

Stack

At the time the statement sequence of a procedure is activated, memory for the *local variables* (including parameters) is allocated. This memory is tied up only during the time the procedure is active. The combined local memory of the procedures active at a given time is known as *stack* – owing to a standard method of implementation. It grows and shrinks with the nesting of procedure calls. The memory allocation for the stack is called *dynamic*.

Heap

The storage for pointer variables is managed like any other variable – it is either allocated globally or on the stack. However, memory for the objects pointed to by pointers is only reserved at the time of a call to NEW. Since calls of NEW may occur at any time, it is advantageous to allot a third kind of memory known as the *heap*.

Garbage collection

Without special measures, the heap grows monotonically in time. However – as the term implies – dynamic data structures may grow and shrink. Computing systems differ in the way the heap is kept under control. It is still customary to relegate this task to the programmer. Such systems afford a predeclared function FREE(p) or DEALLOCATE(p). The task to free unused nodes of dynamic data structures is not only a burden on the programmer – it is also *error prone*. Suppose a node is freed up, but pointers which referenced that node are still in existence. Any attempt at dereferencing such a pointer will result in a catastrophic error. Oberon advocates the use of automatic cleanup of the heap, known as *garbage collection*, and thereby relieves programmers from the burden of keeping track of allocation problems while, at the same time, eliminating a source of errors that are difficult to pinpoint.

9.2 Lists

9.2.1 Simple or linear lists

In the last section, we developed the tools necessary to deal with dynamic data structures. The list structure provides a suitable first example. Lists appear in a variety of applications, spanning the breadth from commercial programming over system simulations to operating systems. A list is a chain of records, linked together through pointers.

We recapitulate the type declaration of a list node, for simplicity named *Node* (rather than *ListNode* as before):

```
TYPE
   Node = POINTER TO NodeDesc;
   NodeDesc = RECORD
      key: Key;
      next: Node
   END;
```

Note that the node type (*NodeDesc*) must be explicit to avoid an illegal recursive type definition of the form

Node = POINTER TO RECORD key: Key; next: Node END;

Since we want to concentrate on the essentials, we do not carry data fields in the list nodes – the field *key* stands for the data stored in the list node. The name *key* suggests a special usage: the list is searched for a record matching a given key. For that purpose, lists are frequently sorted according to increasing or decreasing key values. In real applications, a node usually has a variety of data fields of different type. *Key* denotes the type of the key. It may by any type that is compatible with the relations 'less than', for example INTEGER, REAL or ARRAY n OF CHAR.

Create node

Declaration of a pointer of type *Node* does *not create a list*. The list has to be *built dynamically during program execution*.

Let us start with the empty list *x*, which is represented by *x* = NIL. A longer list is most conveniently constructed by inserting new nodes at its front. An instance *new* of type *Node* with key *k* is created as follows:

NEW(new); new.key := k; new.next := NIL;

9.2 Lists

These three statements produce a structure that may be viewed itself as a small list composed of one single element (see Figure 9.5).

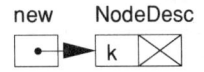

Figure 9.5 A newly created list node.

Insert

The simplest operation is to insert a newly created node at the beginning of a list. Let the variable *new* denote such a node and *first* be a pointer that provides a link to the first node of the list. The pointer *first* is also termed the *anchor of the list*. Two assignments suffice to add the new node to the list as shown in Figure 9.6 and in the sample procedure *Insert*:

```
PROCEDURE Insert(VAR first: Node; new: Node);
BEGIN (* new # NIL, no test for duplicate nodes *)
    new.next := first;  first := new
END Insert;
```

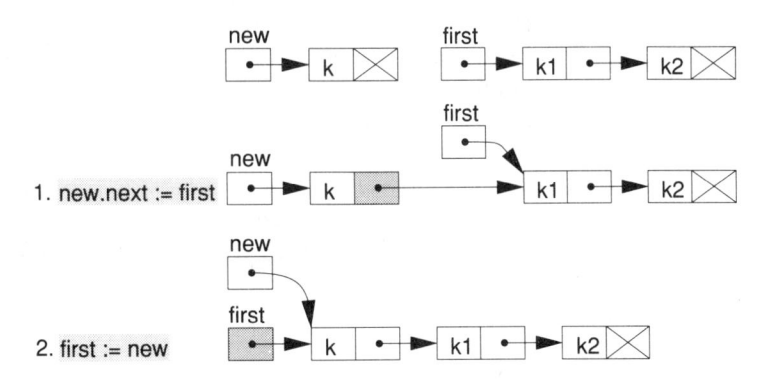

1. new.next := first
2. first := new

Figure 9.6 Insertion of a node at the head of the list.

Remove first node

Removal of the first node of a list is also an easy operation.

```
PROCEDURE FirstNode(VAR first: Node): Node;
VAR n: Node;
BEGIN
    n := first;  IF  n # NIL THEN  first := n.next  END;
    RETURN n
END FirstNode;
```

Note the guard *n* # NIL that is necessary to avoid potential dereferencing of a NIL pointer. As subsequent examples will reveal, it is quite typical that the empty list needs to be treated as a special case. Also observe that *first* is a VAR parameter through which procedure *FirstNode* produces a side-effect.

List traversal

A basic operation on dynamic data structures is their traversal. Each node *n* is visited exactly once in a specified order, and a certain operation, *P(n)* say, is applied. For example, the node's key is listed or the node itself is copied. The following example of procedure *Enumerate* traverses a list and applies procedure *P* to every node:

```
PROCEDURE Enumerate(first: Node);
BEGIN
    WHILE first # NIL DO  P(first);  first := first.next  END
END Enumerate;
```

The while statement expresses list traversal both naturally and efficiently. Observe that the formal parameter *first* also serves as local variable used in the while-loop. This is permitted, since *first* is a value parameter. Hence the actual parameter passed to *first* remains unchanged, as is required for a proper operation of *Enumerate*.

Insert at tail

Adding a node at the head of the list is particularly simple, since the anchor points directly to the first node. No such direct link exists to the last element. Adding a node there requires first a *traversal of the list* – an operation whose complexity is proportional to the number of list elements

```
PROCEDURE InsertLast(VAR first: Node; new: Node);
VAR n: Node;
BEGIN  (* new # NIL *)
    IF first = NIL THEN  new.next := first; first := new
    ELSE
        n := first;
        WHILE n.next # NIL DO  n := n.next  END;
```

9.2 Lists

```
        new.next := n.next; n.next := new
    END
END InsertLast;
```

In this example, *first* is a VAR parameter — hence an additional local variable *n* is needed for list traversal.

Insert ranked

Lists are sometimes sorted, for example in order of ascending key values. If a new node is inserted in such a *ranked list*, it should be done such that the order is preserved. Procedure *InsertRanked* fulfills this requirement:

```
PROCEDURE InsertRanked(VAR first: Node; new: Node);
VAR n: Node;
BEGIN (* new # NIL *)
    IF (first = NIL) OR (new.key < first.key) THEN
        new.next := first;  first := new
    ELSE
        n := first;
        WHILE (n.next # NIL) & (new.key >= n.next.key) DO
            n := n.next
        END;
        new.next := n.next;  n.next := new
    END
END InsertRanked;
```

If no node with the specified key exists, NIL is returned. Again, the list is traversed until the appropriate element is found. It is essential that the compound condition be written as (*first* # NIL) & (*first.key* # *k*) and not the other way around, otherwise dereferencing of a NIL pointer may take place and the computation will abort.

Search a key

Another frequent operation is the extraction of an element with a given key:

```
PROCEDURE Search(first: Node; k: Key): Node;
BEGIN
    WHILE (first # NIL) & (first.key # k) DO first := first.next END;
    RETURN first
END Search ;
```

If no node with the specified key exists, NIL is returned. The list is traversed until the appropriate element is found.

Delete

As a final example, we will study how a given node is deleted from the list:

```
PROCEDURE Delete(VAR first: Node; node: Node);
VAR n: Node;
BEGIN (* node # NIL *)
   IF first # NIL THEN
      IF first = node THEN  first := node.next
      ELSE
         n := first;
         WHILE (n.next # NIL) & (n.next # node) DO
            n := n.next
         END;
         IF n.next # NIL THEN n.next := n.next.next END
      END
   END
END Delete;
```

Summary

We could give many more examples of procedures operating on simple lists. They all turn out to be variations on the themes that we encountered previously and that we summarize as follows:

(1) Operations at the head of the list are simple. Their execution is fast and independent of the size of the list. In contrast, operations at the end of the list require that the list be traversed. Their execution time is therefore proportional to the size of the list.

(2) The programmer must always ensure that dereferencing pointers whose value is NIL is excluded. Typically, the NIL case is a special branch in an if statement.

9.2.2 FIFO lists

Lists are a natural representation of waiting lines or *queues*. Such lines always form if a serially reusable resource is shared among many requests that arrive at arbitrary points in time. If requests are served in order of arrival the line is said to be operating under the *first-in, first-out* discipline – in short, FIFO.

FIFO operation is achieved if procedures *InsertLast* and *FirstNode* are used in combination. However, adding an element at the end of a linear list is an expensive operation. In implementing a FIFO queue, therefore, we strive for a special optimization of that operation. For this purpose, we will introduce an additional record type that comprises two pointers designating the last and the first node in the waiting line:

```
TYPE
    FIFO = RECORD
        first, last: Node
    END
```

Figure 9.7 depicts the dynamic data structure of a FIFO queue.

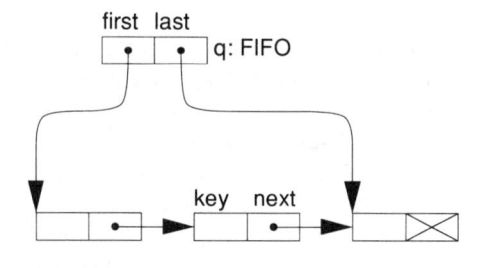

Figure 9.7 Structure of a FIFO queue.

Hint

The information afforded by field *last* is redundant. It is already contained in the pointer *first*. The extra field, should therefore be considered as a *hint*, to be used to improve the performance of the append operation.

Enqueueing and dequeueing of entries is performed by the following pair of procedures:

```
PROCEDURE Enqueue(VAR q: FIFO; n: Node);
BEGIN
    n.next := NIL;
    IF q.first # NIL THEN q.last.next := n ELSE q.first := n END;
    q.last := n
END Enqueue;
```

At first sight, the guard *q.first* # NIL seems perplexing – *q.last* # NIL seems the logical choice. A study of *DequeuedNode* reveals that *last* is not set to NIL when the queue empties out. This is permissible, since *last* is only considered a hint. It is, of course, possible to make last more precise – at the cost, however, of an additional if statement:

```
PROCEDURE DequeuedNode(VAR q: FIFO): Node;
VAR n: Node;
BEGIN
    n := q.first;
    IF n # NIL THEN q.first := n.next END;
    RETURN n
END DequeuedNode;
```

9.3 Trees

The use of an array to represent a table was introduced in Section 8.2.5. It is easy to see that lists may serve the same purpose – the data attached to each list node is an entry in the table.

The disadvantages of the array structure to represent tables are the need to specify a maximum size and the fact that to insert an element at a given position, one has to move entries to make room. Experienced programmers know the dilemma of choosing a maximal table size: every choice – however well reasoned – is wrong in some applications. The list structure neither has an upper limit nor is there a need to shift elements around. When it comes to sorted (static) tables, however, the array structure scores well, because of the fast binary search algorithm.

Binary search tree

Our goal, is to design therefore a dynamic data structure that admits fast search and sort algorithms. The essence of the binary search is the possibility of accessing the middle and deciding whether the test key is in the left or right half. Obviously, if the nodes are arranged in an ordered tree, the same procedure can be formulated. An example of such a tree is given in Figure 9.8.

A search tree is an *ordered binary tree*. A binary tree is said to be ordered if every node has two successors for which the key value of the node at left is smaller than the key value of the node at right.

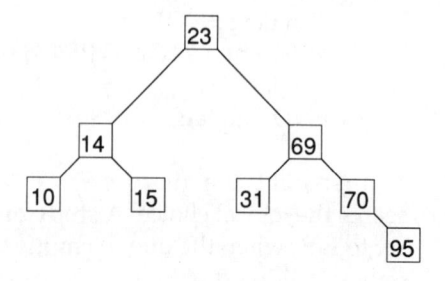

Figure 9.8 A binary search tree.

9.3 Trees

Other trees The tree structure also occurs naturally in many other contexts. One does not have to be a programmer to know the pedigree (or family) tree. Closer to computer science are parsing trees, which are at the heart of compilers. Another example is furnished by game-playing programs, which are typically based on a tree representation of the future moves emanating from a given position.

Type definitions Let us recapitulate the type definitions of a *binary* tree:

> TYPE
>   Node = POINTER TO NodeDesc;
>   NodeDesc = RECORD
>   key: Key;
>   left, right: Node
>   END;

As in Section 9.2, we call a tree node simply *Node*, rather than *TreeNode*. Similarly, the field *key* represents all the data stored in a tree node. A diagram in the same style adopted for lists is presented in Figure 9.9.

The tree definition is again recursive. The pointer *root* serves as anchor and provides a link to the first node which is also known as the root node. The pointer fields *left* and *right* point themselves to tree nodes which are the roots of *sub-trees*. The data recursion stops at NIL pointers. Nodes without links to sub-trees are termed *leaves*.

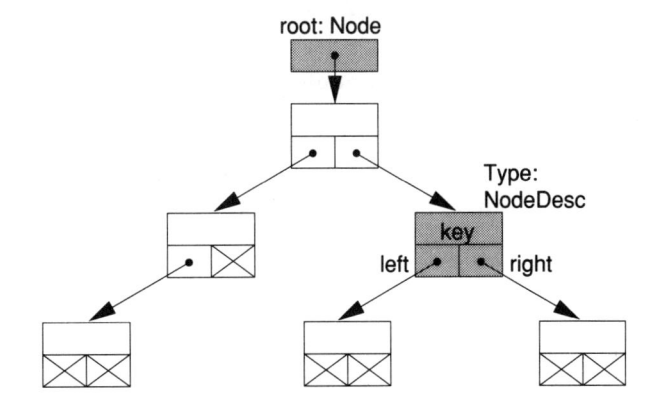

Figure 9.9 Data structure of a binary tree.

9.3.1 Inherently recursive procedures

The fundamental type definitions of both the list and the tree are recursive. Therefore one would expect that their processing also leads naturally to recursive procedures. In the realm of trees, this is indeed the case. A first example is furnished by the fundamental operation of traversing an ordered (binary) tree.

Tree traversal To each node n of a given ordered tree, a specific procedure $P(n)$ is applied. Often it is desirable to sequence the operations in order of increasing key values.

If we look at the preceding diagram, we realize that tree traversal is not simply expressible as a loop. We follow all the left branches to the first leave. Then we have to *backtrack* to the first node with a right branch, which we take, just to repeat the whole procedure. This informal description again points to the recursive nature of the problem.

Assume that *root* is a pointer providing a link to the root node. If the tree is empty (that is, if *root* = NIL) then no work has to be done. If not, we know that all nodes in the sub-tree pointed at by *root.left* have key values that are smaller than *root.key*. Hence we apply the whole procedure to *root.left* first. Once this is done, it is the root's turn. The action is applied to the node pointed at by *root*. Subsequently, it is the turn of all keys bigger than or equal to *root.key* – hence the whole procedure is applied again to *root.right*. In Oberon notation, this recursive algorithm is translated into the procedure:

```
PROCEDURE Enumerate(root: Node);
BEGIN
    IF root # NIL THEN
        Enumerate(root.left); P(root); Enumerate(root.right)
    END
END Enumerate;
```

We observe that the recursive data definition leads naturally – one might say effortlessly – to the recursive algorithm. The same, of course, is also true for lists. Recursion is used in the following variant of list traversal:

```
PROCEDURE Enumerate(first: ListNode);
BEGIN
    IF first # NIL THEN
        P(first); Enumerate(first.next)
    END
END Enumerate;
```

In the case of lists, the recursive formulation is not really simpler than the iterative one. Since each procedure call requires some *overhead for bookkeeping operations*, the iterative formulation, using a while statement, will execute faster, and hence is the method of choice.

No simple iterative formulation exists for traversing a tree. In fact, a close examination reveals that non-recursive formulations closely mimic the mentioned bookkeeping of recursive procedure calls (method of local stacks). Therefore recursion is the appropriate method for tree traversal.

Insert a node

Another inherently recursive operation is the insertion of a new node into an ordered tree, such that the order is preserved. For the special case of the empty tree (that is, *root* = NIL), the insert operation is easily solved: the new node, *new* say, simply becomes the root. This is stated as follows:

>   root := new;

In the case of a non-empty tree, we have to find the appropriate place to add the new node. Being at the root, all we know is whether the node will go to the left or to the right sub-tree. Therefore, we simply apply the whole procedure to the appropriate sub-tree until an empty tree is found. Using the facilities of Oberon, this idea is expressed in the following procedure:

```
PROCEDURE Insert(VAR root: Node; new: Node);
BEGIN (* new # NIL *)
  IF root = NIL THEN (* stop recursion *)
    root := new; root.left := NIL; root.right := NIL
  ELSIF new.key < root.key THEN Insert(root.left, new)
  ELSIF new.key > root.key THEN Insert(root.right, new)
  ELSE (* duplicate key, add desired action *)
  END
END Insert;
```

Deletion of a node

Deletion of a given node – also a recursive operation – is somewhat more complicated than insertion.

First, the node to be deleted has to be found. If it turns out to have only one descendant, the task is easy. However, if two sub-trees are present the situation is more involved – one pointer cannot point to two objects! In this case, a node further down in the tree has to be promoted to replace the node being deleted. It is the node with the maximum key

150 *Dynamic data structures and pointer types*

value in the left sub-tree of the node being deleted as clarified in Figure 9.10. Procedure *RemoveMax* locates this node.

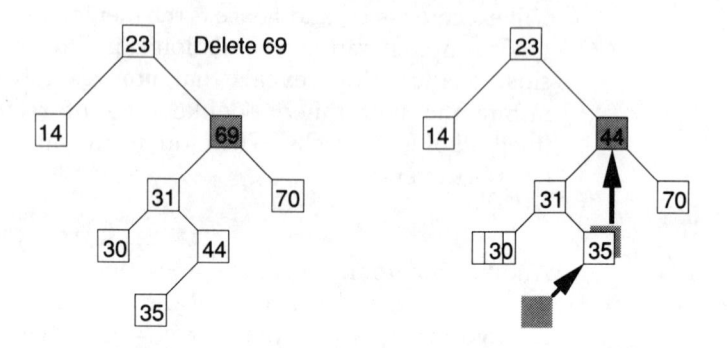

Figure 9.10 Deletion of a node in a binary search tree.

```
PROCEDURE RemoveMax(VAR root, max: Node);
BEGIN
   IF root.right # NIL THEN RemoveMax(root.right, max)
   ELSE max := root;  root := max.left
   END
END RemoveMax;
```

Using *Remove Max*, we formulate the program text of procedure *Delete*:

```
PROCEDURE Delete(VAR root: Node; key: Key);
VAR node: Node;
BEGIN
   IF root # NIL THEN
      IF key < root.key THEN Delete(root.left, key)
      ELSIF key > root.key THEN Delete(root.right, key)
      ELSE (* delete root *)
         IF root.left = NIL THEN root := root.right
         ELSIF root.right = NIL THEN root := root.left
         ELSE (* root has two sub-trees *)
            RemoveMax(root.left, node);
            node.left := root.left;  node.right := root.right;
            root := node
         END
      END
   END
END Delete;
```

9.3.2 Searching in trees

We introduced the tree with the motivation of a fast search algorithm in a table represented by a dynamic data structure. Such an algorithm is now simple to formulate:

```
PROCEDURE Search(root: Node; key: Key): Node;
BEGIN
    WHILE (root # NIL) & (root.key # key) DO
        IF key < root.key THEN root := root.left
        ELSE  root := root.right
        END
    END;
    RETURN root
END Search;
```

It is noteworthy that while the previous procedures are intrinsically recursive, *Search* is presented as an iterative algorithm. The reason is that to search a node, *no backtracking takes place*. The algorithm simply chooses between the left and right branches of the binary tree. While a recursive formulation is easily possible, it is not simpler but less efficient.

Balancing search trees

A crucial question is the speed of procedure *Search*. The answer depends on the structure of the tree. A tree is said to be *perfectly balanced* if, for each node, the number of nodes in its left and right sub-trees differ by at most one. Ordered binary trees are not balanced a priori. Figure 9.11 shows two extreme cases.

If N denotes the number of nodes then it is easily verified that the number of levels in a perfectly balanced binary tree is of order $\log_2 (N)$. On the other hand, an ordered binary tree may be extremely unbalanced. The number of levels in such an unbalanced tree may be as large as the order of N.

In a given tree, the worst-case performance of the search algorithm is proportional to the number of levels. Hence the magnitude of the number of iterations of procedure *Search* is between $\log_2 (N)$ and N. To ensure *logarithmic search performance*, the tree has to be balanced. Our procedures *Insert* and *Delete* do not achieve balance. Fortunately, if the keys are drawn randomly between minimum and maximum values, it can be shown that the resulting tree has a very high probability of being reasonably balanced.

152 *Dynamic data structures and pointer types*

```
                         root                                          root
              level 1    [4]                                level 1    [7]
        level 2  [2]         [6]                         level 2   [6]
   level 3  [1]  [3]     [5]   [7]                  level 3   [5]
                                                level 4   [4]
                                             level 5  [3]
                                          level 6  [2]
   Balanced:                          level 7  [1]
   Number of levels ≈ log N                           Unbalanced:
                                                     Number of levels ≈ N
```

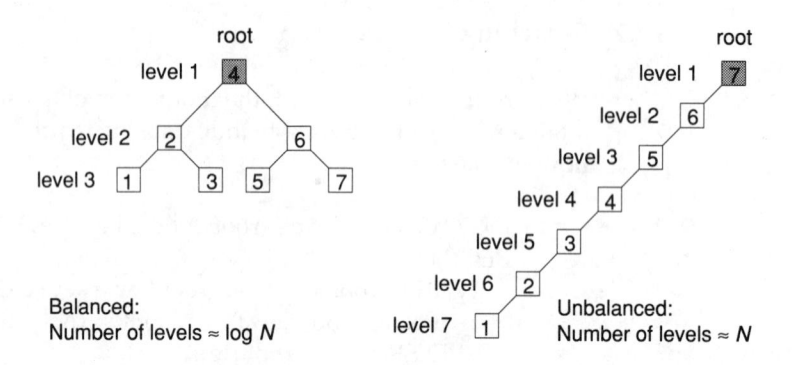

Figure 9.11 Balanced and unbalanced binary search trees.

In most applications, we know little about actual key distribution. We therefore have to take measures to rebalance the search tree. Balancing an ordered tree perfectly is a complex operation – both with respect to the length of the program text and the number of operations. The practical trade-off is therefore between the number of balancing steps and the increased length of the search paths, arising from imbalance. How often and how perfectly one balances the search tree depends on the frequency of insert and delete operations compared with the frequency of searches. If searches are highly predominant, it pays to balance the tree quite well. On the other hand, if updates predominate, balancing is hardly worthwhile.

To strike a practical balance, the perfect balance criterion can be relaxed – with the goal of reducing the balancing overhead. Several such schemes have been published.

Detailed coverage is beyond the scope of this book and we refer to the literature (Wirth, 1976; Smith, 1987; and Sedgewick, 1988).

Summary

Trees are among the most important dynamic data structures. Some of their properties are summarized below:

(1) The tree data structure arises in many practical situations: tables with efficient search algorithms, compilers, game playing programs, to mention just a few.

(2) Tree traversal is most appropriately formulated with a recursive algorithm that takes care of backtracking.

(3) Ordered trees composed of N nodes admit search algorithms of the complexity $\log(N)$ if they are balanced.

(4) Most tree algorithms are naturally expressed recursively. Those procedures, however, that do not backtrack also have usually a

simple iterative solution using the while statement. An iterative formulation of backtracking procedures is possible but cumbersome and its speed advantage marginal.

(5) In search trees, the trade-off between the gain in search performance and balancing cost leads to a variety of schemes that allow a measured degree of imbalance in order to reduce the number of balancing steps.

9.4 Other dynamic data structures

Linear lists and binary trees are just two important examples of dynamic data structures. Many more exist – some with the aim of improving the performance of certain operations, others reflecting genuinely more complex models. Subsequently, we will give an example of each category.

Alternative list representations In the examples of Section 9.2, we used the simplest list representation. The empty list is a NIL pointer and the list is accessed through an anchor. There exist a variety of other representations with the aim of simplifying and optimizing certain procedures. One such representation always contains two (virtual) nodes as shown in Figure 9.12. These nodes are sometimes dubbed *sentinels*. If the key of the sentinel is the supremum of all possible keys, the condition of the search loop can be abridged. The use of a *tail* that points to itself to terminate the list simplifies the delete action.

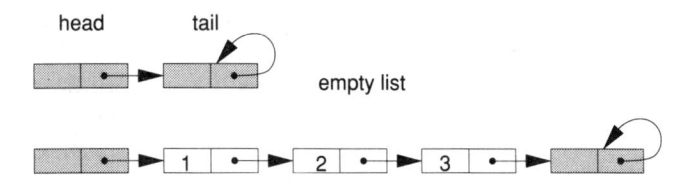

Figure 9.12 Simple list with two permanent virtual nodes.

It is also possible to organize the list node in a doubly linked ring, as Figure 9.13 illustrates. In the doubly linked ring, removal of a node is particularly easy – no traversal of the structure is required. Similarly, FIFO (first-in, first-out) and LIFO (last-in, first-out) operation is efficiently achieved.

154 Dynamic data structures and pointer types

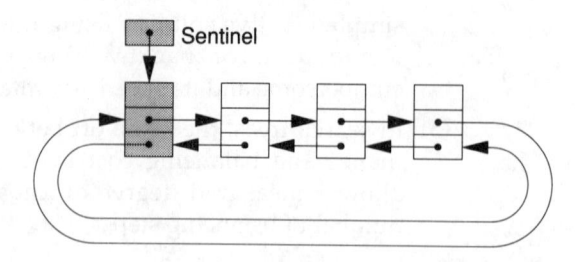

Figure 9.13 A list represented as a doubly linked ring.

n-way tree

Graphs are a powerful mathematical abstraction for many problems. The binary trees discussed in Section 9.3 are a special case of graphs. A simple generalization of the binary tree is the tree of degree *n*. In such a tree, each node has at most *n* successors. If *n* is fixed and reasonably small then the following node declaration can be used (see Figure 9.14):

```
TYPE
    Node = POINTER TO NodeDesc;
    NodeDesc = RECORD
        key: INTEGER;
        descendants: ARRAY n OF Node
    END;
```

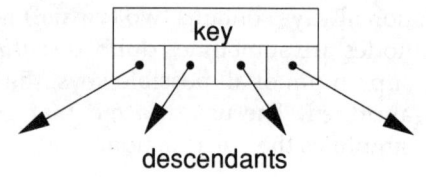

Figure 9.14 Node for a 4-way tree.

There are situations, however, where the number of descendants is variable and may become large. In this case, using an array for the descendants is wasteful and should be replaced again by a list.

9.5 Summary

In many programs, data change their relationship and bulk. Oberon provides a basic tool to construct dynamic data structures: the *pointer type*.

In this chapter, we have introduced the pointer type and the pointer:

a variable whose value is a reference to another object. The following points should be remembered:

(1) A pointer cannot point to any object. The pointer type is bound to a record or array type: the *pointer base type*.

(2) If p is a pointer then the variable to which it points is obtained from the *dereferencing operator* applied to p; that is, $p\uparrow$. As a convenience, Oberon *implies dereferencing* in the case of a record field or array index.

(3) NIL is a value compatible with all pointer types. Dereferencing of a NIL pointer leads to program termination.

(4) An (anonymous) variable $p\uparrow$ of pointer base type is created with the predeclared procedure NEW(p); at the same time, p is initialized. The variable $p\uparrow$ is allocated on the *heap* memory.

A dynamic data structure is composed of *nodes* that are of record type and themselves contain pointer fields. The definition of the dynamic data structure is thus *recursive*. One of the simplest (but most versatile) dynamic structures is the *list*: a chain of nodes. We have given a number of examples of inserting and deleting nodes in lists. A key observation is that accessing the last element requires list traversal, which is an expensive operation.

Since access to the last element occurs frequently in a *first-in, first-out* list, a special *hint* has been introduced to deal with the insert operation efficiently. The hint is a pointer providing a link to the last element.

Another useful dynamic structure is the *binary tree*. In contrast to the list, the tree allows search of a given node in logarithmic time. We have given examples of tree processing using *recursion*. Trees provide a good example of how recursive data definition and recursive processing may complement each other.

9.6 Exercises

9.1 Which of the following declarations are correct:

(a) VAR p: POINTER TO REAL;
(b) VAR q: POINTER TO RECORD END;
(c) VAR v: POINTER TO ARRAY OF REAL;
(d) VAR a: POINTER TO ARRAY N, N OF REAL;
(e) VAR b: ARRAY 100 OF REAL; p: POINTER TO b;
(f) TYPE A: ARRAY 100 OF REAL; a: POINTER TO A;

9.2 Find the errors in the following procedure:

```
PROCEDURE Search(VAR first: Node; k: Key): Node;
BEGIN
    WHILE (first.key # k) & (first # NIL) DO first := first.next END;
    RETURN first
END Search ;
```

9.3 [**Lists**] Implement a module *Lists* with definition

```
DEFINITION Lists;
IMPORT Out;
TYPE
    Data, Key = INTEGER;
    Node = POINTER TO NodeDesc;
    NodeDesc = RECORD
        key: Key; data: Data; next: Node
    END;

    PROCEDURE Insert(VAR first: Node; new: Node);
    PROCEDURE InsertLast(VAR first: Node; new: Node);
    PROCEDURE InsertRanked(VAR first: Node; new: Node);
    PROCEDURE FirstNode(VAR first: Node): Node;
    PROCEDURE Search(first: Node; k: Key): Node;
    PROCEDURE Delete(VAR first: Node; node: Node);
END Lists.
```

Using modules *In* and *Out* compose a module *UseLists* that is a client of module *Lists*. The commands exported by *UseLists* are

- Make: creates an instance of a list.
- *Add*: reads key and data values from the input stream, creates an instance of a node and adds it to the list.
- *Query*: reads a key value from the input stream and prints the corresponding data value if the key is found, "not found" otherwise.
- *Delete*: reads a key value from the input stream and deletes the corresponding list node.

9.4 Repeat Exercise 9.3 for the list representation with virtual head and tail elements (Figure 9.12). In the procedures of 9.3, the formal VAR parameter *first* is replaced by a value parameter *head*, for example

```
PROCEDURE Insert(head: Node; new: Node);
```

Provide

```
PROCEDURE New(): Node;
```

which creates an empty list. Why are no VAR parameters required? Why is there a need for a procedure *New* now but not previously?

Hint: study the following implementation of *Delete*:

PROCEDURE Delete(head: Node; k: Key);
VAR y: Node;
BEGIN
  y := head;
  WHILE (y.next # tail) & (y.next.key # k) DO y := y.next END;
  y.next := y.next.next
END Delete;

9.5 Repeat Exercise 9.3 for doubly linked rings (Figure 9.13).

9.6 [**Trees**] Write a module *Trees* that implements the procedures *Insert*, *Search*, *Delete* of Section 9.3. Implement a module *UseTrees* analogously to *UseLists*.

9.7 [**Tree enumeration**] Expressions can be conveniently represented by trees called *parse trees*. Write procedures that traverse the parse tree of Figure 9.15 in the following order:

  (a) Preorder: $* + a / b c - d * e f$
  (b) Inorder: $a + b / c * d - e * f$
  (c) Postorder: $a b c / + d e f * - *$

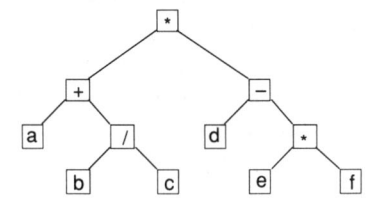

Figure 9.15 Tree representation of the expression $(a + b/c)*(d - e*f)$.

Hint: consider procedure *Enumerate* of Section 9.3.1 with modified order of the statement sequence

Enumerate(root.left); P(root); Enumerate(root.right).

References

Sedgewick R. (1988). *Algorithms*, 2nd edn. Reading, MA: Addison-Wesley.
Smith H. F. (1987). *Data Structures, Form and Function*. New York: Academic Press.
Wirth N. (1976). *Algorithms + Data Structures = Programs*. Englewood Cliffs, NJ: Prentice-Hall.

10 Stepwise refinement and data abstraction

When tackling a complex programming task, it is easy to get swamped by the details of the data structures or the intricacies of the algorithms. It is therefore advisable to proceed on carefully chosen levels of abstractions, first drawing a broad outline of the task in terms of subtasks, then specifying the actions of the subtask, possibly again pushing details to a further round of refinements. In this process of *stepwise refinement*, the procedure is an indispensable tool (Wirth, 1971, 1974; Dahl et al., 1972). If the subtasks are performed by appropriately named procedures, the inherent structure of the program remains visible, and the tasks may be performed by different groups of programmers. The module adds a further level of structure through carefully chosen interfaces and import relations.

In this chapter, we will discuss a realistic example: the simulation of a waiting line. We will practice stepwise refinement and illuminate the role of the procedure and more importantly of the module in creating *abstractions*. The scenario is the simulation of a waiting line, an example from the class of discrete event simulation programs.

10.1 Discrete event simulation of a waiting line

The digital computer is a new and powerful analytical tool in the hands of scientists and engineers. The graphical capability of modern workstations is a great help in visualizing complex results. The computation of the fractal fern is a good example. Who would see the structure of the limiting set by pondering over piles of 7-digit floating-point numbers?

Many systems elude a formulation as a set of deterministic equations. Consider a waiting line in front of a ticket counter. The arrival of customers and their departure is the collective result of the individual decisions of a large number of persons.

10.1 Discrete event simulation of a waiting line

The only model we may use in such a situation is a statistical one. Random numbers are used to generate events such as customer arrivals and departures. The state changes only at discrete time epochs such as arrivals and departures. Nothing happens between events. Thus when evolving the waiting line on the computer, *time jumps from event to event*. We speak therefore of a discrete-time, discrete-event simulation.

To simulate the waiting line, we need two sequences of random numbers: one to measure the times between arrival events and the other to determine the time needed to serve a customer. The properties of these sequences are described by their *distribution*. For simplicity, we will work with the exponential distribution (see Box 10.1).

Events and the calendar

The operation of the waiting line is governed by two types of event: the *arrival* and the *departure* of a customer. Each event has an associated time – its *due time*. An algorithmic description of the operation of the waiting line rests on the notion of a *calendar* of such events. The calendar is defined by two actions: an event may be *scheduled* and the most imminent event may be *retrieved*.

Operation of the queue

Using these concepts, the operation of the waiting line can be expressed more rigorously in an algorithmic notation similar to Oberon:

```
REPEAT
   "Retrieve event from the calendar";
   IF event = arrival THEN
      "Schedule a new arrival event";
      "If the queue is empty, schedule a departure event,
       else join queue "
   ELSIF event = departure THEN
      "Remove head of the queue. If the queue is not empty,
       schedule a new departure event"
   END
UNTIL "Simulation time exceeds given limit";
```

Box 10.1
The distribution of random numbers

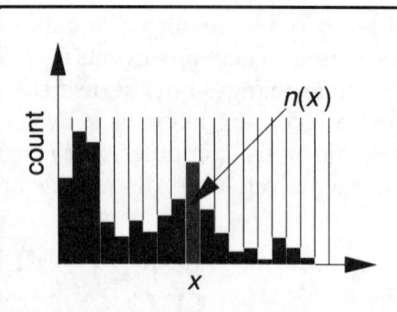

Assume that we have made a large number of observations of a random phenomenon. A good way to characterize the set of observations is to plot a *histogram*. The abscissa is divided into equal intervals, and the number $n(x)$ of observations falling into the interval beginning at x is graphed as a bar chart.

If we decrease the width of the intervals and simultaneously increase the number of observations we call the normalized limiting function (if it exists) the *distribution* of the random observations.[1]

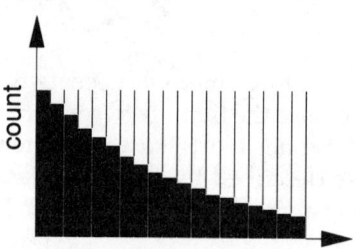

Sometimes such a chart looks like the diagram on the left: the shape approaches a negative exponential curve – we speak of a *negative exponential distribution*. The time between arrivals of phone calls is an example where the exponential distribution is found in practice.

An exponential random number rn_{exp} can be obtained from a uniform random number rn_{uni} according to the simple formula:

$$rn_{exp} = -\ln(rn_{uni})/\mu$$

where $1/\mu$ is the mean value of the random numbers. If the random variables are used to measure the time between events, the parameter μ is also the *rate* (in events/s).

System state

The state of the queue is an integer n that measures the number of customers in the waiting line and in service. The action

- 'join queue' means incrementing n;
- 'remove head of the queue' means decrementing n.

---

[1] Technically distribution of *random variable*.

10.2 Putting the operation of the queue into Oberon terms

The last section provides a description of the queueing operation that is quite rigorous. However, it is still far from an executable Oberon program. The specification of such a program will require

(1) a data representation of the system state (queue, events and so on);
(2) a precise definition of the calendar, in particular the actions 'schedule an event' and 'retrieve an event';
(3) translation of the algorithmic description of the queue's operation into an Oberon procedure;
(4) specification of further procedures that initialize the model, gather statistical results and produce output;
(5) embedding all procedures in one (or several) modules.

The difficulty in attacking a complex programming task is to decide where to start – and how to proceed in a methodological fashion. Many problems of data design and procedural specification are interrelated – it seems all has to be done at once.

Abstraction is the key technique that allows the programmer to break the vicious cycle. To abstract means to leave out detail. The procedure is a powerful concept in this respect: *we can write down a procedure call without need to specify the text of that procedure right away*. Having this in mind, our plan to attack the queueing simulation is to start with task (1), defer (2) and proceed with (3), then return to (2) and complete (4) and (5) subsequently. The methodology behind this approach is known as *structured programming* or *stepwise refinement*.

10.2.1 Data representation of the system state

The entities of the queueing systems are the *events*, the *calendar*, the *queue* and a *random number generator*. Also required to describe the global state is the notion of the simulation time.

Events

Mathematically, the events are labels on the time axis. In our example, there are two kinds of events: arrivals and departures. It is expedient to represent event types as integers. Therefore an event is a tuple (e, t), where e serves as event label (or identifier) and t is the event's due time.

Stepwise refinement and data abstraction

Calendar

In order to specify the queueing simulation, we also need the calendar. One possibility is to now focus on that problem. This is not the course we have chosen. However, we have to make an assumption about the actions supported by the calendar. We postulate the following procedures:

> PROCEDURE GetNextEvent(VAR e: INTEGER; VAR t: REAL);
> PROCEDURE Schedule(e: INTEGER; t: REAL);

At this point, the calendar remains abstract – a lot of detail is hidden behind those two procedures. A data structure that is defined solely by procedures acting on it is known as an *abstract data structure* – a concept that we will refine in Section 10.3.

Queue

Recall that since customers have no identity, the state of the queue is simply an integer. This compact state description greatly simplifies the program.

Random numbers

Random numbers, finally, are already available through module *RandomNumbers*, which we assume to be part of the program library of our workstation. We will use the procedure *RandomNumbers.Exp*. Two parameters have to be specified: the *arrival rate* λ (in customers/s) and the *mean service time* $1/\mu$.

Global variables

With these preliminaries, we are ready to list the declarations of the global variables needed in our simulation program:

```
CONST arrival = 0; departure = 1;
VAR
    event: INTEGER;    (* The current event type *)
    time: REAL;        (* The current time *)
    n: INTEGER;        (* The number of customers in the queue *)
    lambda: REAL;      (* The arrival rate *)
    mu: REAL;          (* The service rate *)
```

The named constants *arrival* and *departure* will render the resulting program text readable. Their use should be considered essential and not just a nicety.

10.2.2 A first round of refinement of the queueing algorithm

The preparations are now complete to make a first round of refinement of the algorithm stated in Section 10.1:

10.2 Putting the operation of the queue into Oberon terms

```
REPEAT
    GetNextEvent(event, time) (* retrieve event from calendar *)
    IF event = arrival THEN  ProcessArrival
    ELSIF event = departure THEN  ProcessDeparture
    END
UNTIL time > tEnd;
```

Clearly, the description of the simulation task has been made in terms of subtasks, emphasizing the dominant structure and suppressing details.

Of course, suitable data structures must be chosen, and the subtasks *ProcessArrival* and *ProcessDeparture* must now be further described with all the necessary details. *GetNextEvent* is part of the calendar operation and its specification awaits one more round of refinement.

Instead of replacing the descriptive English words with more or less elaborate Oberon program texts, we may consider these words as *procedure identifiers*, and we will proceed to write their program texts.

Let us first focus on the processing of an arrival event. With the preceding discussion, the 'pseudocode' of Section 10.1 translates easily into a formal Oberon procedure:

```
PROCEDURE ProcessArrival;
BEGIN
    Schedule(arrival, time + RandomNumbers.Exp(lamda));
    IF n = 0 THEN
        Schedule(departure, time + RandomNumbers.Exp(mu))
    END;
    INC(n)
END ProcessArrival;
```

The actions taken upon a departure event are similarly simple:

```
PROCEDURE ProcessDeparture;
BEGIN
    DEC(n)
    IF n > 0 THEN
        Schedule(departure, time + RandomNumbers.Exp(mu))
    END
END ProcessDeparture;
```

The actions corresponding to the subtasks are now specified except for the calendar and the embedding into a final module, which we consider in a second and a third round of refinements.

10.3 Hiding of details

10.3.1 Implementation of module *Calendar*

The calendar is a central component of every discrete event simulation. Therefore we will encapsulate it in its own module, which we name *Calendar*. Such a module may support many particular simulation models – it will serve as a *service module* in the computer's library.

In the preceding section, we described the calendar abstractly as a repository of timed events, admitting the operations *GetNextEvent* and *Schedule*. We are now at the stage where the abstract definition has to be concretized; that is, a data representation for the calendar needs to be chosen and the actions specified.

To store events, we need a table. Events in the calendar have a natural order defined by their due time. It is therefore an obvious choice to maintain a *ranked list*, with the head of the list being the most imminent event.

For the purpose of module *Calendar*, the definition of the type *Node* of Section 9.2 has to be modified. There we deliberately omitted application specific fields. In our case, we need such 'data' fields for the integer that serves as *event identifier*. The application-specific meaning of the key is the *due time*. Therefore it is of type REAL.

To render the program text more readable, we also rename the type *Node* as *Event* and *key* as *time*. The text of the procedures *FirstNode* and *InsertRanked* can be easily adapted – the program text of module *Calendar* should be quite self explanatory.

```
        MODULE Calendar;
        CONST deadlock* = MAX(INTEGER);
        TYPE
           Event = POINTER TO EventDesc;
           EventDesc = RECORD
              id: INTEGER;
              time: REAL;
              next: Event
           END;
(1)  →  VAR clndr: Event;

        PROCEDURE GetNextEvent*(VAR id: INTEGER; VAR t: REAL);
        BEGIN
           IF clndr # NIL THEN
              id := clndr.id;  t := clndr.time;
              clndr := clndr.next
```

10.3 Hiding of details

```
(2) →         ELSE id := deadlock
            END
        END GetNextEvent;

        PROCEDURE Schedule* (id: INTEGER; t: REAL);
        VAR x, y: Event;
        BEGIN
(3) →       NEW(x); x.id := id; x.time := t;
            IF (clndr = NIL) OR (t < clndr.time) THEN
                x.next := clndr; clndr := x
            ELSE
                y := clndr;
                WHILE (y.next # NIL) & (t >= y.time) DO  y := y.next  END;
                x.next := y.next; y.next := x
            END
        END Schedule;

        PROCEDURE Reset*;
        BEGIN  clndr := NIL
        END Reset;

        BEGIN
(4) →       Reset
        END Calendar.
```

Notes

(1) Global variable *clndr* is the anchor of the calendar list.

(2) If the calendar is empty, a deadlock is said to have occurred. A special event identifier is returned, the time is undefined. The client of module *Calendar* has to test for this event, if it is not guaranteed that the simulation remains active.

(3) An instance of type *Event* is created and initialized. Subsequently, the event is inserted into the calendar list such that it remains ranked with respect to time.

(4) In the body of module *Calendar*, the calendar list is initialized.

Besides the familiar procedures *GetNextEvent* and *Schedule*, a third one is added, namely *Reset*. It empties an existing calendar and is useful when a new simulation run is started.

There is little more to explain about module *Calendar*, except for the *choice of exports*. Module *Calendar* performs no computations on its own.

It is a service module that exports procedures to be used in a client module.

Clearly, we have to export the procedures *Reset*, *GetNextEvent* and *Schedule*. But do we also have to export the calendar – that is, the global variable *clndr*? At first sight, this clearly seems necessary.

But we already know that the importing module is perfectly served if it has access to the procedures *Reset*, *GetNextEvent* and *Schedule*.

We deliberately opt for export of those procedures only. The consequence is that we *hide the dynamic data structure that represents the calendar*. The client has no access to that data structure. The exported declarations, seen from a module that imports *Calendar*, are in the style of a definition module:

```
DEFINITION Calendar;
    CONST deadlock = MAX(INTEGER);
    PROCEDURE GetNextEvent(VAR id: INTEGER; VAR t: REAL);
    PROCEDURE Schedule(id: INTEGER; t: REAL);
    PROCEDURE Reset;
END Calendar.
```

Abstract data structure

We call a data structure that is not visible outside of a module but that can be created and changed by a set of exported procedures an *abstract data structure*.

It is abstract in the sense that only its properties are known – not its implementation. The properties of the data structure that are visible in a client module are called the *interface*. In our example, the interface is composed of the constants *deadlock* and the procedures *Reset*, *GetNextEvent* and *Schedule*.

What is hidden is the type *Event* as well as the anchor of the calendar list (the global variable *clndr*). An importing module is thus unable to traverse the list, to enter events on its own or to remove events.

Increased safety

What purpose is served by data hiding? Could the client not do more if it had full access to the dynamic data structure of the calendar? Yes it could – and this may be an advantage as well as a bane.

For example, an already scheduled event could be removed or a group of almost simultaneous events could be inserted at once, thereby saving execution time. But it is as easily possible to introduce errors, for example to insert an event at the wrong place in the ranked list and – as a consequence – completely annihilate the results of the simulation.

The notion is that a service module affords a set of carefully validated functions. The data structure is protected, and thus its *integrity is guaranteed* – no tampering with it can invalidate the results of the procedures operating on it.

10.3 Hiding of details

Simplification of documentation

We are all aware that the documentation of programs is a tedious and hence often neglected duty of the programmer. Using data abstraction, implementation details remain hidden, and their documentation (or lack thereof) does not affect others whose work depends on availability of our module. Only the interface needs documentation. If the names of variables and parameters are well chosen, the interface almost documents itself – a significant advantage of deliberately chosen *thin interfaces*.

Freedom of implementation

Data hiding – or data abstraction – has a third important benefit: the implementer is free to *change the data structure* without affecting any of the importing modules.

For example, instead of a linear list, an array could as well serve as basis for the calendar, using the declaration

    VAR clndr: ARRAY max OF RECORD
        id: INTEGER; time: REAL
    END;

An implementation based on arrays admits the *heap structure*, which allows insertion in log (n) operations (where n measures the number of calendar entries); see Wirth (1976). The heap algorithms work similarly to the binary search (Section 8.2.5). An implementation of the procedure *Schedule* using such a binary search to pinpoint the insertion point may hold a speed advantage over its cousin working on lists. Another possibility is the use of a tree structure that also allows insertion in $\log(n)$ time rather than in linear time. In any case, such improved implementations will show a significant gain only for large simulation models whose calendars grow really big. For small models, they may even be counter-productive.

Using data abstraction, it is possible to substitute a new and improved implementation of a service module in a program library. None of the clients will have to be modified or even recompiled, as long as the interface remains the same.

10.3.2 Computing statistics: module *Paths*

We have now all the elements in place to complete the simulation program. However, running the algorithm as stated in Section 10.2 would not be too exciting – its only result is a busy computer. Clearly, the simulation experiment has to be instrumented with the goal of gathering statistics about the system's behavior.

It turns out that in practice, a great deal of the size of a simulation program is devoted to instrumentation and data analysis. Therefore it is a good idea to provide some tools to facilitate this task. Our goal, again, is to provide a *service module* usable for many applications.

In order to compute the mean value of a queue, one has to analyze its *path* (see Box 10.2). In a realistic simulation, there is not only one but many different queues with their respective paths that the investigator wants to analyze. We therefore need a mechanism that allows the user of the service module to declare an *open-ended number* of paths and gather data about them.

Box 10.2
Mean and path of a queue

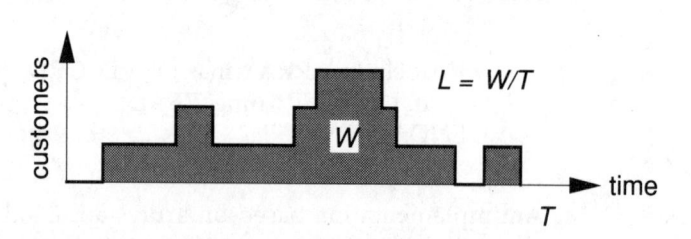

One of the simplest statistics that we can compute for our queue is the mean number of customers found waiting or in service over a given period of length T. This mean number, L say, is computed according to the formula

$$L = W/T$$

where W denotes the *cumulative waiting time* defined as the area under the graph 'customers in queue versus time' measured from time 0 to T. Such a graph is also known as the *path* of the queueing process.

In Oberon, that mechanism is the type – our goal is to design a module that *exports a type* called *Path*. Clients are then able to declare multiple instances of that type in the customary manner.

Each time the path jumps one unit up or down, the accumulated waiting time W is updated. In order to do this, we need a record of the path value n at the time of the last change, as well as the epoch t of that change. Thus a path is an instance of the following record type:

10.3 Hiding of details

```
TYPE Path = RECORD
    n: INTEGER;
    W, t: REAL
END;
```

It is now easy to write the program text of module *Paths*:

```
MODULE Paths;
TYPE Path* = RECORD
    n*: INTEGER;
    W, t: REAL
END;

PROCEDURE Init * (VAR p: Path);
BEGIN  p.W := 0;  p.n := 0;  p.t := 0
END Init;

PROCEDURE Up* (VAR p: Path; t: REAL);
BEGIN  p.W := p.W + p.n*(t – p.t);  INC(p.n);  p.t := t
END Up;

PROCEDURE Down* (VAR p: Path; t: REAL);
BEGIN  p.W := p.W + p.n*(t – p.t);  DEC(p.n);  p.t := t
END Down;

PROCEDURE Mean* (p: Path; tEnd: REAL): REAL;
BEGIN  RETURN (p.W + p.n*(tEnd - p.t))/tEnd
END Mean;

END Paths.
```

The actions of the procedures are so simple that a few comments suffice:

- *Init*:   Initializes the fields of a path.
- *Up*:   At time t, the path makes a jump of one unit in the upward direction.
- *Down*: Like *Up*, but jump is downward.
- *Mean*: Returns the mean value of the path variable for the time interval starting at 0 and ending at *tEnd*.

Abstract data type

As in the case of the calendar, the choice of exports justifies further discussion.

The client of module *Paths* is not interested in the accumulated waiting time W or in the time stamp t. It is the mean queue length that really matters. With this in mind, module *Paths* only exports the record type *Path* and field n measuring the instantaneous value of the path. Since details remain hidden from the client, we speak of an *abstract data type*. The visible declarations that provide the interface to module *Paths* are

```
DEFINITION Paths;
TYPE Path = RECORD
    n: INTEGER
END;

PROCEDURE Init (VAR p: Path);
PROCEDURE Up (VAR p: Path; t: REAL);
PROCEDURE Down (VAR p: Path; t: REAL);
PROCEDURE Mean (p: Path; tEnd: REAL): REAL;
END Paths.
```

Instances of an abstract data type are *initialized and manipulated exclusively through procedures*. Each one of the procedures needs a *formal parameter that identifies the particular instance of the abstract data type*, upon which actions are performed. It is good practice to start the parameter list with this identification parameter.

The data structure itself is hidden. The advantage of hiding details are no different in the case of an abstract data type from the abstract data structure: simplicity of the interface, security and freedom of implementation. The disadvantage is also the same, namely a possible restriction of operations that the client may legitimately want to perform.

10.4 Completion of the simulation example

We have now all the elements in place to list the complete program text of the simulation program. We know that this means to create a module, which we call *Model*. We draw on the services of imported modules, namely *Calendar*, *RandomNumbers*, *Paths*, *In* and *Out*.

The following program text should be self-explanatory:

10.4 Completion of the simulation example

```
MODULE Model;
IMPORT Paths, Calendar, RandomNumbers, In, Out;
CONST arrival = 0; departure = 1;
VAR
   event: INTEGER;
   time: REAL;        (* current time *)
```
(1) →
```
   q: Paths.Path;     (* state of queue and statistics *)
   lamda: REAL;       (* arrival rate *)
   mu: REAL;          (* inverse of mean service time *)

PROCEDURE ProcessArrival;
BEGIN
   Calendar.Schedule(arrival, time + RandomNumbers.Exp(lamda));
   IF q.n = 0 THEN
      Calendar.Schedule(departure, time + RandomNumbers.Exp(mu))
   END;
```
(2) →
```
   Paths.Up(q, time)
END ProcessArrival;

PROCEDURE ProcessDeparture;
VAR s: REAL;
BEGIN
```
(3) →
```
   Paths.Down(q, time);
   IF q.n > 0 THEN
      Calendar.Schedule(departure, time + RandomNumbers.Exp(mu))
   END
END ProcessDeparture;

PROCEDURE Simulate(dt: REAL);
VAR tEnd: REAL;
BEGIN
   tEnd := time + dt;
   REPEAT
      Calendar.GetNextEvent(event, time);
      IF event = arrival THEN  ProcessArrival
      ELSIF event = departure THEN  ProcessDeparture
      END
   UNTIL time > tEnd
END Simulate;

PROCEDURE Setup*;
BEGIN
   In.Open; In.Real(lamda); In.Real(mu);
```

```
            Out.Open;
            Out.String("lamda =");  Out.Real(lamda, 10);
            Out.String("  mu =");   Out.Real(mu, 10);      Out.Ln;
            Calendar.Reset;    Paths.Init(q);
            Calendar.Schedule(arrival, 0.0)
        END Setup;

        PROCEDURE Run*;
        VAR dt: REAL;
        BEGIN
            In.Open; In.Real(dt);
            Simulate(dt);
            Out.String("mean =");  Out.Real(Paths.Mean(q, time), 11); Out.Ln
        END Run;

    END Model.
```

Notes

> (1) Instead of employing a simple integer to describe the state, we make use of the abstraction *Path*, which also reflects the number of customers in *q.n*.
>
> (2) The call *Paths.Up* replaces INC(n) in the preliminary version.
>
> (3) The call *Paths.Down* replaces DEC(n) in the preliminary version.

To execute a simulation run, two commands need to be executed in sequence: *Setup* and *Run*. The command *Setup* fixes the basic parameters *lamda* and *mu* and initializes the data structure for a new simulation run. Note that an initial arrival event must be entered into the calendar – otherwise the simulation would never start.

Executing the command *Run* starts a particular simulation. The incremental simulation time *dt* is a parameter. After completion, the command *Run* displays the mean queue length. *Run* has the property that it can be iterated. A second invocation will continue from where the first one stopped.

The division between *Setup* and *Run* is deliberate. Typically, the results of a simulation converge to a stationary state. Whether a result is close to that limit is not known beforehand. Issuing one *Setup* and executing *Run* several times will help the investigator to evaluate the degree to which steady state is reached.

Observe that module *Model* is *mainly composed of declarations and calls to procedures exported by service modules*. This is demonstrated by the predominance of qualified identifiers and is quite typical of a properly modularized Oberon program.

10.5 More on program structuring and abstraction

Structuring and abstracting are the main techniques leading to understandable and hence trustworthy programs. To abstract literally means to pull out the essence from irrelevant details.

The quality of a program is an elusive property, and may mean different things to different groups of people. All would agree, however, that program correctness is of fundamental importance. To demonstrate a program's correctness is ultimately a matter of convincing a person that the program is trustworthy. How can we approach this goal? While great progress was made in proving program correctness through assertions, the method is still far from being a panacea. Provable programs are still a small – albeit growing – minority.

The only salvation for the rest lies in *structure*. A program must be decomposed into partitions that can be considered one at a time without too much regard for the remaining parts. At the lowest level, the elements of the structure are statements; at the next level, procedures; and at the highest level, modules. In parallel with program structuring proceeds the structuring of data. The essence of programming is finding the right – or at least an appropriate – structure.

10.5.1 Decomposition into modules, data hiding

The distinctive property of the module as the largest structuring unit is its capability to hide details and thereby to establish a new level of abstraction. Decomposing a program into modules divides programmers into *providers* and *users*. The provider of an abstraction writes a module and carefully chooses which variables or procedures to export. As we mentioned earlier, those exports are called the *interface* of the module. The provider creates a *service module*. The user deals with the facilities of a service module through the interface only. Since abstraction is a hierarchical concept, every provider is usually also a user of abstractions at a lower level.

Module hierarchy

Partitioning of a program into modules establishes a *hierarchy of abstractions*. The hierarchy is defined by the relation 'module C imports module S.' C is called a *client* of S, which itself is a *service module* for C.

To reveal the structure of a hierarchy of abstractions, the graph consisting of modules as nodes and import relations as edges is useful. Properly structured abstractions avoid mutual dependency – which means that their module graph is *cycle-free*. An example of a module hierarchy is depicted in Figure 10.1.

Even if there does not exist a recipe to determine the most favorable decomposition, there have emerged some criteria separating the good from the bad. A basic rule is that the *connection between modules – the interface – be simple* or 'thin.' A crude measure is the number of items participating in the interface. Naturally, it is difficult to find an optimum, since this number would vanish if the entire program could be collapsed into a single module – clearly an undesirable solution.

We can distinguish the following typical cases:

(1) The module contains no data of its own, but exports a collection of procedures. The typical example is a mathematical subroutine library. Such modules are *packages of procedures*.

(2) The module's essence is a set of data. It hides the details of the data representation by granting access to these data through calls of its exported procedures only. We speak of an *abstract data structure*.

(3) The module exports a data type together with associated procedures. The data type may again represent a dynamic structure. In contrast to (2), the client of such a module may declare multiple instances of the type – now termed an *abstract data type*.

Hiding details has three benefits:

- The user or client of a service module is not bothered with unnecessary characteristics of the implementation. Only the interface must be described – a task that is much easier than a complete documentation of the module.

- In the case of abstract data structures or abstract data types, the user is not only not bothered with detail – but is effectively prevented from tampering with the data structure. If the functions of the service module are carefully tested, their validity is not endangered by inappropriate use. Certain invariants can be guaranteed. *Data abstraction increases the safety of programs.*

- The implementer is free to choose and even change the data representation without bothering or invalidating client modules.

However, data abstraction also prevents the client from performing perfectly correct and sensible operations on the data. The trade-off is not always easy, and has to be made judiciously.

10.5.2 Module *Out*: an example of an abstract data structure

Let us revisit module *Out* that we introduced in Chapter 7 for textual output. It depends on operating system services dealing with files and

10.5 More on program structuring and abstraction

the viewer subsystem. Assuming a standard Oberon operating environment, the provider of module *Out* uses the whole hierarchy of Oberon system modules shown in Figure 10.1. Each module provides an abstraction of its own.

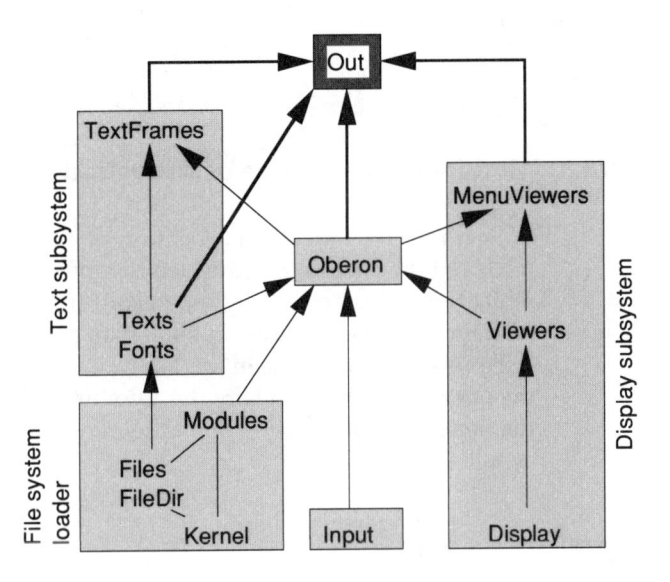

Figure 10.1 Module *Out* embedded into the hierarchy of the Oberon system (there are more import relations – only the major ones are depicted).

Modules *TextFrames*, *Oberon*, *Texts* and *MenuViewers* are directly imported by module *Out*. However, since those modules themselves depend on the lower modules in the hierarchy, almost the entire Oberon operating system is at the service of *Out*.

The user of *Out* deals with all that complexity through six simple procedures only: *Open*, *Char*, *Ln*, *Int*, *Real* and *String*. Behind the six procedures is a single instance of a data structure – the stream – that we know only *through its properties*: (1) it is composed of elements that have a successor and possibly a last element and (2) a position.

The advantage of the abstraction provided by module *Out* is obvious. A simple concept, the stream, and six procedures allow the user to deal with output operations. Furthermore, the abstraction on a level high enough that it can be implemented on any contemporary computer, from PC to a large mainframe.

However, does module *Out* supplant the functions of the foundation comprising the modules *Kernel*, *FileDir*, *Modules*, *Display*, *Input*, *Files*, *Fonts*, *Texts*, *Viewers*, *Oberon*, *MenuViewers* and *TextFrames*? Of course not. Those other modules deliver a wealth of functions that are useful, even essential, but abstracted from (or hidden) by *Out*. *The price of abstraction is therefore a loss of functionality – traded for simplicity of concept, correctness of the functions and freedom of implementation.* Where to draw the line in making this trade-off is always a matter of judgement and debate.

10.5.3 Module *Files*, example of an abstract data type

We came across the abstract data type in Section 10.3.2, where we introduced the type *Path*. Admittedly, module *Paths* is a simple example – while the reason for hiding two record fields *t* and *W* is plausible, some readers may find it somewhat less than compelling.

To illustrate a truly convincing example, we make a digression into the *Oberon file system*, where the amount of hidden detail is massive and the benefits of abstraction overwhelming. The interface definition reads as follows:

```
DEFINITION Files;
TYPE
    File = POINTER TO Handle;
    Handle = RECORD END;

    Rider = RECORD
        res: LONGINT;      (* a result code *)
        eof: BOOLEAN       (* end of the file reached *)
    END;

    (* Procedures operating on the type File *)
    PROCEDURE New(name: ARRAY OF CHAR): File;
    PROCEDURE Old(name: ARRAY OF CHAR): File;
    PROCEDURE Register(f: File);
    PROCEDURE Length(f: File): LONGINT;

    (* Procedures operating on the type Rider *)
    PROCEDURE Set(VAR r: Rider; f: File; pos: LONGINT);
    PROCEDURE Read(VAR r: Rider; VAR ch: CHAR);
    PROCEDURE Write(VAR r: Rider;  ch CHAR);
    PROCEDURE Pos(VAR r: Rider): LONGINT;
    PROCEDURE Base(VAR r: Rider): File;
```

10.5 More on program structuring and abstraction

```
        (* Procedures operating on the directory *)
        PROCEDURE Rename(old, new: ARRAY OF CHAR;
                                VAR res: INTEGER);
        PROCEDURE Delete(name: ARRAY OF CHAR;
                                VAR res: INTEGER);
    END Files.
```

A file is a pointer to a record termed file handle. None of the fields of that handle is visible to the client. Instead, the user needs to know only the following properties of a file:

- A file is an sequence of characters (stored on a permanent medium such as a hard disk).
- A file has, apart from the sequence of characters, a *name*, a *length* and a *creation date*.

Module *Files* also implements the notion of a directory in which files are registered by their name. Procedures *Rename* and *Delete* perform the indicated operations on the directory; the integer parameter *res* is a result code stating termination conditions.

A file (pointer) can be obtained in one of two ways: procedure *New(name)* yields a new file representing the empty sequence; and procedure *Old(name)* yields the file registered under *name* in the file directory, or NIL if this name is not registered.

For the purpose of reading and writing files, the module provides a further abstract data type called *Rider*. As its name suggests, it acts as a rider through the sequence of characters, and advances by one position after each read or write operation represented by procedure *Read(R, ch)* and *Write(R, ch)*. Thus, the properties of the rider are

- a position (hidden);
- an integer field *res* providing a termination (or result) code indicating the success of a read/write operation;
- a Boolean field *eof* that indicates whether read/write operations reach the end of the file.

Procedure *Set(R, F, pos)* places rider *R* onto file *F* at position *pos*. Function procedure *Base(R, F)* yields the file *F* associated with rider *R*. Procedure *Read(R, ch)* reads a character at rider *R*'s position and returns it in *ch*. Similarly, *Write(R, ch)* writes character *ch* at rider *R*'s position. In both cases, the position is incremented.

In the following program template, a registered file named "Laura" is accessed and for each character a procedure *Consume* is invoked:

```
VAR ch: CHAR; F: Files.File; R: Files.Rider;
...
F := Files.Old("Laura");
IF F # NIL THEN
    Files.Set(R, F, 0); Files.Read(ch);
    WHILE R.eof DO Consume(ch); Files.Read(R, ch) END
END;
```

The rider field *eof* indicates whether or not a read operation has reached the end of the file. If it did, the value assigned to *ch* is not a character from the file, it is 0X.

In the next example, characters are produced and written sequentially to a new file that is eventually registered in the directory. We use the same declaration as in the previous example:

```
F := Files.New("Laura");
Files.Set(R, F, 0);
WHILE ~done DO Produce(ch); Files.Write(R, ch) END;
Files.Register(F);
```

Variable *done* is a Boolean set by procedure *Produce* to indicate the end of sequential character generation. Procedure *Register(F)* closes the file and registers its name in the directory. If it already exists, the previously registered file is unregistered.

As a last example, we append a character *ch* at the end of a file *F*:

```
Files.Set(R, F, Files.Length(F)); Files.Write(F, ch);
```

Length(F) yields the length of the file, hence the call statement *Files.Set(R, F, Files.Length(F))* positions rider *R* at the end of file *F*.

We refrain from elaborating on further details of the file concept and its realization in the Oberon system, except for the following remarks:

(1) Procedure *Set* allows the user to place a rider at any position between 0 and the file's length. Access to file elements, therefore, need not be sequential. However, for various reasons it is highly recommended to access files in a sequential manner as shown above. Files are practically always generated sequentially, whereas for reading, the recommendation is somewhat less stringent.

(2) To be exact, files are defined to be sequences of the data type SYSTEM.BYTE (see Appendix A, Section A.12). Similarly, the formal parameter *ch* of the procedures *Read* and *Write* is of type

10.5 More on program structuring and abstraction

SYSTEM.BYTE and not CHAR. However, SYSTEM.BYTE may be replaced anywhere by CHAR, but not vice versa.

The purpose of this example of module *Files* is to demonstrate the extent to which abstraction is successful at reducing the complexity of documenting an interface, and at reserving enough freedom for the implementer to use appropriate techniques. We must be aware that this succinctly described interface rests on a mechanism of substantial complexity, comprising a disk driver, an allocation strategy, a buffering mechanism and a directory management for fast searching, inserting and deleting entries (see Figure 10.2).

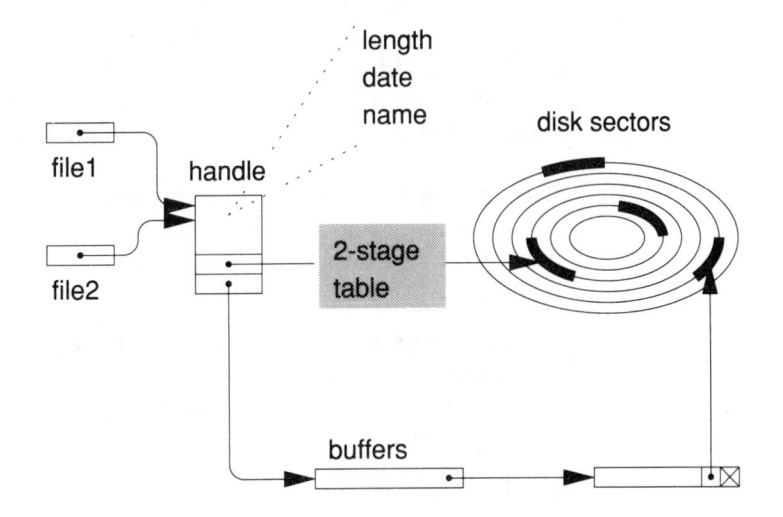

Figure 10.2 Some of the data structures behind the abstract data type *File*.

10.5.4 Textual structure and naming

The textual structure of the program is of essence. This is easily appreciated if we take away the structure of module *Model* – that is, print it as a simple sequence of characters and words:

MODULE Model; IMPORT Paths, Calendar, RandomNumbers, In, Out; CONST arrival = 0; departure = 1; VAR event: INTEGER; time: REAL; (* current time *) q: Paths.Path; (* state of queue and statistics *) lamda: REAL; (* arrival rate *) mu: REAL; (* inverse of mean service time *) PROCEDURE ProcessArrival; BEGIN Calendar.Schedule arrival, time + RandomNumbers.Exp(lamda)); IF q.n = 0 THEN Calendar.Schedule(departure, time + RandomNumbers.Exp(mu)) END; Paths.Up(q, time) END ProcessArrival; PROCEDURE ProcessDeparture; VAR s: REAL; BEGIN Paths.Down(q, time); IF q.n > 0 THEN Calendar.Schedule(departure, time+RandomNumbers.Exp(mu)) END END ProcessDeparture; PROCEDURE Simulate(dt: REAL); VAR tEnd: REAL; BEGIN tEnd := time + dt; REPEAT Calendar.GetNextEvent(event, time); IF event = arrival THEN ProcessArrival ELSIF event = departure THEN ProcessDeparture END UNTIL time > tEnd END Simulate; PROCEDURE Setup*; BEGIN In.Open; In.Real(lamda); In.Real(mu); Out.String("lamda ="); Out.Real(lamda, 10); Out.String("   mu ="); Out.Real(mu, 10); Out.Ln; Calendar.Reset; Paths.Init(q); Calendar.Schedule(arrival, 0.0) END Setup; PROCEDURE Run*; VAR dt: REAL; BEGIN In.Open; In.Real(dt); Simulate(dt); Out.String("mean ="); Out.Real (Paths.Mean (q, time), 11); Out.Ln END Run;BEGIN Out.Open END Model.

Although still perfectly well formed and hence accepted by the compiler, without textual structure, the program *Model* is next to unintelligible. In all the examples presented so far, we have adopted a strongly recommended style:

- Generally restrict the number of statements to one or a small number per line.
- Use indentation to exhibit the recursive nature of structured statements.

The appropriate choice of names is also of great importance, and either elucidates or obscures the action of a program. From long practice, we recommend the use of

- *Verbs* for proper procedures such as *Insert, Delete, Search* and *Schedule*.
- *Nouns* for variables (except variables of type BOOLEAN), for example *time, queue, event*.
- *Adjectives* for Boolean variables and function procedures, for example, *empty* and *full*.
- *Nouns* for function procedures such as *NewCustomer, Uniform* and *Exponential*.
- *Nouns* (singular) for modules that export an abstract data structure, for example *Calendar*.
- *Nouns* (plural) for modules that export an abstract data type, for example *Paths, Texts* and *Lists*. Note that the identifier for the

(main) type is normally the singular form of the module name such as *Paths.Path*, *Texts.Text* and *Lists.List*.

It is advisable not to make names cryptic – in the case of doubt opt for a longer name. This may not hold for local objects in short procedures, however, where long names do not serve any purpose except promote verbosity. Again, rigid rules cannot replace good judgement.

10.6 Summary

This chapter has introduced the proper use of data structures, procedures and modules in programming; in particular, it has been about

(1) the programming process at large;
(2) the role of the procedure and of the module to structure programs;
(3) data hiding and the notions of an *abstract data structure* and an *abstract data type*.

The method that we adopt is *stepwise refinement* and *data abstraction*. Formulation of the programming task starts at a high level, using a pseudo-Oberon notation, and is subsequently refined in various rounds. The procedure is a particularly useful structural tool: descriptive English words are replaced by a procedure call. The corresponding procedure definition is formulated later.

One of the most powerful tools is *abstraction: hiding of details*. When the programmer uses a procedure call instead of writing an elaborate stretch of program text, he or she practices abstraction. However, the capability of the module to selectively export certain declarations while hiding others provides even more powerful tools: *the abstract data structure* and the *abstract data type*.

An abstract data structure is hidden in a module, and is accessible only through procedure calls. In the case of the abstract data type, the user can declare multiple instances, each one representing a hidden (hence abstract) data structure.

The benefit derived from *data abstraction* is simplicity of the interface, security and freedom of implementation. A potential drawback is a loss of function, otherwise available (to good use) to the client.

The chapter has concluded with further examples of abstract data structures and abstract data types and with a recommendation for program structuring and naming.

10.7 Exercises

10.1 [Stack] Implement a module *Stacks* that exports the abstract data type *Stack*:

```
DEFINITION Stacks;
TYPE
    Data = INTEGER;
    Stack = RECORD END;
PROCEDURE Push(s: Stack; i: Data);
PROCEDURE Pop(s: Stack): Data;
PROCEDURE Empty(s: Stack): BOOLEAN;
PROCEDURE Open(s: Stack);
END Stacks.
```

A stack is a repository for data element. A data element *i* is stored by means of *Push*. The most recently stored data element is recovered using *Pop*. *Empty* informs whether the stack is empty or not. A stack is initialized through a call to *Open*.

What happens if *Pop* is called when the stack is empty? Two solutions come to mind: (1) a special value *undefined* is returned (for example MIN(INTEGER)) or (2) the program comes to an abnormal termination (HALT). Discuss advantages and disadvantages of the two solutions.

Provide two implementations: one based on the list structure and one using an array. In the latter case, how is index overflow dealt with?

Implement a module *UseStack* with commands *New*, *Push* and *Pop*. *Push* reads an integer from the stream and pushes it onto a stack, *Pop* recovers an integer from the stack and writes it to the output stream.

10.2 [Mean and variance] In simulation, one often encounters *sequences of successive observations*, represented by real numbers $\{x_i : i = 1, 2, 3, \ldots, n\}$. Of interest are the *sample mean* and the *sample variance*, which are defined by

$$\overline{X}_n = (1/n) \sum_{i=0}^{n} x_i, \quad S_n^2 = \frac{1}{n-1} \sum_{i=0}^{n} (x_i - \overline{X}_n)^2, \quad \text{for } n > 1 \quad (1,2)$$

In a simulation, the observations x_i occur one at a time as the run progresses. It is quite fortuitous that the sample mean and the sample variance can be calculated with a recurrence relation, without storing the whole sequence:

$$S_n^2 = S_{n-1}^2 \left(\frac{n-2}{n-1}\right) + \frac{(x_n - \overline{X}_{n-1})^2}{n}, \quad \text{for } n > 1 \quad (3)$$

$$\overline{X}_n = \overline{X}_{n-1} + (x_n - \overline{X}_{n-1})/n, \quad \text{for } n \geq 1 \quad (4)$$

Note that computation of the sample variance by means of (2) should be avoided; the difference of possibly large, but nearly equal quantities may lead to loss of accuracy (cancellation). Besides the amenity of computation 'on the go,' equations (3) and (4) are free from such numerical instabilities.

Write a module *Sequences* that exports an *abstract data type* named *Sequence*. An instance of *Sequence* is used to compute the sample mean and the sample variance of a given sequence of observations. Module *Sequences* has definition:

```
DEFINITION Sequences;
TYPE Sequence = RECORD END;
PROCEDURE Init(VAR s: Sequence);
PROCEDURE Add(VAR s: Sequence; x: REAL);
PROCEDURE Mean(s: Sequence): REAL;
MODULE Var(s: Sequence): REAL;
END Sequences.
```

Why are the fields X, $S2$ and n not exported? The procedures *Mean* and *Var* are rather trivial. What is their purpose?

10.3 [**Path distribution**] Change module *Paths* such that the *sample path distribution*, in addition to the mean is evaluated. The sample path distribution is the set of probabilities

$$P(n) = \Pr\{\text{path is in state } n\} = T(n)/T$$

where

$$T(n) = \text{Cumulative time the path spends at value } n$$
$$T = \text{Length of simulation run}$$

Use an array T to accumulate $T(n)$. Is the index bounded? Make sure no index exceptions occur.

Add a parameter *max* to procedure *Open* that specifies the maximal value of n. Also augment *Paths* with a procedure *Distr* that provides $P(n)$.

10.4 [**Simulation of tandem queues**] Implement a module *Tandem* that simulates *two queues in tandem*, using the services of modules *Calendar* and *Paths*. Tandem queues operate as follows: an arriving customer joins the first queue. After service completion at the first queue, a customer immediately joins the second one – being satisfied there, it leaves the system. All random numbers have exponential distribution. Use the following constants and global variables:

```
CONST
    arrival = 0;        (* arrival event *)
    departure1 = 1;     (* departure event at queue 1 *)
    departure2 = 2;     (* departure event at queue 2 *)
VAR
    event: Calendar.Event;
    time: REAL;         (* current time *)
    q1, q2: Paths.Path; (* state of queue and statistics *)
```

lamda: REAL;   (* arrival rate *)
s1: REAL;   (* mean service times at queue 1 *)
s2: REAL;   (* mean service times at queue 2 *)

Hint: the parameter of the exponential distribution is the inverse of the mean service time.

10.5 [**Files**] Support the phone directory of Exercise 8.7 with a file. The command *Open* takes a name as parameter. If a file of that name exists, initialize the directory from that file, otherwise open an empty directory.

Add a command *Store* to write a (new or changed) directory to disk storage. Retain the old file version as a backup. *Hint*: first rename the file with a backup name (Exercise 8.3). Then create a new file with the original name, write the directory to that file, and register the new file.

References

Dahl O. J., Dijkstra E.W. and Hoare C. A. R. (1972). *Structured Programming*. New York: Academic Press.

Wirth N. (1971). Program development by stepwise refinement. *Communications of the ACM*, **14**, 221–7.

Wirth N. (1974). On the composition of well-structured programs. *Computing Surveys*, **6**, 247–9.

Wirth N. (1976) *Algorithms + Data Structures = Programs*. Englewood Chliffs, NJ: Prentice Hall.

Part III

Type extension
Procedure types
Object–orientation

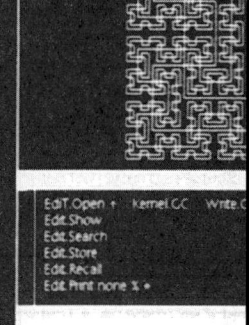

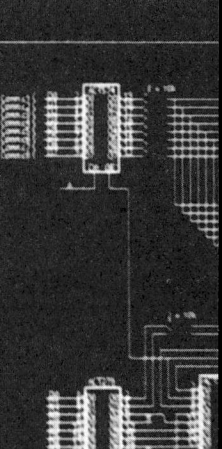

Synopsis

To date, programming remains a craft characterized by the fact that the wheel is re-invented daily. Every experienced programmer has programmed algorithms operating on trees and lists – not once but many times. Why is there this waste in a time where standardization of parts and methods is so successful in other areas such as hardware design?

The answer may not be clear-cut. But a major reason is obviously that traditional languages are deficient in tools that allow the user of an existing object library to bind data or procedures to those afforded by a service module.

To provide the tools to encapsulate standard methods into reusable modules is the object of much current research. In the remaining chapters we will discuss Oberon's answer: *type extension*. As user-definable data types distinguished Pascal from its ancestor, Algol, and as modules and information hiding separated Modula-2 from Pascal, type extension is the most important feature differentiating Oberon from its predecessor.

11 Type extension and procedure types

In Chapter 9 we learned how complex dynamic data structures can be composed from nodes that contain pointers to other nodes of the structure. A node is an (anonymous) instance of a record type – as such, it is the *static* constituent of the structure. While these dynamic structures may be arbitrarily complex in the relation among the nodes, they are *homogeneous* as far as the node type is concerned. This is a serious restriction that is overcome by *type extension*. The notion of type extension is simple in concept: from any existing record type, new types can be derived that have additional fields but remain *compatible* with the existing type (Wirth, 1988).

We will subsequently introduce the concept of a *procedure variable*. In Chapter 6, we defined the procedure as a named statement sequence. A procedure declaration is in a sense like a constant declaration – a fixed relationship between name and value is established. It is not difficult to visualize the concept of a procedure variable whose value is a statement sequence. Its type, the *procedure type*, is specified by the parameter list of the procedure.

Both type extension and the procedure variable have one thing in common: they allow the creation of service modules that lack certain information that has to be provided if programming is conducted according to Chapter 10. The missing part – that is, data fields or specific actions – is furnished by the client module later. Type extension allows late addition of data fields, the procedure variable of actions.

Extension of record types

For an introductory example of type extension, we revert to the declaration of the list node as used in Section 9.2.1, namely

```
TYPE
    Node = POINTER TO NodeDesc;
    NodeDesc = RECORD
        key: Key;
        next: Node
    END;
```

Type extension and procedure types

A list composed of such nodes may serve as a *directory*, with the key representing the name of persons. Rather than adding further data fields such as a phone number to the node directly, we may extend the type *Node* elsewhere. The declaration of such an extended type reads as follows:

```
TYPE
    Entry = POINTER TO EntryDesc;
    EntryDesc = RECORD (NodeDesc)
        phone: ARRAY 16 OF CHAR
    END;
```

An instance of type *Entry* is comprised of three fields: *key*, *next*, and *phone*. Field *phone* is declared directly, whereas the fields *key* and *next* are inherited from *NodeDesc*. Type *NodeDesc* is called the base type of *EntryDesc* that is said to be an extension of *NodeDesc*. Syntactically, the base type is listed in parentheses after the reserved word RECORD.

```
User interface part
MODULE PhoneBook;
IMPORT Directories;
TYPE
Entry = POINTER TO EntryDesc;
EntryDesc = RECORD (Directories.NodeDesc)
    phone: ARRAY 16 OF CHAR
END;
...
```

```
List processing algorithms
MODULE Directories;
TYPE
Key* = ARRAY 32 OF CHAR;

Node* = POINTER TO NodeDesc;
NodeDesc* = RECORD
    key* = Key;
    next: Node
END;
...
```

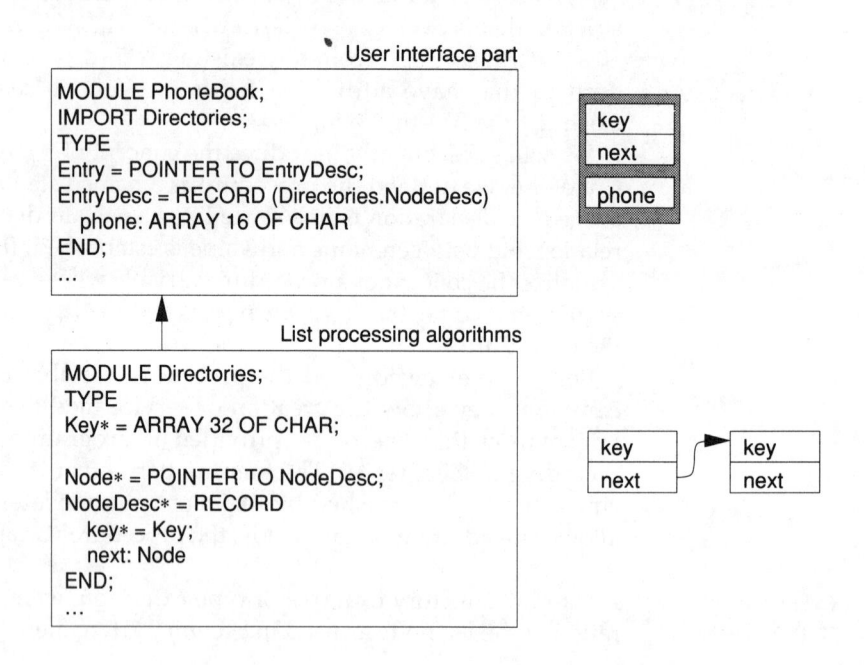

Figure 11.1 Adding 'data' fields in a client module.

It is essential that the *extended type remain compatible with the base type*. Suppose that *base* is a pointer of type *Node* and *ext* one of type *Entry*.

Compatibility means that an assignment *base := ext* is possible. Moreover, the concept of type is made dynamic. That means that after the assignment, the pointer *base* 'remembers' the type of *ext*. We shall say more about the use of this concept later.

Type extension is especially powerful if the declaration of the base type and the extension are in different modules. For example, assume that module *Directories* implements the function of searching and updating a directory. *PhoneBook* is a client module that yields phone numbers for given names. The task is split in two independent parts. Module *Directories* works on a dynamic data structure whereas the client, in our example module *PhoneBook*, implements the application-specific parts, most notably the user interface. This frees the service module from all application-specific details – it serves a potentially large class of directory applications – we may truly speak of a *generic module* (see Figure 11.1).

Procedure types

Like type extension, procedure types help to decouple a service module from its client. A good example is furnished by numerical routines for extracting roots of equations, integrating functions or solving differential equations. Consider a procedure *Bisection* that finds the root of an equation $f(x) = 0$. Instead of passing the function through a global identifier f, we may use a formal parameter of procedure type as shown in the following heading:

TYPE RealFunct = PROCEDURE (x: Real): REAL;
PROCEDURE Bisection(f: RealFunct; x1, x2: REAL): REAL;

As in the previous example, the procedure *Bisection* may be part of a service module. The particular function is provided in the client, where its root needs to be calculated.

Objects

Our introductory examples show how type extension and procedure variables are instrumental to realize the notion of a generic module. Through their combination, however, an even more powerful concept emerges – that of an *object*.[1] This is a record with procedure fields that can be regarded an instance of an abstract data type. More about this follows in Chapters 12 and 13.

---

[1] In the specific sense of object-oriented programming.

11.1 Extension of record types

11.1.1 Declaration of an extended type

In Oberon, record types are extensible. The syntax of Section 8.3.1 needs generalization, the boldfaced terms are added:

```
RecordType = "RECORD" [ "(" BaseType ")" ]
             FieldListSequence
             "END".
BaseType = qualident.
FieldListSequence = FieldList { ";" FieldList }.
FieldList = [ IdentList ":" type ].
IdentList = ident ["*"] { "," ident ["*"] }.
```

If a record type definition extends another type, that type is called *base type* and appears in parentheses after the keyword RECORD. The qualident specifying the base type must itself designate a record type.

The fields defined in the field list sequence are *added to the fields of the base type*. Therefore an instance of the extended type comprises the union of the fields of the base type and those defined in the field list sequence. The fields of the base type are sometimes said to be *inherited*.

Type extensions may be cascaded. Consider the following example of type declarations $T0$, $T1$ and $T2$. $T0$ is the familiar list node, this time without a key or data. $T1$ extends $T0$; the data field a is added. $T2$ further extends $T1$, adding yet another data field b. The diagrams on the right-hand side are a schematic representation of the fields a and b.

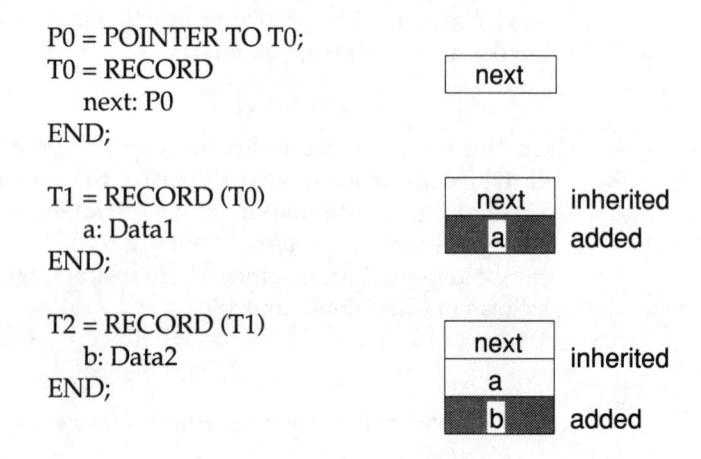

```
P0 = POINTER TO T0;
T0 = RECORD
    next: P0
END;

T1 = RECORD (T0)
    a: Data1
END;

T2 = RECORD (T1)
    b: Data2
END;
```

Both *T1* and *T2* are extensions of *T0*. *T1* is said to be a *direct extension*. Similarly, *T2* is an direct extension of *T1*. Analogously, *T1* and *T0* are base types of *T2*. *T1* is termed a *direct base type* of *T2*, and *T0* is a direct base type of *T1*.

We may regard an extended type as a *specialization* of its base type. It represents those instances to which additional attributes apply, namely the attributes expressed by the added fields.

Typically, extensions are declared in a module different from the one containing the declaration of the base type. In this case, the base type is a qualified name. Only the public fields of the base type are visible in the client module.

It is useful to define the relation '*T1* extends *T0*' to be transitive. In other words, *T1* extends *T0* if it is either equal to *T0* or it is a direct extension of an extension of *T0*.

11.1.2 Record designators and assignments

All the fields of a record variable of an extended type can be referenced in the usual manner. Consider

VAR   x0, y0: T0;   x1, y1: T1;   x2, y2: T2;

Then

x2.next   x2.a   x2.b

are designators referencing the three fields of the record variable *x2*. Similarly, *x1.next* and *x1.a* comprise the fields of *x1*. The variable *x0* has only one field, *x0.next*.

What about assignments? The essence of a language featuring strong typing is that the type of the expression on the right-hand side of ":=" must be *assignment-compatible* (see Table 4.3) with the type of the designator on the left-hand side. The compiler enforces that compatibility, even across module boundaries.

Can a base type be compatible with its extension or vice versa? Consider the assignment y2 := x2, where both participating variables are of identical type (Figure 11.2). This assignment is equivalent to the assignments of the three fields

y2.next := x2.next;
y2.a := x2.a;
y2.b := x2.b;

192 Type extension and procedure types

which are all necessary to establish pre-condition P in

$$(* P *) \ y2 := x2 \ (* R *)$$

as the predicate R in which all occurrences of $y2$ were replaced by $x2$.

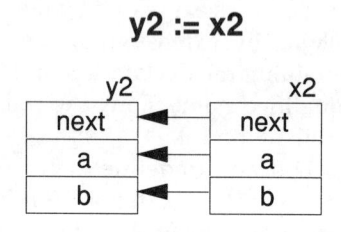

y2 := x2

y2		x2
next	←	next
a	←	a
b	←	b

Figure 11.2 Assignment of records of equal type.

We now contemplate $y1 := x2$, the case where the type $T2$ of $x2$ extends the type $T1$ of $y1$. Figure 11.3 depicts this assignment in a diagram like the previous one.

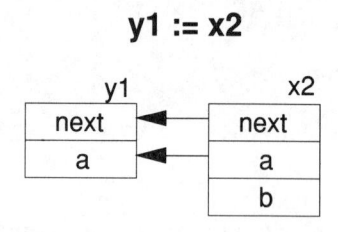

y1 := x2

y1		x2
next	←	next
a	←	a
		b

Figure 11.3 Assignment of a record of extended type to its base type.

This assignment may be defined as being equivalent to

  y1.next := x2.next;
  y1.a := x2.a;

Only those fields that comprise type $T1$ participate in the assignment. $T1$ is a base type of $T2$; that is, $x2$ is not only an instance of $T2$, but has also all properties of a $T1$. Therefore it is assured that there always exists a one-to-one correspondence.

Projection

This definition has an analogy in mathematics: the projection of a higher-dimensional vector onto a lower-dimensional space; see Figure 11.4. Using this analogy, we say that the *assignment is a projection of type T2 onto type T1*.

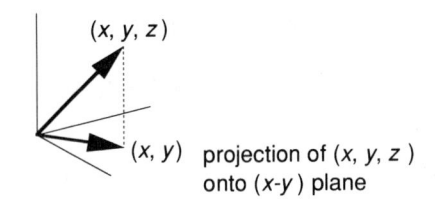

Figure 11.4 Projection.

Finally, visualize the reverse case $y2 := x1$. The type of the assigment target extends the type of the variable being assigned. From Figure 11.5, we infer that there is not enough information to unambiguously specify $y2$. Such an assignment is *illegal in Oberon*. An attempt at an artificial definition, such as 'field b remains unchanged' cannot be reconciled with the axiom of assignment.

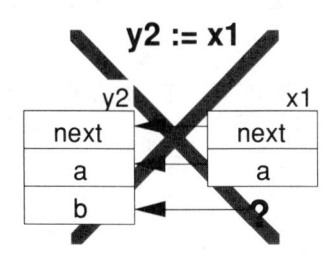

Figure 11.5 Illegal assignment of a record to an extended type.

Type compatibility, VAR parameter

We can now summarize the modified type compatibility rule. Type $T2$ is compatible with $T1$; that is, an assignment of an expression of type $T2$ to a designator of type $T1$ is possible if

(1) $T2$ is an extension of $T1$
(2) $T2$ is included in $T1$ (such as INTEGER in REAL)

Recall that (1) includes the case where *T2* is identical with *T1* or declared equal to *T1*.

The type rule for VAR parameters is relaxed: the type of the actual parameter can be an extension of the type of the formal VAR parameter. For example, a procedure

PROCEDURE Proc(VAR t0: T0);

can be called as *Proc(x2)*, where *x2: T2*.

11.2 Pointers, type guards and type tests

11.2.1 Extension of pointer types

Record variables accessed through pointers are the basic ingredient of dynamic data structures. In Section 9.1.2, we learned how a call of the predeclared procedure NEW(*p*) allocates an anonymous instance of the pointer base type on the heap and, at the same time, assigns a pointer to the new instance to variable *p*. Exactly the same mechanism applies if the pointer base type is an extension of another record type. Consider the type declarations

```
P0 = POINTER TO T0;   P1 = POINTER TO T1;   P2 = POINTER TO T2;
T0 = RECORD            T1 = RECORD (T0)      T2 = RECORD (T1)
       next: P0                a: Data1              b: Data2
     END;                    END;                  END;
```

Let *p2: P2*. The effect of NEW(*p2*) is depicted in Figure 11.6. As we would expect, an instance of *T2*, including all the inherited fields is created and allocated on the heap. The pointer *p2* now points to the new (anonymous) instance of *T2*.

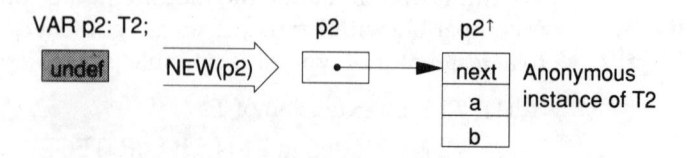

Figure 11.6 Creation of an instance of an extended type.

11.2 Pointers, type guards and type tests

A pointer is bound to its pointer base type. Programmers often regard the pointer and the dereferenced record variable as synonyms, a fact enhanced by the implied dereferencing afforded by Oberon. Recall that implied dereferencing, for example, allows us to abbreviate *p2↑.b* by *p2.b*. It is therefore appropriate to generalize the concept of type extension to pointers. Consider again the previous declaration, in particular

- *P0* is a pointer type with base type *T0*;
- *P1* is a pointer type with base type *T1*;
- *T1* extends *T0*.

In this case, we say that pointer type *P1 extends P0*.

Extension of pointer type, definition

In general, a pointer type *P1* extends a pointer type *P0* if its base type *T1* extends the base type *T0* of *P0*. As in the case of records, *P1* is said to be a (direct) extension of *P0* and *P0* is a (direct) base type[1] of *P1*.

With our sample declaration, it follows that *P2* is a direct extension of *P1* and an extension of *P0*.

11.2.2 Static and dynamic type, type guard, type test

The rule governing the assignment of records is also governing the assignment of pointers: a pointer of type *P1* can be assigned to a pointer of type *P0* if *P1* extends *P0*.

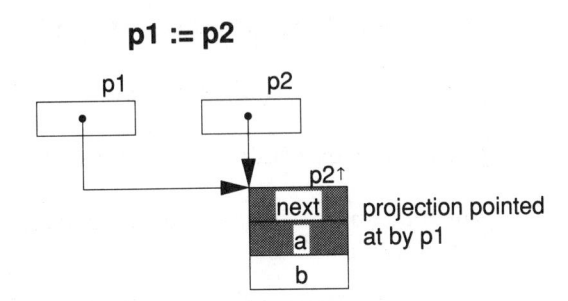

Figure 11.7 Assignment of pointers referencing the same record variable.

Let *p1*: *P1* and *p2*: *P2* according to the type declarations of the last section. The effect of the assignment *p1* := *p2* is depicted in Figure 11.7. We assume that an instance of type *T2* was created previously. After the assignment, both pointers afford access to the same anonymous

---

[1] Note the difference between pointer base type and base type in the sense of type extension.

Type extension and procedure types

variable p2↑. Nevertheless, since p1 is of type P1, it yields a *projected view* of p2↑; the field b cannot be referenced through p1.

However, if we know that p1 points to an instance of T2, then field b could be unambiguously accessed – if only the type rules could be generalized from the static view to a dynamic one, accounting for the actual state of the computation.

Dynamic type

Oberon provides such a generalization. After the assignment p1 := p2, p1 is said to be of *dynamic type P2*, and field b can be referenced. The dynamic type is distinct from the declared or *static type*, which is still P1. We must assert, however, that p1 can be assumed to be of an appropriate dynamic type through a *type guard* expressed as

    p1(P2)

The dynamic type is indicated in parentheses immediately following the pointer's identifier. Under the provisions of a type guard, the following assignments are legal:

    y2 := p1(P2)↑;   d2 := p1(P2).b;

where y2: T2 and d2: Data2. The type guard asserts that currently p1↑ is of type T2. If, during the execution of a program, the *type guard is violated*, the program comes to an abnormal halt.

General designator

We are now ready to list the syntax of the designator in full generality:

```
designator = qualident {"." ident   | "[" ExpList "]"
                                    | "(" qualident ")" | "↑"}.
ExpList = expression {"," expression}.
```

The type guard is highlighted in boldface. A type guard of the form v(T) is applicable only if

(1) T extends the declared (or *static*) type of the variable v; and
(2) variable v is a pointer or a formal VAR parameter of record type.

Type test

The use of extended pointer types can only come to full bloom if a test can be applied that reveals the dynamic type of a pointer variable. The relation operator "IS" performs such a *type test*:

    v IS T

which is satisfied if the actual (or dynamic) type of v is an extension of T; that is equal to T or a proper extension of T. Variable v and type T must satisfy the same two conditions listed above for the type guard $v(T)$. If v = NIL the result of the type test remains undefined.

For example, consider

>   VAR p0; T0; p1: T1; p2: T2;
>   ...
>   NEW(p1); p0 := p1;

where $T0$ and $T2$ are those of Section 11.2.1. Then the following holds:

$$(p0 \text{ IS } P0) = \text{TRUE} \quad (p0 \text{ IS } P1) = \text{TRUE} \quad (p0 \text{ IS } P2) = \text{FALSE}.$$

Unless it is assured a priori that a type guard is satisfied, the guarded designator must be within the protection of an IF statement. For example, take the previous statement sequence $y2 := p1(P2)\uparrow$; $d2 := p1(P2).b$. If it is not certain that $p1$ is of the dynamic type $P2$, we have to write

>   IF p1 IS P2 THEN
>   y2 := p1(P2)↑; d2 := p1(P2).b
>   END

11.2.3 With statement, regional type guard

It is quite typical that in a statement sequence, the same type guard appears a number of times. Therefore a type guard with a bigger textual scope is desirable to aid clarity and avoid unnecessary clerical work. The with statement provides such a *regional guard*. Using a with statement, the above example can be expressed as

>   IF p1 IS P2 THEN
>   WITH p1: P2 DO
>   y2 := p1↑; d2 := p1.b
>   END
>   END;

In formal syntax notation,

WithStatement = "WITH" guard "DO" StatementSequence
            "END".
guard = qualident ":" qualident.

In a statement

WITH v: T DO S_1; S_2; ... S_n END

v is a variable and T a type. The rules of type guards apply as described in Section 11.2.2. Within the statement sequence, v is regarded as if it had been declared of type T.

Records with variant parts

Programming languages such as Pascal and Modula-2 feature special language constructs for *records with variant parts*. Oberon deals with variant records through type extension. The timeworn personnel record should serve a last time as an example:

```
TYPE
    Person = RECORD
        first, last: Name;
        idno: INTEGER;
        birth: Date
    END;

    Pilot = RECORD (Person)
        hoursInFlight: INTEGER
    END;

    Clerk = RECORD (Person)
        jobCode: INTEGER
    END;
```

Two variants – that is, extensions or rather specializations of *Person* are defined, namely pilots and clerks. In a procedure processing records of type *Person*, we can distinguish the variants using a type test, for example

```
PROCEDURE ProcessPerson(VAR p: Person);
BEGIN
    ... (* process common Person data name, idno and birth *)
    IF p IS Pilot THEN
        WITH p: Pilot DO
            ... (* process pilot specific data *)
        END
```

```
        ELSIF p IS Clerk THEN
            WITH p: Clerk DO
                ... (* process clerk specific data *)
            END
        END
    END ProcessPerson;
```

Note that it is essential that the formal parameter of the procedure *ProcessPerson* be a variable parameter, otherwise the type tests are not legal.

11.3 Procedure types

11.3.1 The procedure type and procedure variables

So far, we have regarded procedures exclusively as named statement sequences. They specify actions to be performed on variables. However, we may take the view that procedures are themselves objects that can be assigned to variables. In this light, a procedure declaration appears as a special kind of a constant declaration, the value of the constant being a statement sequence and a parameter mechanism, for example

```
    CONST white = 0;

    PROCEDURE Init;
        NEW(list); list.next := NIL
    END Init;
```

The first declaration binds the identifier *white* to the integer 0. The second declaration associates *Init* with the statement sequence NEW(list); list.next := NIL.

If we allow procedure variables, in addition to procedure constants, it must be possible to declare types whose instances are procedures. These are called *procedure types*. A procedure type declaration specifies the number and the types of the formal parameters and, in the case of a function procedure, the type of the result.

Consider the examples

```
    RealFunct = PROCEDURE (x: REAL): REAL;
    Quadratic = PROCEDURE (a, b, c, x: REAL): REAL;
    Handler = PROCEDURE (obj: Object; VAR msg: Message);
```

The identifiers that appear in the formal parameter list of the procedure type declaration are *dummy names* – they serve only as a mnemonic indicating the purpose of the parameter. It is merely their type that is important.

The formal syntax of the procedure type declaration is

| ProcedureType = PROCEDURE [FormalParameters].

Matching parameter lists

Two procedure types are *compatible* with each other if their *formal parameter lists match*; that is, if the following three conditions are satisfied:

(1) they have the same number of parameters;
(2) they have the same function result type, or none;
(3) corresponding parameters have equal types and are either both VAR parameters or both value parameters.

Variables of procedure type can be declared in the usual manner, for example

```
VAR
    f, g, trig: RealFunct;
    combinatorial: PROCEDURE (x: INTEGER): INTEGER;
    q: Quadratic;
    handleFigure: Handler;
```

11.3.2 Expressions and assignments

Procedure variables can be *compared for equality or inequality*. They receive their values through normal *assignment statements*. Ultimately, values assignable to procedure variables are defined through normal procedure declarations. Oberon imposes the following restriction on an assignment $v := procId$, where *procId* is a procedure identifier:

(1) *procId* must represent a procedure that is neither local to other procedures nor predeclared;
(2) the parameter list of *procId* must match the one of the type of v.

NIL

A special value, NIL, specifies abortion, and is compatible with all procedure types; that is, NIL may be assigned to or compared with every procedure variable. NIL is typically used to initialize a procedure variable at a time when no definite action is yet determined.

Consider the procedure declarations:

PROCEDURE Square(x: REAL): REAL;
BEGIN RETURN x*x END Square;

PROCEDURE Quadratic(a, b, c, x: REAL): REAL;
BEGIN RETURN a*x*x + b*x + c END Quadratic;

The following assignments are possible (the declaration of the variables is given above):

f := Square;   g := f;   q := Quadratic;   handleText := NIL;
trig := Math.sin;

The assignment $f := q$, however, is illegal, since the types of the variables f and q are incompatible.

11.3.3 Call of procedure variables

A procedure variable *may be called*. If it is a proper procedure, the call is a statement – in the case of a function procedure, a factor in an expression. If the type of the procedure variable specifies formal parameters, actual parameters must be specified. Syntactically, the actual parameters are specified in the same way as in the case of procedure constants, namely

> factor = designator [ActualParameters].
> ProcedureCall = designator [ActualParameters].
> ActualParameters = "(" ExpList ")".
> ExpList = expression { "," expression}.

where the designator stands for the procedure variable. The call of a procedure variable binds actual parameters to formal ones and evaluates the statement sequence associated with the variable. The rules are identical to the call of a procedure constant (see Chapter 6). Note that an attempt to call a procedure variable whose value is NIL results in abnormal program termination.

The variables defined in the earlier examples can be called in the following ways:

y := f(x);   a := g(3.14);   s := q(1, 2, c, y);

An evaluation of a function procedure is characterized by always having a parameter list (possibly empty).

11.3.4 Formal parameters of procedure type

Variables and formal parameters of procedure type free the programmer from having to provide a procedure declaration *prior* to the call.

A good example is given by numerical routines for finding roots, integrating functions, or solving differential equations, for example

PROCEDURE Bisection(f: RealFunct; x1, x2: REAL): REAL;

If the only reason for a named procedure type, such as *RealFunct*, is to specify a formal parameter, Oberon admits the short cut

PROCEDURE Bisection(f: PROCEDURE (x: REAL): REAL;
x1, x2: REAL): REAL;

The EBNF definition of FormalType is therefore augmented as follows:

| FormalType = { "ARRAY OF" } qualident | **ProcedureType**.

The important benefit from using a procedure parameter is the fact that *Bisection* can be part of a *service module*, while the declaration of the function, whose root we seek, is contained in the context of the client module. The service module can be compiled once and put in the computer's library of object modules.

Another good example of the use of a procedure parameter is the traversal of dynamic data structures with the purpose of applying a procedure, *P* say, to each node. For example, consider the procedure *Enumerate* from Section 9.2.1. Passing the action *P* as a parameter makes it general-purpose – the algorithm used for traversing the list structure is decoupled from the action to be performed on each node:

```
PROCEDURE Enumerate(first: Node; P: PROCEDURE (n: Node));
BEGIN
   WHILE first # NIL DO  P(first); first := first.next END
END Enumerate;
```

11.3.5 Up-calls

Typically, a module provides an abstraction and a programming task is divided into a hierarchy of such abstractions. A client module imports a service module and makes use of the exported data structures and procedures. For example, if a random number is needed, module *RandomNumbers* is imported and *RandomNumbers.Uniform*() called. Modules higher up in the hierarchy use objects of modules that are further down.

Using procedure variables, we can invert the relationship of the service module and its client: a module can call a procedure defined higher up in the hierarchy. Such a call is known as an *up-call*. Up-calls are instrumental in object-orientation, a methodology that we will introduce in the remaining chapters.

Here we will introduce the notion of an up-call by means of an example. An application is found in Section 12.4.3. The scenario is a service module *S* that generates an object in a procedure *Generate*. In order to create that object, a procedure variable *new* is called. The value of that variable originates from an assignment made in the client module *C*. Hence, the statement sequence of a procedure declared in a module that is not imported by *S* is executed:

```
          MODULE C;
          IMPORT S;
          ...
(1) →     PROCEDURE New; ...END New;
          ...
          PROCEDURE Set*;
          BEGIN
(2) →         S.new := New
          END Set;
          ...
          END C.

          MODULE S;
(3) →     VAR new*: PROCEDURE;
          ...
          PROCEDURE Generate*;
          BEGIN
              ...
```

(4) →   **new**;
          ...
   END Generate;
   ...
   END S.

Notes

(1) Procedure *New* is declared. We assume that it generates a certain object.

(2) Within the statement sequence of the command *Set*, the procedure *New* is assigned to procedure variable *S.new*. This is an assignment to a global variable exported by S.

(3) Here *new* is declared as a global procedure variable exported by module S.

(4) In procedure *Generate*, the procedure variable *new* is called. It is assumed that prior to that call, *new* was initialized through execution of the command *C.Set*. The call of *new* is an up-call, since the statement sequence that is executed is declared in module C (namely that of procedure *New*).

11.4 Summary

This chapter has introduced three new concepts:

(1) From a given record type, an *extended type* may be derived that *adds new data fields* to its base type. Variables of extended types may be assigned to variables of their base types, but not vice versa. Such an assignment is called a *projection* – only the record fields of the base type participate in the assignment.

(2) A pointer to an extended type is said to extend the pointer to the base type. The same assignment rule applies to pointers: extended pointers may be assigned to instances of their base types. After such an assignment, the base pointer assumes a *dynamic type* differing from the declared type. Under the auspices of a type guard, the extended fields may be accessed. A type test allows guarding of such references. The with statement affords a type guard of extended textual scope: it is a *regional* type guard.

(3) The *procedure type* defines a parameter list and a result type. A procedure may be assigned to such a variable if that procedure's

formal parameter types and result type match those declared in the procedure type of the variable.

The aim of type extension and the procedure variable is to make programs *extensible*. A program is said to be extensible if addition of new functions is textually localized – ideally by simply adding a new module to an existing module hierarchy, without needing to change or recompile any of the existing parts.

Through type extension, record fields may be added to a given base type later, usually in a different module. In this manner, generic modules operating on lists and trees may be composed without determining the 'data fields.' The procedure variable allows placement of a call *prior* to specifying the actions of the procedure. For example, in a scientific subroutine library, a function to be integrated may be called that is provided later by the client.

But it is really the *combination* of type extension and procedure variables that advances extensibility in the most significant way. The technique is known as *object-orientation*, a topic explored in depth in Chapters 12 and 13.

11.5 Exercises

11.1 Consider the declarations

> TYPE
> LN = POINTER TO LND; LND = RECORD next: LN END;
> TN = POINTER TO TND; TND = RECORD right, left TN END;
> M = RECORD END;

Identify legal extensions:

(a) LN1 = POINTER TO LN1D; LN1D = RECORD(LN) a: Data END;
(b) LN2 = POINTER TO LN2D; LN2D = RECORD(LND) a: Data END;
(c) LN3 = POINTER TO LN3D; LN3D = RECORD(M) a: Data END;
(d) LN4 = POINTER TO LN4D; LN4D = RECORD(LND); next: LN4 END;
(e) TN1 = POINTER TO TN1D; TN1D = RECORD(LND) a: Data END;
(f) TN2 = POINTER TO TN2D; TN2D = RECORD(TND) a: Data END;
(g) M1 = RECORD: M; a: Data END;
(e) M2 = POINTER TO RECORD(M) c: Data END;

11.2 Assume the type declarations of Exercise 11.1 and

> LN1 = POINTER TO LN1D; LN1D = RECORD(LN) a: Data END;
> TN1 = POINTER TO TN1D; TN1D = RECORD(TN) b: Data END;

M1 = RECORD(M) x, y: Data END;
VAR a: LN; b: LN1; c: TN; d, t: TN1; e: M; f, m: M1; g: Data;

Which of the following assignments and relations are legal?

a := b;   b := a;   a := c;   a↑ := b↑;   f := e;   a(LN1).a := d.a;
c.a := f.x;   d(TN1).a := g;   WITH a: LN1 DO g := a.a END;
a IS b   a IS LN1   a IS TN1   e IS M   e IS M1

11.3 Given the declaration of Exercise 11.2 and

PROCEDURE H(t: TN; VAR m: M);
VAR msg: M;
BEGIN c := t; msg := m; IF m IS M1 THEN g := m(M1).x END
END H;

Assuming a call $H(t, m)$, what is the dynamaic type of c and msg? Is the assignment $g := m(M1).x$ executed?

11.4 [**Directory based on lists**] Implement a module *Directories*. A directory is a repository of entries that can be entered, deleted and recovered according to a key. Use a list (Section 9.2) to represent a directory.

DEFINITION Directories;
TYPE
    Key = ARRAY 32 OF CHAR;
    Entry = POINTER TO EntryDesc;
    EntryDesc = RECORD key: Key END;
    Directory = Node;
    NodeProc = PROCEDURE(n: Node);
PROCEDURE Insert(VAR dir: Directory; new: Node);
PROCEDURE Search(dir: Directory; k: Key): Node;
PROCEDURE Delete(VAR dir: Directory; k: Key);
PROCEDURE Enumerate(dir: Directory; P: NodeProc);
PROCEDURE New(): Directory;
END Directories.

11.5 [**Phone directory**] Write a module *PhoneDir* that is a client of module *Directories*. Design a suitable user interface with commands *Open, Add, Delete* and *Query*. *Hint*: use a type *PhoneEntry* that extends *Directories.Entry*, for example

TYPE
    PhoneEntry = POINTER TO PhoneEntryDesc;
    PhoneEntryDesc = RECORD (Directories.Entry)
        phone: ARRAY 10 OF CHAR
    END;

11.6 [**File support**] Support the phone directory with a file *PhoneDir.Open* opens the directory from the file, if one exists. Otherwise a new directory is created. *PhoneDir.Store* writes the directory back to the file.

11.7 [**Directories based on trees**] Base module *Directories* on a tree data structure. Leave the interface unchanged. Show that the new module can substitute for the old one without affecting its client.

11.8 [**Phone and address directory**] Expand the functionality of the phone directory. Some (but not all) of the entries list not only the phone number but also addresses. *Hint*: use a type *PhoneEntry* that extends *Directories.Entry* and a type *AddrEntry* that extends *PhoneEntry*.

11.9 [**File support**] Support the phone and address directory with a file. *Hint*: Define a type flag, for example a character 0X means 'Type is *PhoneEntry*' and 1X means 'type is *AddrEntry*.' Organize the file such that each entry is preceded by a type flag. Reading the flag first enables you to create the appropriate variable.

Reference

Wirth N. (1988). Type extension. *ACM Transactions on Programming Languages and Systems*, **10**, 204–14.

12 Object-orientation

Structuring and abstraction are major software design techniques. Chapter 10 introduced these concepts using a realistic example. Proper structure is essential to make a program text readable – and ultimately trustworthy. Abstraction – in particular the notion of the abstract data type – aids in the specification of clearly defined *interfaces* between modules and helps in *dividing* a large programming task into different areas of concern that may be tackled by different programmers or programming teams.

Since its inception some twenty years ago, structured programming has become a well-known programming technique. If programming is practiced as described in Chapter 10, at the time a module is ready for compilation, all variables are declared and all procedures fully specified. The declarations may reside in imported modules – in this case, those modules must be compiled first. As we will see shortly, this imposes limitations on the extensibility of programs – limitations that a programming technique, known as *object-orientation*, will remove or diminish.

Localized upgrade

It is a common experience that programs need maintenance. If they are useful, their capabilities will expand over time. Unfortunately, even excellent structuring often fails to make the addition of a feature a mere local change in the program text. Instead, the places that need change are numerous and spread over many modules. Making a change in such a program is not only tedious – it is also error-prone. All too easily, one of the necessary changes is overlooked or one of the consequences of a change is ignored. Clearly, a design technique that helps to make feature upgrades a *localized* task is of utmost value. The ultimate goal is a system that allows adding of features by simply adding modules to the library – without even having to recompile the existing modules of a system.

Reusing modules   The term module is also encountered in hardware design, where it is used as a synonym for a common part – typically, a VLSI component. Hardware modularization is highly successful through a proper choice of the building blocks and standardization of their interfaces.

While in programming, the module concept is well over a decade old, similar success is still quite elusive. The goal is a *standard library of service modules*, provided by experts and available in object form. It is essential for the success of this concept that the user of such service modules have *no need to modify their source code*. Programmers have a well-justified hesitation in opening somebody else's source code and modifying it. It either solves their problem – then it can be used – or the function will be re-created, even though only slightly different from already existing code. Moreover, for practical or commercial reasons, source code is often unavailable.

The earliest and still one of the most successful examples of reusable procedure libraries is furnished by *scientific subroutine packages*. Fortunately, those programmers who still insist on producing their own sine or exponential functions are becoming quite rare. A second success story is the use of *abstract data structures and abstract data types in operating systems*. On the other hand, good list and tree processing programs are still rare.

The primary reason for the difficulty in localizing functional extensions and the lack of success of the concept of reusable libraries stems primarily from the fact that in traditional programming languages[1]

- data fields are bound statically to their record variable;
- procedures are associated statically with a module – hence the procedures of an abstract data type are bound statically to the type.

Substantial progress in the direction of reusable and extensible programming systems is being made – the methodology is known as *object-orientation*. In Oberon, object-orientation is achieved through use of type extension and procedure variables.

This chapter is an introduction to the key notions of object-orientation, namely

- the *generic module*;
- the *heterogeneous data structure*;
- the *object* and its representation;
- the *dynamic binding* of procedures;
- the *module structure* of an object-oriented program.

[1] Such as PL/I, Pascal or Modula-2.

We will develop and motivate the object-oriented concepts with examples rather than in a deductive style. However, in order not to drown in a sea of details, we refrain from presenting large programs, and concentrate on the essential ideas of the design of data structures and types.

One of those examples is a graphics editor. Editors in general are good cases for programs that benefit from object-orientation. Other applications are found in the area of system software[1] and simulation. A complete simulation package based on object-oriented design principles is presented in Chapter 13.

12.1 Generic modules

To amplify the concept of the generic module, we consider the example of a FIFO queue that we encounted in Chapter 9. The definition of a module *FIFOs* may read as follows:

```
DEFINITION FIFOs;
TYPE
    FIFO = RECORD END;

    Node = POINTER TO NodeDesc;
    NodeDesc = RECORD END;

    PROCEDURE Enqueue(VAR q: FIFO; n: Node);
    PROCEDURE DequeuedNode(VAR q: FIFO): Node;
    PROCEDURE Open(VAR q: FIFO);
END FIFOs.
```

In this interface, the data types *FIFO* and *Node* are abstract.

A possible implementation is that of Section 9.2.2. In this case the initialization procedure *Open* is particularly simple:

```
PROCEDURE Open(VAR q: FIFO);
BEGIN q.first := NIL
END Open;
```

Prior to type extension, such an interface, while syntactically correct,

---

[1] In particular, the window subsystem of graphic based workstations. An example is the Oberon system itself (see Wirth and Gutknecht, 1992).

would be pretty pointless. To make *FIFOs* useful, the type *Node* would have to make *application-specific fields visible*. But this violates the condition that a service module should not have to be modified and recompiled by its user.

Type extension, however, makes a module *FIFOs* immediately useful in many applications that need FIFO lists: *the application-specific 'data' fields are added by the client.* Paying tribute to its generality, we call *FIFOs* a *generic module*.

Client of module FIFOs

An excerpt of a client of *FIFOs* follows. It is a simulation program where customers are queueing for a resource.

```
MODULE Sim;
IMPORT FIFOs, ... ;
TYPE
   Customer = POINTER TO CustomerDesc;
   CustomerDesc = RECORD (FIFOs.NodeDesc)
      priority: INTEGER
   END;
...
VAR c: Customer;  q: FIFOs.FIFO; temp: FIFOs.Node;
...
```

A customer *c* is created and enqueued in FIFO queue *q* as follows:

```
NEW(c); c.priority = 0; FIFOs.Enqueue(q, c); ...
```

It is essential that *c* be a variable of the extended type *Customer*. This type will be 'remembered' in the list, since the appropriate list pointer will assume *Customer* as its dynamic type.

The following statement sequence retrieves a customer *c* from the waiting line *q*:

```
temp := FIFOs.DequeuedNode(q);
IF (temp # NIL) & (temp IS Customer)
   c := temp(Customer); ...
END;
```

We need an ancillary variable *temp* of type *FIFOs.Node* that matches the result type of *FIFOs.DequeuedNode*. The reason is that a type guard cannot be applied to function calls. A type guard is required because *FIFOs.DequeuedNode* returns a result of type *FIFOs.Node*, not *Customer*.

Summary

A generic module is one to be used by many clients, typically involving type extension. In the case of dynamic data structures, it is possible to separate (into different modules) the algorithm operating on the pointers from the processing of the 'data.'

(1) Often, the generic module encapsulates the algorithms operating on a dynamic data structure such as list and tree processing. Such data structures are hidden and represented as abstract data types.

(2) The client module adds application-specific fields to the node type of the generic module.

(3) It is the task of the client to generate instances of data items and to add them to the data structure using its procedures.

(4) When items are retrieved, appropriate type guards are required.

(5) It is the task of the generic module to initialize instances of its abstract types (typically, the procedure is termed *Open* or *Init*).

12.2 Heterogeneous data structures

The dynamic data structures that we know from Chapter 9 are composed of static elements – or nodes – linked by pointers. Since the pointers refer to the node type, the entire data structure is composed of nodes of the same type. In many cases, this is an unacceptable restriction.

Type extension is the tool for building *heterogeneous dynamic structures*; that is, structures composed of different (but related and compatible) node types. The key idea is to *declare a common base* type that incorporates the links and possibly data common to all node types and *add 'private data' by extending that base type*.

Consider module *FIFOs*. Different customers may be declared as extensions of base type *FIFOs.Node*, for example

```
Customer1 = POINTER TO C1D;
C1D =
RECORD (FIFOs.NodeDesc)
    priority: INTEGER
END;
```

```
Customer2 = POINTER TO C2D;
C2D =
RECORD (FIFOs.NodeDesc)
    timeStamp: REAL;
    workDemand: REAL
END;
```

Both types, *Customer1* and *Customer2*, are extensions of *FIFOs.Node*; hence they can be enqueued in the same FIFO queue. It is important that the *dynamic type not be lost upon retrieval* – a type test will reveal it and allow type-specific processing of the customers.

To make the last point more transparent, we will study a list of graphical objects or figures used by a graphics editor. The editor uses such a list to keep track of the shapes displayed on the screen. Typical items in that list are straight lines, rectangles, circles, ellipses, polygons, spline curves and captions.

We base our figure descriptors on the type *Figure* that contains only structure information:[1]

```
TYPE
    Figure = POINTER TO FigureDesc;
    FigureDesc = RECORD
        next: Figure
    END;
```

Each specific figure is represented by an instance of a type that extends the base type *Figure*. From the many possibilities, we give two examples, namely the types *Line* and *Rect* that define the corresponding figures:

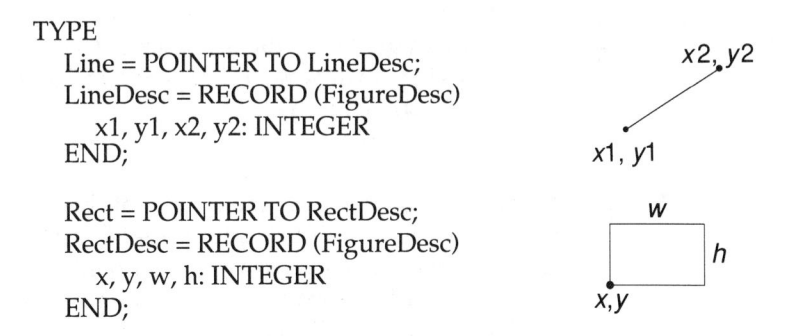

```
TYPE
    Line = POINTER TO LineDesc;
    LineDesc = RECORD (FigureDesc)
        x1, y1, x2, y2: INTEGER
    END;

    Rect = POINTER TO RectDesc;
    RectDesc = RECORD (FigureDesc)
        x, y, w, h: INTEGER
    END;
```

A heterogeneous list composed of two lines and two rectangles is depicted in Figure 12.1.

---

[1] The type *Figure* assumes the role of *Node* in Section 9.2.

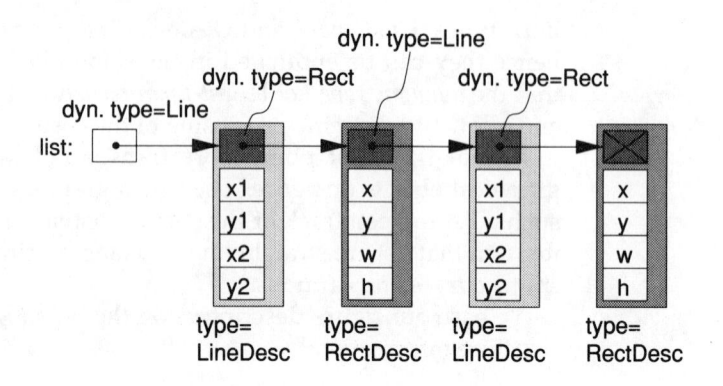

Figure 12.1 A list of heterogeneous records. The *dynamic* type of the pointers is shown.

We will discuss two typical actions: the creation of a new figure and processing all the elements of a heterogeneous list of figures.

An instance of the type *Line* is created and inserted into the list of figures as follows:

    PROCEDURE NewLine(list: Figure; x1, y1, x2, y2: INTEGER);
    VAR l: Line;
    BEGIN
      NEW(l);   (* Create instance of *Line* *)
      l.x1 := x1; l.y1 := y1; l.x2 := x2; l.y2 := y2;   (* Initialize fields *)
      InsertLast(list, l)
    END NewLine;

Formal parameter *list* is the anchor of the list of figures that comprise the graph. The text of procedure *InsertLast* is found in Section 9.2 (with the difference that here it works on the base type *Figure* rather than *Node*). Similar initialization procedures are required for each shape such as *NewRect* and *NewCircle*.

Another action typically performed by graphics editors is to draw all the figures contained in the list. A procedure *DrawAll* does this. It traverses the list structure and acts according to the type of a particular figure:

    PROCEDURE DrawAll(list: Figure);
    VAR f: Figure;
    BEGIN
      f := list;

12.2 Heterogeneous data structures

```
        WHILE f # NIL DO
          IF f IS Line THEN  DrawLine(f(Line))
          ELSIF f IS Rect THEN  DrawRect(f(Rect))
          ELSIF ... (* Other shapes *)
          END;
          f := f.next
        END
      END DrawAll;
```

where *DrawLine* and *DrawRect* are procedures that produce the respective figures on the display. They have headings

```
        PROCEDURE DrawLine(l: Line);
        PROCEDURE DrawRect(r: Rect);
```

Typical for a procedure processing a heterogeneous list is the selection based upon the dynamic type of the list node.

Summary Heterogeneous dynamic data structures usually occur when object-oriented program designs are pursued. The following points are typical of the processing of heterogeneous data structures and should be noted:

(1) Operations involving pointers are performed on the *base type*, in our example type *Figure*.

(2) Elements of the heterogeneous data structure are created as instances of the *extended type*, *Line* or *Rect*.

(3) When an element is inserted into the list, the assignments insure that the list pointers (variable *list* or field *next*) assume the dynamic type of the object.

(4) When processing the elements of the data structure, their type is determined with a type test and appropriate actions are taken. Typically, a *type guard is required*. The type test guarantees that the type guard is never violated.

12.3 Objects, dynamic binding of procedures

Assume that a new figure, an ellipse say, is being added to the graphics editor. What changes are necessary to the program text? First, a new type has to be defined. Like *Line* and *Rect*, the new type, called *Ellipse*, extends the base type *Figure*:

```
TYPE
   Ellipse = POINTER TO EllipseDesc;
   EllipseDesc = RECORD (FigureDesc)
      x, y: INTEGER;   (* Coordinates of center *)
      a, b: INTEGER    (* Major and minor axes *)
   END;
```

Next, a procedure *NewEllipse* has to be furnished that creates an instance of the type *Ellipse* and inserts it into the list of figures. Similarly, procedures such as *DrawEllipse* need to be specified. Finally, wherever type-specific actions occur, such as in the procedure *DrawAll*, the following statements have to be added:

```
   ...
   ELSIF  f IS Ellipse  THEN
      WITH f: Ellipse DO
         ... (* handle ellipse *)
      END
   ELSIF ...
```

As we said in the introduction, such modifications can be expected to be numerous and dispersed throughout the program text – defying the stated goal to localize the modifications to a single place. Localization can only be achieved if operations can be performed on the list of objects that are applicable to *all figures* irrespective of their dynamic type.

The key idea is to *augment the state description of the figure with procedure variables*. Our example considered drawing of figures; we therefore add a procedure field *draw* to the type *Figure*:

```
TYPE
   Figure = POINTER TO FigureDesc;
   FigureDesc = RECORD
      draw: PROCEDURE (f: Figure);
      next: Figure
   END;
```

Additions over the previous version are shown in boldface. Using the redefined type *Figure*, we can now provide a general *type-independent* procedure that draws all the members of a list of figures:

```
PROCEDURE DrawAll(list: Figure);
VAR f: Figure;
BEGIN
   f := list;
   WHILE f # NIL DO  f.draw(f);  f := f.next  END
END DrawAll;
```

Note that the new procedure *draws the figures abstractly*. It is valid for all possible figures handled by the editor – now and in the future. In fact, the new figure is more than just an item in a list, it is an instance of an abstract data type *Figure*. Its properties are a next figure (or none) and the ability to draw itself. The data necessary to describe the figure, as well as the detailed drawing action is hidden to *DrawAll*.

For this general scheme to work, the appropriate type-specific procedures must be assigned to the field *draw* when a figure is created. Each figure type has its initialization procedure – that for the newly added ellipse reads:

```
PROCEDURE NewEllipse(list: Figure; x, y, a, b: INTEGER);
VAR e: Ellipse;
BEGIN
   NEW(e);  e.x := x;  e.y := y;  e.a := a;  e.b := b;
   e.draw := DrawEllipse;
   InsertLast(list, e)
END NewEllipse;
```

What is different from the initialization routines of the previous section is only the assignment of *DrawEllipse* to *e.draw* (marked in bold face). This assignment statement associates the type-specific procedure with the graphical object; that is, to the instance *e* of type *Ellipse*. We also use the term 'the procedure *DrawEllipse* is installed in the object.'

Dynamic binding

Suppose we revert to the previous way in which we handled the heterogeneous list and write a guarded call to the procedure *DrawEllipse*:

```
...
ELSIF  f IS Ellipse  THEN
   WITH f: Ellipse DO
      DrawEllipse(f)
   END;
```

The compiler has all the necessary information to pass parameter and control directly to the statement sequence of the procedure *DrawEllipse*.

Compare this with a call of the procedure variable *draw* in *DrawAll*:

f.draw(f)

The statement sequence to which control should be passed is not available to the compiler. It is determined *at run time* and consists of the action performed by the procedure assigned to the field *draw* in the record variable *f↑*. If *f* is an ellipse then this action is the statement sequence of *DrawEllipse*; if *f* is a rectangle, it is *DrawRect* and so on. The binding of a specific action at run time is known as *dynamic binding*, as opposed to static binding, which takes place at compile time.

Object

So far, we have dealt with the term 'object' rather informally. For example, we used to say that variables and types are objects of the Oberon language. From now on, *object* will have a precise meaning: *a record with procedure fields, accessed through a pointer*. The object may have other fields that define its state. The procedure variable (or variables) governs the object's behavior in the same way as procedures define the abstract data type. The object is an *instance of an abstract data type with dynamic binding* of the procedures (see also Section 12.4).

Finally, let us focus on the specific procedure that has to be assignable to the field *draw* of a graphics object. The formal parameter of the procedure type of *draw* is of base type *Figure*. The text of specific procedures such as *DrawLine*, *DrawRect* or *DrawEllipse* therefore requires a *type guard over their entire scope*, as shown schematically for *DrawEllipse*:

```
PROCEDURE DrawEllipse(f: Figure);
BEGIN
    WITH f: Ellipse DO
    ...
    END
END DrawEllipse;
```

What have we gained by supplying the graphics objects with an individual procedure? Primarily, we have a decoupling of the actions performed with all objects in the list from the definition of individual actions that apply to a specific type of object. The addition of a new type of object therefore becomes a *localized* addition of program text, declaring

- a type extension, for example *Ellipse*;
- type-specific procedures such as *DrawEllipse*;
- a procedure to create an instance of the new object.

In the preceding discussion, the only action considered was to draw a figure. Of course, this is a deliberate oversimplification. Other typical operations performed by graphics editors on their figures are selecting and deselecting, copying, moving, shading, changing size and so on. A more realistic declaration of a figure therefore shows a number of procedure variables, each one representing a specific operation. The following object 'knows' how to draw, clear, mark and move itself:

```
TYPE
    Figure = POINTER TO FigureDesc;
    FigureDesc = RECORD
        draw, clear, mark: PROCEDURE (f: Figure);
        move: PROCEDURE (f: Figure; dX, dY: INTEGER);
        next: Figure
    END;
```

Summary

The following essential points are worth remembering:

(1) An object is represented by a pointer to a descriptor record that, among other state information, contains *fields of procedure type*. The values of these procedure variables define the operations that can be applied to the object. The object is an instance of an abstract data type.

(2) The type of an object is commonly extended in various ways such as in our example, *Figure* is extended to *Line*, *Rect* and *Ellipse*.

(3) The object pointer is a parameter of the action procedures. The type of the formal parameter is the *base type of the object*. Within the text of a specific action procedure, a regional type guard is required to allow access to the state variables defined in the extension of the base type.

(4) Procedure variables enable the programmer to write general procedures that *operate abstractly on all the objects* contained in a heterogeneous data structure without having to declare – or even anticipate all the extensions.

(5) The benefit is that new extensions can be added without changing many procedures that comprise an application. The modification is *textually localized*. The extension can even be within the scope of another module – a most important structuring concept explored in the next section.

12.4 Objects and modules

Heterogeneous data structures and dynamic binding of procedures are the technical essence of object-orientation. The concept, however, comes to full bloom only if paired with proper modularization of a large program or system. In Oberon, it is the module that controls visibility of declarations and hence defines levels of abstraction.

Let us return to the graphics editor. If programmed in the traditional style, such an editor may be broken down into modules as shown in Figure 12.2. Each shape, such as a line, a rectangle, or a circle is handled in its own module. Actions on all shapes such as a procedure *DrawAll* are carried out in module *Draw* that is also responsible for the user interface.

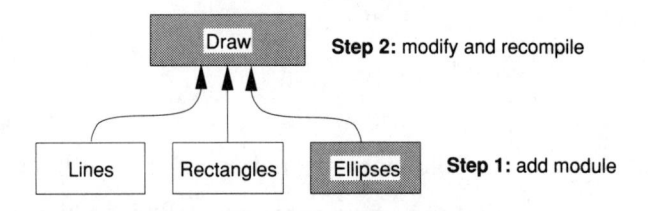

Figure 12.2 Normal module hierarchy.

If a new shape is added, a new shape module is provided, and the main module *Draw* has to be modified and recompiled. As stated, it is precisely this modification of module *Draw* that makes such a system hard to maintain and even harder to extend in functionality.

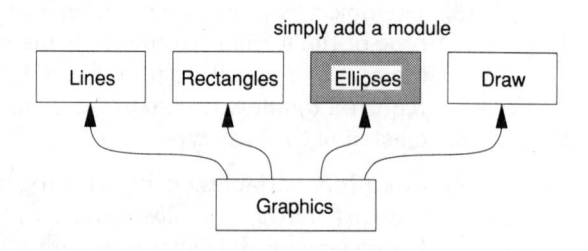

Figure 12.3 An extensible module hierarchy.

Desirable is a module structure that puts Figure 12.2 upside down. Such an extensible structure is depicted in Figure 12.3. Adding a new shape, an ellipse for example, simply means *adding a module Ellipses* to the system's library. No changes to the other modules are needed, in particular *no recompilation*. This implies that an extension is possible without requiring availability of the source text of the base.

The overall work is divided as follows between the modules of Figure 12.3:

- Module *Graphics* declares the fundamental data type *Figure* and data structures comprising a graph. It deals with the *ensemble of figures abstractly* (such as in *DrawAll*) and maintains the heterogeneous list of figures.
- Module *Lines, Rectangles, Ellipses* etc. declare all data structures and procedures that are *shape-specific* such as *DrawLine* and generate an instance of the figure (such as in *NewLine*).
- Module *Draw* handles the *user interface* – especially mouse and keyboard and their semantics.

An interesting framework of abstract data types and up-calls is behind the extensible structure of Figure 12.3. Of special interest is the way *Draw* creates new figures. We will explore the essential features of this framework in the sequel.

12.4.1 Module *Graphics*

Module *Graphics* defines two basic abstract data types: *Graph* and *Figure*. We are already familiar with *Figure*. Instances of type *Figure* are objects in the sense of object-orientation.

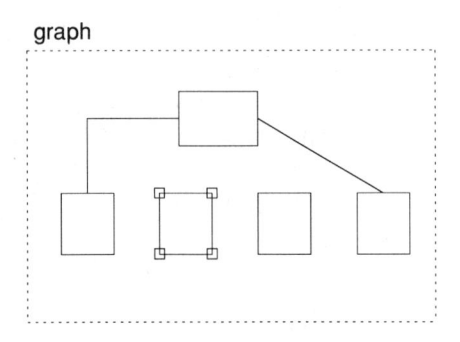

Figure 12.4 A graph composed of lines and rectangles, one being selected.

A graph represents a Cartesian plane as depicted in Figure 12.4. Graphs are instances of the abstract data type *Graph*. In this simple version, the only property of *Graph* is a list of figures. In a realistic implementation, there would be other properties such as a selection and a scrolling position. The type declaration for *Graph* is therefore

>TYPE
>   Graph = POINTER TO GraphDesc;
>   GraphDesc = RECORD list: Figure END;

The familiar procedure *DrawAll* is a typical action applicable to a graph. Other procedures encompass *Select*, *Deselect*, *DeleteSelection* and *MoveSelection*, with obvious meaning.

With these preliminaries in mind, we state an abbreviated version of module *Graphics*:

>MODULE Graphics;
>TYPE
>   **Figure*** = POINTER TO FigureDesc;
>   **FigureDesc*** = RECORD
>   **draw***, **clear***, **mark***: PROCEDURE (f: Figure);
>   **move***: PROCEDURE (f: Figure; dX, dY: INTEGER);
>   next: Figure
>   END;
>
>   **Graph*** = POINTER TO GraphDesc;
>   **GraphDesc*** = RECORD list: Figure END;
>
>...(* other type and variable declarations *)
>
>PROCEDURE **DrawAll***(g: Graph);
>VAR f: Figure;
>BEGIN
>   f := g.list;
>   WHILE f # NIL DO f.draw(f); f := f.next END
>END DrawAll;
>
>... (* other procedure declarations *)
>
>PROCEDURE **Open***(VAR g: Graph);
>BEGIN g.list := NIL
>END Open;
>
>END Graphics.

We note that *Graph* is an ordinary abstract data type as we know it from

Chapter 10. In particular, its procedures are bound statically through the context of module *Graphics*. That means that in a call *Graphics.DrawAll*, for example, the compiler can generate the transfer of control to the statement sequence of *DrawAll* directly. Each of the procedures has a formal parameter of type *Graph*, identifying the particular instance on which to operate.

Most of the procedures of *Graphics* operate on the (heterogeneous) list of figures. The data type *Figure* is also abstract – however, in a different sense than we are used to. Normally, a data type is abstract in the client but concrete in the service module. Here the reverse is the case. *Figure* is abstract in *Graphics*: the actions *draw*, *clear*, *mark* and *move* are not specified. They are concretized in shape-specific client modules such as *Rectangles* or *Lines*. Thus, wherever a procedure of *Figure* is called, for example *f.draw(f)* in *DrawAll*, dynamic binding takes place and an up-call is enacted.

12.4.2 Shape-specific modules

The task of the shape-specific modules, such as *Rectangles*, *Lines*, *Ellipses* etc. is to implement the abstract type *Figure* – in particular, to

- extend type *Figure* with shape-specific data;
- declare procedures for drawing, clearing, marking and moving figures;
- create an instance of a figure.

Each one of these modules implements a specialization of the abstract data type *Figure*. For example, an excerpt of module *Rectangles* reads as follows:

```
           MODULE Rectangles;
           IMPORT Graphics, ...;
           TYPE
               Rectangle* = POINTER TO RectangleDesc;
(1) →        RectangleDesc* = RECORD (Graphics.FigureDesc)
                   x*, y*, w*, h*: INTEGER
               END;

           PROCEDURE Draw*(rect: Graphics.Figure);
           BEGIN
(2) →          WITH rect: Rectangle DO
```

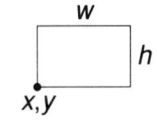

... (* display rectangle on screen *)
            END
         END Draw;

         ...(* Declarations of Clear, Mark and Move *)

         PROCEDURE **New***(): Graphics.Figure;
         VAR rect: Rectangle; x, y, w, h: INTEGER;
         BEGIN
(3) →   NEW(rect);
            rect.draw := Draw; rect.clear := Clear;
            rect.mark := Mark; rect.move := Move;
            (* obtain values x, y, w, h typically using the mouse *);
            rect.x := x; rect.y := y; rect.w := w; rect.h := h;
            RETURN rect
         END New;

      END Rectangles.

Notes

(1) Here the type *Figure* is extended with rectangle-specific data fields x, y, w and h. Other shapes require other data structures, in the case of a polygon, this may even be a list structure.

(2) Note the required type guard in *Draw*: the formal parameter must be of base type *Graphics.Figure*.

(3) An instance of the extended type *Rectangle* is created and the procedure fields are initialized.

The only identifier that must be exported is *New*. The reason that module *Rectangles* also makes the type *Rectangle* and the procedures *Draw*, *Clear*, *Mark* and *Move* visible will be discussed in Section 12.4.4, where the rectangle will be redefined. The majority of the procedures in shape-specific modules deal with programming the display, an intricacy that we shun at this point.

12.4.3 Creation of a new figure

The initiative to create a new figure originates in module *Draw* in reaction to a mouse or keyboard command issued by the user. The information for creating an instance of the appropriate type, however, is contained in the shape-specific modules *Lines*, *Rectangles* and so on. But

12.4 Objects and modules

Draw does not import those modules. How can this predicament be resolved?

An up-call mediated by *Graphics* is the answer. The method is an application of the example given in Section 11.3.5 on up-calls. A procedure variable *newFigure* is declared in module *Graphics*, which also exports a general procedure *CreateFigure* for the use by *Draw*. *CreateFigure* makes the up-call, draws the newly created figure and inserts it into the list of figures.

```
          MODULE Graphics;
          ...
(1) →     VAR newFigure*: PROCEDURE (): Figure;
          ...
          PROCEDURE CreateFigure*(g: Graph);
          VAR f: Figure;
          BEGIN
(2) →       f := newFigure();
            f.draw(f); InsertLast(g.list, f)
          END CreateFigure;

          END Graphics.
```

Notes

(1) *newFigure* is a global procedure variable used to make an up-call to the shape-specific module. Its value must be initialized by those modules.

(2) Here procedure variable *newFigure* is called and the up-call takes place.

We have now discussed all the essential features of module *Graphics*, whose definition we list:

```
DEFINITION Graphics;
TYPE
   Figure = POINTER TO FigureDesc;
   FigureDesc = RECORD
        draw, clear, mark: PROCEDURE (f: Figure);
        move: PROCEDURE (f: Figure; dX, dY: INTEGER);
   END ;

   Graph = POINTER TO GraphDesc;
   GraphDesc = RECORD END;
```

```
VAR newFigure: PROCEDURE (): Figure;

PROCEDURE DrawAll(g: Graph);
PROCEDURE Select(g: Graph; x, y: INTEGER);
PROCEDURE Deselect(g: Graph);
PROCEDURE DeleteSelection(g: Graph);
PROCEDURE MoveSelection(g: Graph; dX, dY: INTEGER);
PROCEDURE CreateFigure(g: Graph);
PROCEDURE Open(g: Graph);
END Graphics.
```

With the initialization of the global procedure variable *Graphics.newFigure*, the final piece of the puzzle falls into place. Clearly, only one of the shape-specific modules can do that. This initialization takes place in a *command* that we call *Set*. For the example of module *Rectangles*, the implementation of *Set* reads as follows:

```
MODULE Rectangle;
...
PROCEDURE Set*
BEGIN  Graphics.newFigure := New;
END Set;

END Rectangles.
```

Each of the modules *Lines, Rectangles, Ellipses* etc. has its own *Set* command. We have now also covered all the functions of the shape-specific modules. Representative of all, let us list the definition of *Rectangles*:

```
DEFINITION Rectangles;
IMPORT Graphics;
TYPE
   Rectangle = POINTER TO RectangleDesc;
   RectangleDesc = RECORD (Graphics.FigureDesc)
      x, y, w, h: INTEGER
   END;

PROCEDURE Draw(rect: Graphics.Figure);
PROCEDURE Clear(rect: Graphics.Figure);
PROCEDURE Mark(rect: Graphics.Figure);
PROCEDURE Move(rect: Graphics.Figure; dX, dY: INTEGER);
PROCEDURE New(): Graphics.Figure;
PROCEDURE Set;
END Rectangles.
```

Graphics modes   Execution of a *Set* command puts the graphics editor into a *mode*: all subsequently created figures are of the particular shape. In commercial graphics editors, this mode is usually termed a 'tool.'[1] The user selects the 'rectangle tool,' for example, and subsequently draws a number of rectangles with the mouse. The selection of such a tool is typically done by clicking at an icon.

The suitability of modes in user interfaces is controversial. While modes are not deficient per se, there are many bad examples. The graphics 'tool' modes are well tried in practice. An important condition, however, that renders modes acceptable is their *visibility*. Graphics editors usually use iconic buttons to make the selected 'tool' visible.

12.4.4 Redefining a dynamically bound procedure

Considerations of easy extensibility of the graphics editor led to the remarkable structure of Figure 12.3. All actions having to do with the user interface are completely isolated in module *Draw*. Adding a new figure shape such as a spline, for example, simply requires the writing of a module *Splines*, compiling it, and adding the object module to the computer's library.

Here we want to demonstrate an even more striking feature of objects with dynamically bound procedures: *the ability to re-use a module only partially* – yet without modification of the source text. We are going to add a new figure to the editor: a *filled rectangle*.

A filled rectangle

The filled rectangle consists of a solid line around its perimeter that is filled in with a pattern. *FilledRectangles* is the name of the module that exports the shape-specific procedures.

The essential observation is that only the drawing of a filled rectangle differs from an ordinary rectangle. All the other actions such as *Mark*, *Clear* and *Move* are identical. But even drawing a filled rectangle is not completely different from the base shape. The filled rectangle consists of a 'wire frame' and a filled interior. The first part is already handled in module *Rectangles*, and need not be re-created.

The key idea leading to an implementation that re-uses all the existing functions is to make the type *FilledRect* an extension of the type *Rectangles.Rect* and to redefine only those type-bound procedures that change. We now understand why module *Rectangles* exports its type and procedures. Thus module *FilledRectangle's* text reads as follows:

[1] Not to be confused with the use of the term 'tool' in Oberon.

MODULE FilledRectangles;
IMPORT Graphics, Rectangles, …;
…
TYPE
(1) →   **FilledRect**∗ = POINTER TO FilledRectDesc;
   FilledRectDesc∗ = RECORD (Rectangles.RectDesc)
     pat∗: Pattern
   END;

PROCEDURE **Draw**∗(rect: Graphics.Figure);
BEGIN
   WITH rect: FilledRect DO
(2) →   **Rectangles.Draw(rect);**
     … (∗ fill perimeter of rect with a pattern ∗)
   END
END Draw;

PROCEDURE **New**∗(): Graphics.Figure;
VAR fr: FilledRect; x, y, w, h: INTEGER; pat: Pattern;
BEGIN
(3) →   NEW(fr);
   fr.draw := Draw;   fr.clear := Rectangles.Clear;
   fr.mark := Rectangles.Mark; fr.move := Rectangles.Move;
   (∗ obtain values x, y, w, h, and pat ∗);
   fr.x := x; fr.y := y; fr.w := w; fr.h := h; fr.pat := pat;
   RETURN fr
END New;

END FilledRectangles.

Notes

(1) *FilledRect* extends *Rectangles.Rectangle*. Field *pat* identifies a fill pattern.

(2) *Draw* from module *Rectangles* is invoked to draw the 'wire frame.' Subsequently, the pattern is filled in.

(3) An instance of *FilledRect* is created. The procedures fields *draw*, *clear*, *mark* and *move* are initialized. Note that *draw* receives the modified procedure *Draw*, whereas the other procedures are from module *Rectangles*.

12.4.5 Summary

In Oberon, object-orientation results in module hierarchies that are 'upside-down' (Figure 12.3) and rely heavily on *up-calls*. In particular, we note

(1) The heterogeneous data structure plays a central role.
(2) This data structure is typically abstract, in particular an instance of an *abstract data type* (*Graph* in our example). The module exporting that type (for example *Graphics*) is at the basis of the module hierarchy. The procedures of that type fall in three broad classes: (1) actions dealing with the ensemble of objects (for example *DrawAll*), (2) the procedure initializing the type (for example *Open*) and (3) creation of new objects and insertion into the heterogeneous structure (in our case, *CreateFigure.*) Sometimes class (4) is reduced to merely insert objects into the data structure.
(3) The elements of the heterogeneous structure are objects; that is, instances of a record type with procedure fields, also termed *methods*. The procedures of type (1) such as *DrawAll* make use of the methods to deal with the ensemble of objects abstractly. In the base module, the methods are often left unspecified, or abstract. Alternatively, a common basic behavior of the objects could be implemented.
(4) The implementation of the methods (or specialization if methods are already implemented in the base) is provided in modules higher up in the hierarchy, such as in *Rectangles*. These modules import the base module. Different specializations of the object, such as rectangles and lines, are implemented in different modules. An important task of such an implementation module is to *create an instance of the specialized object*.
(5) Often the user interface can also be isolated in its own module. The creation of objects, their initialization and insertion into the heterogeneous data structure require careful design, possibly relying on additional up-calls.
(6) Sometimes, a new specialization of the object differs only slightly from an existing implementation. In this case, that implementation can be re-used without recourse to its source text. Only the method that differs has to be programmed and assigned when the object is created.

The benefit of object-orientation is the *isolation of different concerns in different modules*. Most importantly, those modules can be added without recompilation of any of the other parts of the system. Through redefinition of some methods, further specializations of the object can often be obtained by reusing existing code.

12.5 Message and handlers

An object is an instance of an abstract data type represented by a record variable containing procedure fields. These procedure variables define the actions admitted by the object – in the sense of the abstract data type.

We recapitulate the declaration of the type *Figure* from Section 12.3:

```
TYPE
    Figure = POINTER TO FigureDesc;
    FigureDesc = RECORD
        draw, clear, mark: PROCEDURE (f: Figure);
        move: PROCEDURE (f: Figure; dX, dY: INTEGER);
        next: Figure
    END;
```

A figure has a next figure and four procedure fields *draw*, *clear*, *mark* and *move*. The basic assumption is that the *number of procedures and their parameters is invariant*.

There are programming tasks where neither number nor meaning of all the actions of an object are known a priori. A good example is a simulation event. We recall from Chapter 10 that such an event is always paired with a specific action – that action may be the procedure of an object. We will pursue this idea in Chapter 13.

We will now introduce a different way of representing the actions; that is, we will unite them with only *a single universal procedure field*, termed *handle*. The procedure assigned to this field is called the *handler*. A simulation event, for example, can be visualized as an instance of

```
TYPE
    Event = POINTER TO EventDesc;
    EventDesc = RECORD
        handle: Handler;
        time: REAL;
        next: Event
    END;
```

The simulation event has a due time, a pointer *next* that admits the event to the calendar list and the procedure field *handle* of type *Handler*.

The problem that at first sight seems to render this idea impracticable is the fact that an open-ended set of actions requires an open-ended number of parameters of possibly different type – a facility that is not part of the Oberon procedure definition. Type extension, however, comes to our rescue and allows just such a parameter.

12.5.1 Message and handler

The key idea is simple and elegant: *the formal parameter is a record that contains the identification of the individual action to be performed and its parameters*. We dub such a record containing parameters a *message*.

How type extension and type tests work hand in hand to create handlers that accept a variable number of messages is best explained by continuing with the example of the graphics editor – now cast in terms of objects with handlers. We start by introducing an empty record as base type for messages:

TYPE Message = RECORD END;

Specific messages are defined as extensions of the type *Message* as need arises. Each action performed on our graphics objects is characterized by its own message type, for example

```
TYPE
   DrawMsg  = RECORD (Message) END;
   ClearMsg = RECORD (Message) END;
   MarkMsg  = RECORD (Message) END;
   MoveMsg  = RECORD (Message) dX, dY: INTEGER
END;
```

The example makes it clear how the formal parameter sections, which appeared in the previous procedure headings, now emerge as record fields in message types. Procedures without parameters lead to extensions of the type *Message* still being empty. The procedure *Move* with two formal parameters of integer type corresponds to a message type *MoveMsg* with two integer fields.

The new figure is an instance of the following type:

```
TYPE
   Figure = POINTER TO FigureDesc;
```

```
FigureDesc = RECORD
    handle: Handler;
    next: Figure
END;
```

The type *Handler* can now be stated:

```
TYPE Handler = PROCEDURE (f: Figure;  VAR msg: Message);
```

The handler procedure therefore has access to its object (here assumed to be of type *Figure*) and to the message. Note that it is essential that *msg* is a VAR parameter, since the handler will apply type tests and type guards to it.

As before, specific shapes have types that extend *Figure*, for example

```
TYPE
    Rectangle = POINTER TO RectangleDesc;
    RectangleDesc = RECORD (FigureDesc);
        x, y, w, h: INTEGER
    END;
```

The structure of a handler for a rectangle is

```
PROCEDURE HandleRect(rect: Figure; VAR msg: Message);
BEGIN
    WITH rect: Rectangle DO
        IF msg IS DrawMsg THEN
            WITH msg: DrawMsg DO
                ... (* draw rectangle *)
            END
        ELSIF msg IS ClearMsg THEN
            WITH msg: ClearMsg DO
                ... (* clear rectangle *)
            END
        ELSIF msg IS MarkMsg THEN
            WITH msg: MarkMsg DO
                ... (* mark rectangle *)
            END
        ELSIF msg IS MoveMsg THEN
            WITH msg: MoveMsg DO
                ...(* move rectangle by vector msg.dx, msg.dy *)
            END
        ELSE
            ... (* message not understood, typically no action *)
```

>   END
>   END
>   END HandleRect;

Which action is to be performed is deduced from the type of the message. The parameters for the action, such as the displacement vector for the move operation, are found in the message fields. Note the global type guard asserting that the object is of dynamic type *Rectangle* and the type guard on the message. For the message-based design to be of full generality, it is essential that an else clause be present. Typically, it is empty, but guarantees that the handler can be called with any message that extends the base type *Message*.

A rectangle *rect*, which is an instance of type *Rectangle,* is created as follows:

>   NEW(rect); rect.handle := HandleRect;
>   rect.x := x; rect.y := y; rect.w := w; rect.h := h;

The assignment of the procedure *HandleRect* to the field *handle* is termed *installation of the handler*.

Finally, let us show how to move a rectangle represented by the variable *rect*. First, the displacement (dX, dY) is determined. Then the message fields are filled and the handler is called, viz.

>   VAR m: MoveMsg; rect: Rect;
>
>   ... (* determine the displacement dX, dY *)
>   m.dX := dX; m.dY := dY; rect.handle(rect, m);

Sending a message

The above operation is known as *sending a message m* to the object *rect*, or sending a *move message* to the rectangle *rect*.

12.5.2 Message broadcast

Objects are typically members of a dynamic data structure. For example, figures are contained in a figure list and events in the simulation calendar. Frequently, operations are performed on the whole ensemble of objects. Procedures performing such operations have to traverse the data structure. *DrawAll* is a good example.

In the case of objects with handlers, the list traversal can be isolated in a procedure *Broadcast* that sends a given message to all objects. For the list of graphics objects, such a broadcast is executed as follows:

```
PROCEDURE Broadcast(g: Graph; VAR msg: Message);
VAR f: Figure;
BEGIN
   f := g.list;
   WHILE  f # NIL DO  f.handle(f, msg)  END
END Broadcast;
```

Using the broadcast, *DrawAll* is considerably simplified:

```
PROCEDURE DrawAll;
VAR m: DrawMsg;
BEGIN  Broadcast(m)
END DrawAll;
```

12.5.3 Generality of handlers

Objects with handlers can do exactly the same as our earlier objects with procedure variables. However, *handlers are more general*. Assume that, without changing the definition of type *Figure* of Section 12.4.1, a call statement

   f.rotate(f, angle)

would appear somewhere in the source text. The compiler would reject such a module.

The analogous situation in the paradigm of handlers is the sending of a rotate message to the object *f*, in Oberon notation,

```
TYPE RotateMsg = Record(Message) angle: INTEGER END;
VAR m: RotateMsg;
...
m.angle := 45;  f.handle(m);
```

Clearly, the compiler accepts such a program without need to redefine the type *Figure*. Note that the type *RotateMsg* as well as the actual sending of a message of that type can be added in later modules. The message broadcast allows such modules to address all objects in the heterogeneous structure. All objects therefore do not necessarily 'understand' all messages.

We summarize by stating that handlers will accept any message that extends the common base type *Message*, but will 'understand' and therefore react only to those message types that appear explicitly in the IF...ELSIF...ELSIF...ELSE...END statement of their statement sequence.

12.5.4 Summary

In this section, we have introduced a special class of objects: those with a handler. The following points are worth recapitulating:

(1) The object is represented by a pointer to record. The record has only one procedure field, typically termed *handle*. The procedure assigned to *handle* is termed *handler* and has two formal parameters. The first designates the object on which the handler operates. The second, a VAR parameter, identifies the operation to be performed. Its type is the base type *Message*, representing a record (usually empty).

(2) The handler defines the semantics of the object. A handler is typically called with an extended object type. A regional type guard is therefore required (WITH *f: Rectangle* in our example).

(3) The actual parameter paired with the second formal parameter of the handler is an extension of the (record) type *Message*. It is known as *message*. Its type specifies the action, its fields contain the parameters that pertain to that action. Their number is variable.

(4) The handler, in essence, comprises a big IF...ELSIF... ELSIF...ELSE...END statement. Type tests discriminate between messages of different types.

(5) Assigning the handler procedure to the field *handle* is called *installation of the handler*.

(6) Assigning values to the fields of a particular message and calling the handler of a given object is referred to as *sending a message to the object*.

(7) Messages may be broadcast to all objects of a heterogeneous data structure; that is, the message is sent to each object in turn. The use of such broadcast often simplifies the procedures that act on the ensemble of objects.

12.6 Conclusions and outlook

The concepts type extension, procedure variable and abstract data type advance the state-of-the-art in program extensibility in a major way. The programming methodology is called *object-orientation*. If successful, object-oriented designs allow augmenting functionality by a mere addition of modules. The normal module hierarchy is thus turned upside-down, as we saw in the example of a graphics editor. Figure 12.5 recapitulates the new module structure.

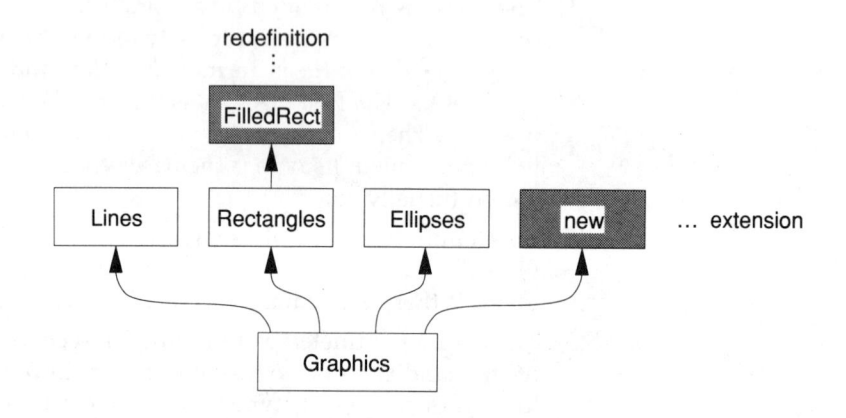

Figure 12.5 Module hierarchy from object-orientation.

Extension may take place in two ways: through addition of entirely new functions and through specialization of existing ones.

The technical foundation is the notion of the *object*, an instance of an abstract data type with dynamically bound procedures. Objects typically belong to a heterogeneous data structure that is managed in the base module (for example *Graphics* in Figure 12.5).

Historically, the techniques of object-orientation were first introduced in the area of discrete event simulation (Dahl and Nygaard, 1966). Currently, it is permeating most problem domains: operating systems, word and graphics processors, and last but not least data bases.

12.6.1 Two categories of Oberon objects – a comparison

In this chapter we have introduced two categories of objects: those with a number of procedure variables and those with a single handler. There follows a brief comparison. In summary, we will conclude that both types of objects have advantages and disadvantages, and should be used where appropriate.

Multitude of procedure variables

The operations that can be applied to the object are defined as procedures in the same way as in the case of an ordinary abstract data type. The difference is dynamic binding: in a call, the specific procedure is

12.6 Conclusions and outlook

selected at run time rather than at compile time. The number of the procedures and their type is fixed and specified at the place where the object's type is declared. The storage demand grows with the number of procedures; their call, however, is as efficient as any call of a procedure variable. New functionality is confined to the scope provided by the set of procedures. Extending that scope means a recompilation of the entire module structure. For example, in our graphics editor, new functions must be expressed in terms of *draw*, *clear*, *mark* and *move*. A function *copy*, for example, would lead to a global change.

In all procedures that deal with the ensemble of objects, an *individual structure traversal* needs to be programmed explicitly (see the while loop in the example *DrawAll*).

Handlers   The object has only one general procedure – hence is likely to consume less memory. At the place of the type declaration, the actions that the object may perform are not defined – neither in terms of number, name nor parameters. That specification is only made in the *implementation of the handler*. An object may be called with *any* message compatible with the base message type. If the message is 'understood' the requested action is performed; otherwise nothing happens. Message broadcasting is an effective way of dealing with the ensemble of objects; sparing the programmer the chore of coding many structure traversals.

Obviously, all objects need not understand the same basic set of messages. Using the broadcast mechanism, it is possible to send any message to all objects of the structure. In fact, such broadcasts may take place from an arbitrary part of the system – they are not confined to the base module. Similarly, new message types can be defined in any module. This generality is sometimes quite useful. For example, the Oberon operating system bases the viewer subsystem on objects with handlers (Wirth and Gutknecht, 1992). The handler is the command interpreter that operates behind the viewer.

The added generality has its price, however. At each call of the handler, the action has first to be re-determined, executing the IF...ELSIF...ELSIF...ELSE...END statement and performing type tests, an overhead not incurred with the first kind of object.

The fact that the compiler cannot check whether a message is 'understood by the object' may be an advantage or a disadvantage, depending on the type of the application.

12.6.2 On the object-oriented programming paradigm

The programmer practicing object-orientation needs appropriate language tools. Object-orientation in its current sense was introduced as a paradigm by *Smalltalk-80* (see for example Goldberg and Robson, 1983). Similar to Oberon, Smalltalk is not merely a language but an entire system. In other respects, however, Smalltalk is at the opposite end of extremes – in particular it lacks strong typing and uses peculiar terminology. In the wake of Smalltalk, a number of languages appeared that emulate its terminology but reintroduce typing. Some are additions to existing languages (Tesler, 1985; Stroustrup, 1986); some are new creations, for example, the language Eiffel (see Meyer, 1988).

This is not a text on the history of object-orientation. For the reader familiar with the subject, we establish briefly the correspondence between object-oriented programming terminology (OOP) and Oberon concepts in Table 12.1.

Table 12.1 Standard object-oriented terminology.

OOP terminology	Oberon terminology
Class	Record type[1] with procedure variable(s), defining an abstract data type
Object	Variable of that type
Method	One of the procedures of the record type
Message	A call of a procedure, for example *rect.draw(rect)*
Sub-class	Extension of the base record type
Super-class	The base type of such an extension
Inheritance	Type extension
Overriding a method	Changing the procedure assigned to a field in an extension
Self	The object passed as actual parameter to a procedure, for example *rect* in *rect.draw(rect)*
Super call	Call of a procedure in the module defining the base of an extension
Dynamic binding	Call of a procedure variable

In Table 12.1 we assumed languages that feature typing such as *C++* or *Eiffel*. Smalltalk-80 is even more general. In a sense, it corresponds

---

[1] More precisely, a pointer type bound to a record with one or several procedure variables, defining an abstract data type.

more to the second kind of Oberon object, that with a handler. The term 'method' is not so well defined in the case of the handler. In a sense, the *method is embodied by the message type and the corresponding program segment in the handler procedure*. We should stress, however, that an Oberon program employing handler objects is still *substantially more efficient* than all Smalltalk implementations known to date.

12.7 Exercises

12.1 [**Object-oriented calculator**] Implement an extensible stack-based calculator. The calculator comprises the four modules *Calc*, *Integers* and *FPNs*. *Calc* contains the stack and exports the basic calculator commands. *Integers* and *FPNs* (floating-point numbers) are supported number types.

The base module *Calc* has definition

```
DEFINITION Calc; (* Basic Calculator *)
IMPORT Out;
TYPE
   Number = POINTER TO NumberDesc;
   NumberDesc = RECORD
      add, sub, mult, div: PROCEDURE(a, b: Number): Number;
      display: PROCEDURE(n: Number)(* display a number *)
   END;
   PROCEDURE Add;
   PROCEDURE Sub;
   PROCEDURE Mult;
   PROCEDURE Div;
   PROCEDURE Clear;
END Calc.
```

The stack is not limited in size and not defined, unless numbers are explicitly entered (note that this stack definition differs from Exercise 7.5). Numbers are implemented as objects.

The commands *Add*, *Sub*, *Mult* and *Div* operate on the two topmost stack elements, which are replaced by the result. Make sure that the program does not abort if the stack is empty (display an error message in that case).

Module *Integers* implements integer numbers based on the type INTEGER. It exports the command *Enter* that reads an integer from the input stream and pushes it onto the stack. An error message is displayed if the input is invalid.

```
DEFINITION Integers;
IMPORT Calc, In, Out;
TYPE
   Integer = POINTER TO IntegerDesc;
   IntegerDesc = RECORD(Calc.NumberDesc) n: INTEGER END;
PROCEDURE Enter;    (* Push an integer onto the stack *)
END Integers.
```

Similarly module *FPNs* handles floating-point numbers based on the type REAL.

12.2 Extend the calculator with module *Fractions* defined by

```
DEFINITION Fractions; (* rational numbers *)
IMPORT Calc, Integers, In, Out;
TYPE
   Fraction = POINTER TO FractionDesc;
   FractionDesc = RECORD(Calc.NumberDesc)
       num, denom: Integers.Integer
   END;
PROCEDURE Enter;  (* Push a rational number onto the stack *)
END Fractions.
```

Rational numbers are pairs of integers. Use the syntax *integer"/"integer* to display rational numbers.

A key design principle is the requirement that module *Integers* may be exchanged without consequences for *Fractions*. This requires that module *Fractions* work exclusively with resources exported by module *Integers*, in particular with the type *Integers.Integer* and the procedures *Integer.Add* and so on. To eliminate common factors, *Integers* has to provide a procedure

   PROCEDURE gcd(Calc.Number, Calc.Number): Calc.Number;

that computes the greatest common divisor. Also, reading an integer from the input stream should be handled by *Integers*, not by *Fractions*, for example with a function *Integers.Read()*.

12.3 Extend the calculator with a module *Complex* operating on complex numbers.

12.4 [**Object-oriented directory**] The generality of the generic type *Entry* in Exercise 11.4 is limited by the fact that the type of the key must be specified. Use object-orientation to make that type client-defined.

Hint: In module *Directories* the key is an empty record to be extended in the client. The object *Entry* has two procedure variables called *eq* (equal) and *lt* (less than) that compare an entry with a key. Don't forget to make *key* a VAR parameter to allow type tests, for example PROCEDURE *Search(dir: Directory; VAR k: Key)*.

12.5 [**Very tiny graphics editor**] Implement a *very tiny graphics editor* that draws rectangles. The modules are *Graphics*, *Rectangles* and *Draw*, with definitions

```
DEFINITION Graphics;
TYPE
    Figure = POINTER TO FigureDesc;
    FigureDesc = RECORD  draw: PROCEDURE (f: Figure) END;
    Graph = POINTER TO GraphDesc;
    GraphDesc = RECORD  END;
VAR
    newFigure: PROCEDURE (g: Graph): Figure;
    spanVect: PROCEDURE (VAR x1, y1, x2, y2: INTEGER);
PROCEDURE DrawAll(g: Graph);
PROCEDURE CreateFigure(g: Graph);
PROCEDURE Open(g: Graph);
END Graphics.

DEFINITION Rectangles;
IMPORT Graphics, Display;
TYPE
    Rectangle = POINTER TO RectangleDesc;
    RectangleDesc = RECORD (Graphics.FigureDesc)
        x, y, w, h: INTEGER;
    END;
PROCEDURE Draw(rect: Graphics.Figure);
PROCEDURE New(): Graphics.Figure;
PROCEDURE Set
END Rectangles.

DEFINITION Draw;
IMPORT Graphics, XYplane, In;
PROCEDURE Open;
PROCEDURE DrawAll;
PROCEDURE New;
END Draw.
```

Procedure variable *spanVect* in module *Graphics* returns start and end point of a vector. It is called in *Rectangles.New* to define the location and extent of a rectangle. The procedure assigned to *spanVect* is declared in *Draw*. What is the reason to introduce *spanVect*?

In a real graphics editor, *spanVect* would use the mouse to define the vector. To avoid this complication, read the vector from the input stream, for example

```
PROCEDURE SpanVect(VAR x1, y1, x2, y2: INTEGER);
BEGIN In.Open; In.Int(x1); In.Int(y1); In.Int(x2); In.Int(y2)
END SpanVect;
```

Use module *XYplane* to open a drawing area. For drawing horizontal and vertical lines, consult Exercises 7.7 and 7.8. The commands exported by module *Draw* are:

- *Draw.Open* opens an *XYplane* viewer
- *Draw.DrawAll* draws all figures. To test *DrawAll*, erase the *XYplane* (*XYplane.Clear*) and restore the drawing.
- *Draw.New* creates a figure (depending on the most recently issued *Set* command).

12.6 Write module *Lines* and add it to the very tiny graphics editor (see Exercises 7.9 and 7.10).

12.7 Write module *FilledRectangles* and add it to the very tiny graphics editor. Use the technique of Section 12.4.4. Produce a grey pattern by drawing a checkerboard pattern of black and white pixels. *Hint*: more efficient than a loop invoking *XYplane.Dot* is the use of the procedures:

VAR pat: Display.Pattern;
pat := Display1.Pattern(3); (* a grey pattern *)
Display.ReplPattern(Display.white, pat, x, y, w, h, Display.replace)

12.8 [**Mouse-based control**] *Oberon system knowledge a prerequisite* (Reiser, 1991). Provide a version of module *Draw* that *uses the mouse* to create figures. Make a graph (instance of *Graphics.Graph*) a proper *Oberon viewer*. Figures are created under mouse control: dragging the mouse over the drawing area while the *left key* is pressed defines the diagonal of a rectangle or the end-points of a line. After the dragging operation ceases, the figure is drawn.

Hint: The type *Graph* extends type *Display.Frame*. Write a handler compatible with a *menu viewer*. The command *Draw.Open* first creates a graph and installs the handler. Then it opens a menu viewer and installs the graph in the new menu viewer.

Module *XYplane* is no longer a suitable base for programming the display. The library of many Oberon systems has a module *GraphicOps* that draws some geometric shapes and performs *clipping*. Use module *GraphicOps* or, if not available, module *Display1* or *Display*. In the latter case, clipping has to be taken care of explicitly.

12.9 [**Tiny graphics editor**] Add the following functions to the very tiny graphics editor, making it a *tiny graphics editor*.

- One figure can be *selected* and thus singled out to be operated on by subsequent commands. If a selection exists, a new selection neutralizes the existing selection. The command *Draw.Select x y* selects the (oldest) figure that is close to the point (x, y).
- The selection can be neutralized (command *Draw.Neutralize*)
- The selected figure can be deleted (command *Draw.Delete*)
- The selected figure can be moved (command *Draw.Move dX, dY*).

Hint 1: Types *FigureDesc* and *GraphDesc* are augmented as follows:

```
TYPE
  FigureDesc = RECORD
    isClose(f: Figure; x, y: INTEGER): BOOLEAN;
    draw, clear, mark: PROCEDURE(f: Figure);
    move(f: Figure; dX, dY: INTEGER);
    next: Figure
  END
  GraphDesc = RECORD
    selection, list: Figure
  END
```

Method *isClose* reports whether a point (x, y) is close to the figure. It is used to determine which figure is selected. Method *mark* makes the selection visible (see Figure 12.4) Method *clear* removes a figure or the selection markings from the display.

Hint 2: If a figure or its markings is removed, a hole is left behind. The easiest way to restore the graph is to invoke *Graphics.DrawAll*.

12.10 [**Mouse control for tiny graphics editor**] *Oberon system knowledge a prerequisite* (Reiser, 1991). Provide mouse control for the tiny graphics editor. A click with the right mouse key will select a close figure $(isClose(f, x, y) = TRUE)$. An interclick[1] with the left mouse key while selecting will delete the selected figure. A vector spanned on the middle mouse key will move the selected figure.

12.11 [**Message-based tiny graphics editor**] Rewrite the tiny graphics editor using objects with handlers and messages. Discuss the two versions – which do you prefer?

12.12 [**File support for graphics editor**] *Oberon system knowledge a prerequisite* (Reiser, 1991). Amend procedure *Graphics.Open* with the ability to read a graph from a file. Provide a procedure *Graphics.Store* that externalizes a graph.

To store a graph, endow the figure object with an additional method *store*. To read a graph from a file, the approriate shape-specific module may have to be (dynamically) loaded first.

Hint: On the file, each figure section is preceded with a string that contains a command name such as "Rectangles.Load" or "Lines.Load". This command string is read by module *Graphics*. Then that command is executed via dynamic loader using the call

   Oberon.Call(cmd, Oberon.Par, FALSE, res)

where *cmd*: ARRAY 32 OF CHAR holds the command string and *res*: INTEGER is a result code.

---

[1] Clicking the left mouse key while dragging on the right key.

References

Dahl O.-J. and Nygaard K. (1966). Simula – an Algol-based simulation language. *Communications of the ACM*, 9, 671–8.

Goldberg A. and Robson D. (1983). *Smalltalk-80: The Language and its Implementation*. Reading, MA: Addison-Wesley.

Meyer B. (1988). *Object Oriented Software Construction*. Englewood Cliffs, NJ: Prentice-Hall.

Reiser M. (1991). *The Oberon System: User Guide and Programmer's Manual*. Wokingham, England: Addison-Wesley.

Stroustrup B. (1986). *The C++ Programming Language*. Reading, MA: Addison-Wesley.

Tesler L. (1985). Object Pascal report. *Structured Language World*, 9, 10–14.

Wirth N. and Gutknecht J. (1992). *Project Oberon*. Wokingham: Addison-Wesley.

13 A simulation example

Chapter 12 introduced the concepts of object-orientation, and their expression in terms of Oberon. The concepts are introduced using program excerpts. In line with Chapter 10, we wish to conclude with the development of a complete example – a *framework of abstract data types and modules* serving as a simulation package.

We are familiar with the fundamentals of discrete event simulation from Chapter 10. Simulation is indeed a classical area for the use of abstract data types – in particular, objects. We wish to demonstrate the usefulness of generic modules and of objects with handlers. Again we aim at a structure that is extensible in the sense that adding functionality means simply adding modules to the library – without change or recompilation of those parts of the package that were conceived earlier.

13.1 Generic module *Qs*

In Chapter 10, customers do not occur explicitly – nor does the waiting line. This is possible in very simple situations only. In general, both customers and queues must be represented by appropriate data structures of the simulation program. The goal of this section is a generic queue module to be used by the simulation package.

Module *Qs* implements the three basic queueing disciplines FIFO, LIFO and ranked as abstract data types. The contents of queues, also called *items*, have to be compatible with queues operating under all three disciplines. That means, for example, that an item may be dequeued from a FIFO queue and subsequently enqueued in a ranked queue. We also require that the implementation make the *queueing discipline an invariant* – the client is assured that the FIFO, LIFO or ranked properties cannot be violated. The invariant is guaranteed against incompetent and even malicious use by the client.

13.1.1 Definition

Fundamental to module *Qs* are two abstract data types: *Queue* and *Item*. The property of a queue is its queueing discipline. Each item has a *key* that is used by the ranked discipline. There are two basic operations: enqueueing and dequeueing of items.

A queue – an instance of type *Queue* – belongs to one of the classes FIFO, LIFO or ranked. In traditional programming, the finer characterization is often implemented with a *type flag*, typically an integer. Type extension, however, affords a much more elegant solution: *FIFO*, *LIFO* and *Ranked* are types that extend the base type *Queue*. Instances of the extended types are compatible with the formal parameter of type *Queue* in the procedures *Enqueue* and *DequeuedItem*. The action taken therein can be discriminated using a type test. This type design is depicted in Figure 13.1.

```
     FIFO      LIFO     Ranked
        \       |       /
         \      |      /
              Queue
```

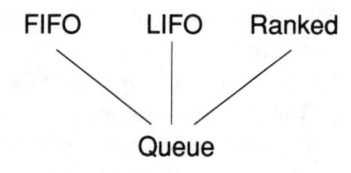

Figure 13.1 The queue types of module *Qs*.

With this design in mind, we state the definition of module *Qs*:

```
DEFINITION Qs;
TYPE
   Key = REAL;
   Item = POINTER TO ItemDesc;
   ItemDesc = RECORD
      key: Key
   END;

   Queue = POINTER TO QueueDesc;
   QueueDesc = RECORD  END;

   FIFO = POINTER TO FIFODesc;
   FIFODesc = RECORD (QueueDesc)  END;

   LIFO = POINTER TO LIFODesc;
   LIFODesc = RECORD (QueueDesc)  END;
```

```
Ranked = POINTER TO RankedDesc;
RankedDesc = RECORD(QueueDesc) END;

PROCEDURE Enqueue(q: Queue; i: Item);
PROCEDURE DequeuedItem(q: Queue): Item;
PROCEDURE Empty(q: Queue): BOOLEAN;
PROCEDURE Enumerate(q: Queue; P: PROCEDURE (i: Item));
PROCEDURE Open(q: Queue);

END Qs.
```

The names of the procedures are self-explanatory; in particular,

- *Enqueue* puts item *i* into queue *q*.
- *DequeuedItem* removes the head of queue *q*.
- *Empty* returns TRUE if the *q* is empty, FALSE otherwise.
- *Enumerate* traverses *q* and applies procedure *P* to every item.
- *Open* initializes instance *q* of type *FIFO*, *LIFO* or *Ranked*.

13.1.2 Implementation

To implement module *Qs*, we must first decide on a data representation. For simplicity, we revert to the linear list – the groundwork for module *Qs* was laid in Section 9.2.

We wish to be able to infer the queueing discipline from the dynamic type of the queue. We therefore represent each queue by a record (type *Queue*) that contains the anchor in a field *first*.

The optimized method of Section 9.2.2 is employed for FIFO queues. The pointer to the last element is in the extension *FIFO* of base type *Queue*.

The text of module *Qs* is as follows:

```
MODULE Qs;
TYPE
   Key = REAL;
   Item* = POINTER TO ItemDesc;
   ItemDesc* = RECORD
     key*: Key;
     next: Item
   END;
```

248 A simulation example

```
            Queue* = POINTER TO QueueDesc;
            QueueDesc* = RECORD
  (1) →       first: Item
            END;

            FIFO* = POINTER TO FIFODesc;
            FIFODesc* = RECORD (QueueDesc)
  (2) →       last: Item
            END;

            LIFO* = POINTER TO LIFODesc;
            LIFODesc* = RECORD (QueueDesc) END;

            Ranked* = POINTER TO RankedDesc;
            RankedDesc* = RECORD (QueueDesc) END;

         PROCEDURE InsertFIFO(q: FIFO; i: Item);
         BEGIN
            i.next := NIL;
            IF q.first # NIL THEN q.last.next := i
            ELSE q.first := i
            END;
            q.last := i
         END InsertFIFO;

         PROCEDURE InsertLIFO(q: LIFO; i: Item);
         BEGIN  i.next := q.first;  q.first := i
         END InsertLIFO;

         PROCEDURE InsertRanked(q: Ranked; i: Item);
         VAR x: Item;
         BEGIN
            IF (q.first = NIL) OR (i.key < q.first.key) THEN
               i.next := q.first;  q.first := i
            ELSE
               x := q.first;
               WHILE (x.next # NIL) & (i.key >= x.next.key) DO
                  x := x.next
               END;
               i.next := x.next;  x.next := i
```

```
            END
        END InsertRanked;
        PROCEDURE Enqueue*(q: Queue; i: Item);
        VAR x: Item;
        BEGIN
(3) →       IF q IS FIFO THEN  InsertFIFO(q(FIFO), i)
            ELSIF q IS LIFO THEN InsertLIFO(q(LIFO), i)
            ELSIF q IS Ranked THEN InsertRanked(q(Ranked), i)
            END
        END Enqueue;

        PROCEDURE DequeuedItem*(q: Queue): Item;
        VAR x: Item;
        BEGIN  x := q.first;
            IF x # NIL THEN q.first := x.next END;
            RETURN x
        END DequeuedItem;

        PROCEDURE Enumerate*(q: Queue; P: PROCEDURE (i: Item));
        VAR x: Item;
        BEGIN  x := q.first; WHILE x # NIL DO P(x); x := x.next END
        END Enumerate;

        PROCEDURE Empty*(q: Queue): BOOLEAN;
        BEGIN  RETURN q.first = NIL
        END Empty;

        PROCEDURE Open*(q: Queue);
        BEGIN  q.first := NIL
        END Open;

        END Qs.
```

Notes

(1) Field *first* is the (hidden) anchor for the list that represents the queue.

(2) Field *last* is added to *first* in the extension *FIFO* of the type *Queue*. It is used to optimize FIFO operations as described in Section 9.2.2.

(3) In this if statement, the type-specific queueing disciplines are invoked. Note the type guards in the call statements.

13.2 An object-oriented simulation calendar

13.2.1 Data type *Actor* and basic module structure

In Chapter 10, we advocated a programming approach that started with a formulation of the action of the program on a high level of abstraction. Successive refinements are aimed at the final specification.

Data-centered design

Here we start with the specification of the most fundamental data type. This view is quite typical when adopting object-orientation. We call this design approach *data-centered*. Stepwise refinement, however, is not invalidated – its application is only delayed to the time when individual module texts are composed.

The simulation program of Chapter 10 is built around the notion of a *calendar of events*. An event can be visualized as a label on the time axis. The main simulation program always pairs an action with an event. This pairing of the event with its action immediately *suggests the use of an object* that makes this association explicit. Since the nature of the action is still open, an object with handler is the natural choice. We call that object an *actor*. Actors can be put into the simulation calendar, and when they are due, their procedure variable *handle* is called with an appropriate message parameter.

In an actual simulation, entities such as customers, sources or servers will be represented by instances of types that extend the base type *Actor*. Therefore actors need to be furnished with the capability to be *members of different queues of types FIFO, LIFO or Ranked*. From Section 13.1 we are familiar with a service module, *Qs*, that provides just that. If *Qs* fulfills the promise of being a generic module, we should be able to use it here.

We will try and declare our type *Actor* as an extension of *Qs.Item*:

```
TYPE
    Actor = POINTER TO ActorDesc;
    ActorDesc = RECORD (Qs.ItemDesc);
        handle: Handler
    END;
```

Let us now specify the basic module structure of our simulation package. From Chapter 10, we remember the service modules *Paths* and *Sequences* (Exercise 10.2) that facilitate the computation of results. They will be as useful here as they were there. The module that implements the abstract data type *Actor* is termed *Sim*. Thus the foundation of the simulation package is the module structure depicted in Figure 13.2.

13.2 An object-oriented simulation calendar

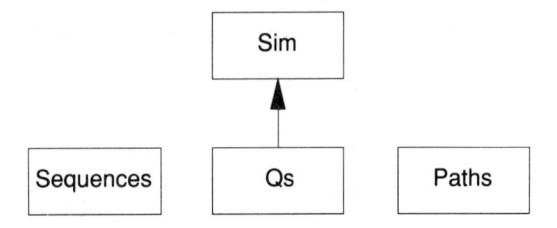

```
              ┌─────┐
              │ Sim │
              └──▲──┘
                 │
┌───────────┐ ┌─────┐ ┌───────┐
│ Sequences │ │ Qs  │ │ Paths │
└───────────┘ └─────┘ └───────┘
```

Figure 13.2 Basic module structure of the simulation package.

13.2.2 Module *Sim*: an abstract simulation

Like its cousin *Calendar* (see Section 10.3.1), module *Sim* embodies the calendar as an abstract data structure. Module *Sim* also exports the definition of the abstract data type *Actor*.
In fact, one design option is to implement *Sim* very much like *Calendar*. Procedures *Schedule* and *GetNextActor* would enter actors into the calendar and retrieve the most imminent actor from there.

However, such an implementation ignores the fact that actors represent 'active' events. In fact, *any particular simulation* can be expressed in the following abstract form:

    REPEAT
        "Retrieve actor from calendar";
        "Set simulation time to actor's time";
        "send calendar message to actor"
    UNTIL "simulation time exceeds given limit" OR "calendar empty"

Module *Sim* is not a specific simulation – hence the actual actions assigned to the procedure variables *handle* are not specified in its scope. Still, all knowledge is present to implement the canonical simulation loop. We may say that *Sim* performs an abstract simulation, the details of which are furnished by its clients, that is modules higher up in the hierarchy. These clients are specified long after *Sim* is completed, compiled and put into the system's library.

Note that this abstract treatment of a simulation is analogous to the way the graphics editor treated all objects abstractly, for example in the procedure *DrawAll*.

After these preliminaries, we present the definition of module *Sim*:

```
DEFINITION Sim;
IMPORT Qs;
TYPE
  Message = RECORD END;
  CalendarMessage = RECORD (Message) END;
  Handler = PROCEDURE (a: Actor; VAR msg: Message);
  Actor = POINTER TO ActorDesc;
  ActorDesc = RECORD (Qs.Item)
    handle: Handler
  END;
VAR time: REAL

PROCEDURE Schedule(a: Actor; t: REAL);
PROCEDURE Simulate(dt: REAL);
PROCEDURE Reset;
END Sim.
```

The simulation calendar is based on the ranked queue exported by module *Qs*:

- *Message* is the prototype of the messages understood by the handlers of actors.
- *CalendarMsg* is the type of a specific message that is sent to the current actor when it is due and removed from the calendar (we say the actor enters its *passive state*).
- *Actor* is the type of the simulation object.
- Variable *time* reports the current global time of the simulation.
- *Schedule* enters actor *a* into the calendar and sets its due time to *time + t*. The actor is said to enter the *active state*.
- *Simulate* performs the (abstract) simulation starting at the current time and ending at *time + dt*. Sets actors into the passive state (i.e. removes them from the calendar) and sends calendar messages to them.
- *Reset* clears the calendar and sets *time* to 0.

All the elements are now in place to list module *Sim*:

```
MODULE Sim;
IMPORT Qs, Out;
TYPE
  Actor* = POINTER TO ActorDesc;
```

13.2 An object oriented simulation calendar

```
        Message* = RECORD END;
        CalendarMsg* = RECORD (Message) END;
        Handler* = PROCEDURE (a: Actor; VAR msg: Message);
        ActorDesc* = RECORD (Qs.ItemDesc)
          handle* : Handler
        END;


      VAR
        time* : REAL;      (* Global simulation time *)
        clndr: Qs.Ranked; (* Abstract data structure *)


(1) →  PROCEDURE Schedule* (a: Actor; t: REAL);
       BEGIN  a.key := t;  Qs.Enqueue(clndr, a)
       END Schedule;

       PROCEDURE Simulate* (dt: REAL);
       VAR
(2) →     cur: Qs.Item;
          msg: CalendarMsg;
          tEnd: REAL;
       BEGIN
          tEnd := time + dt;
          LOOP
(3) →        IF ~Qs.Empty(clndr) THEN
                cur := Qs.DequeuedItem(clndr);
(4) →           WITH cur: Actor DO
(5) →              time := cur.key;  cur.handle(cur, msg)
                END
             ELSE Out.String("empty calendar"); Out.Ln;  EXIT
             END;
             IF time > tEnd THEN EXIT END
          END
       END Simulate;


       PROCEDURE Reset*;
       BEGIN  Qs.Open(clndr);  time := 0
       END Reset;


(6) →  BEGIN  NEW(clndr);  Reset
       END Sim.
```

Notes

(1) Whether the time should be a parameter of *Schedule* or simply a property of the actor (its *key*) is worth some deliberation. Both are valid solutions. We prefer the explicit parameter, since the identifier *key* is not meaningful in the simulation context.

(2) Observe that the variable *cur*, the current actor, must be of base type *Qs.Item* to be compatible with the procedure *Qs.DequeuedItem*.

(3) The test for an empty queue is necessary. An empty simulation calendar means deadlock in the simulated system. When deadlock occurs, *Simulate* terminates.

(4) Do not forget the type guard, *cur* is of base type *Qs.Item*; here we deal with actors. Since the calendar contains only entries of type *Actor* or extensions thereof, no type test is required.

(5) The message *msg* of type *CalendarMsg* is sent to the actor. The message informs the handler that it is current and enters the passive state.

(6) Within the body of module *Sim*, the abstract data structure is created and initialized.

13.3 A simulation based on module *Sim*

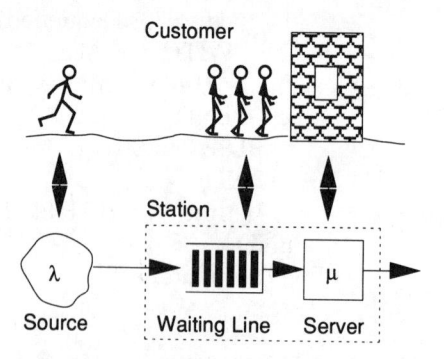

Figure 13.3 A simple queue composed of a single station.

Let us now demonstrate how the new tools can be used to simulate a queueing system. Chapter 10 introduced the basic concepts of the operation of a queue. A broad class of queueing system can be decomposed into the entities *customers*, *sources* and *queueing stations*. Figure

13.3 A simulation based on module Sim

13.3 shows these elements for the case of a single queue. In actual simulation practice, a single waiting line is seldom the object of investigation.[1] Much more common are whole networks of stations through which customers proceed (Figure 13.4).

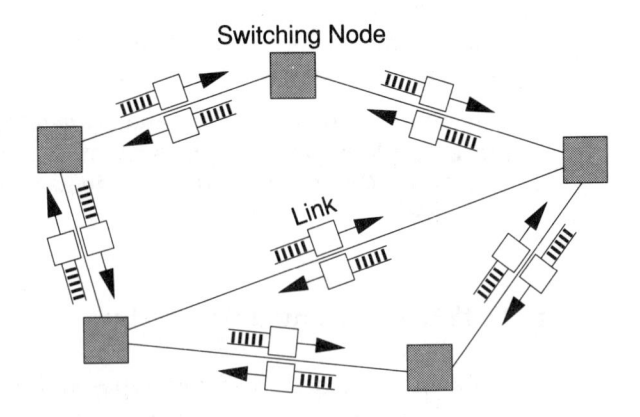

Figure 13.4 A communication network modeled as a system of queues.

More precisely, we have the following:

- *Customers* proceed through the system of queueing stations. They determine the sequence in which the stations are visited and the service demands placed on them.
- *Sources* generate customers according to a given probabilistic rule.
- *Stations* are entities composed of a *server* and a *waiting line*. The station puts customers in the waiting line and schedules them to receive service.

Note that in modeling practice, a number of station types occur that are characterized by the size of the waiting room, the number of servers, and the queueing discipline. In our example, we discuss the simplest case: an unlimited waiting room and a single server that works on customers in order of their arrival (FIFO).

Basic paradigm The interaction of customers with stations can be defined in a variety of ways. We take the following view:

---

[1] The mathematical theory of single queues is well developed. Hence cases are solved analytically instead of experimentally.

(1) The customer decides which station to visit and *requests service* from that station.
(2) The *station notifies the customer* when the server is ready. It is the customer (not the server) that determines the end of the service period.
(3) At the end of the service period, the customer *frees the server* prior to requesting service elsewhere or leaving.

The entities *customer, source,* and *station* appear in multiple instances. But multiple instances of a given entity suggest the introduction of a data type. The design and implementation of such data types is our next task.

13.3.1 Data types and module structure

In Oberon, the design of data types and module structure go hand in hand, since the module is the basis for abstraction. Our goal is to provide three types: *Customer, Source* and *Station*.

Generally, customers, sources and stations are implemented as actors since they have time-dependent behavior. Their types extend the base type *Sim.Actor*.

The types *Customer* and *Source* are intimately related to the details of a specific simulation experiment – also called a *model*. They are therefore naturally declared in the module that implements a particular model, such as a communication network simulation. We call that module simply *Model*.

Queueing stations, on the other hand, come in various well-understood standard versions. The simplest station is one operating the FCFS discipline and having unlimited waiting room. If such a station is implemented as an abstract data type, it can be used by a potentially large number of client modules. We will provide a module *Stations* that exports the type *Station*.

The simple station that we implement has no time-dependent behavior. There is therefore no need to make it an actor. It is not difficult, however, to think of station classes that would need the calendar, for example a station that breaks down from time to time.

The module structure that we have in mind is depicted in Figure 13.5. Our goal is an *extensible simulation package* where new station types can be encapsulated into modules and added to the package without changes or recompilations of existing parts, in particular module *Sim*. It is the object-oriented design that makes this possible.

13.3 A simulation based on module Sim

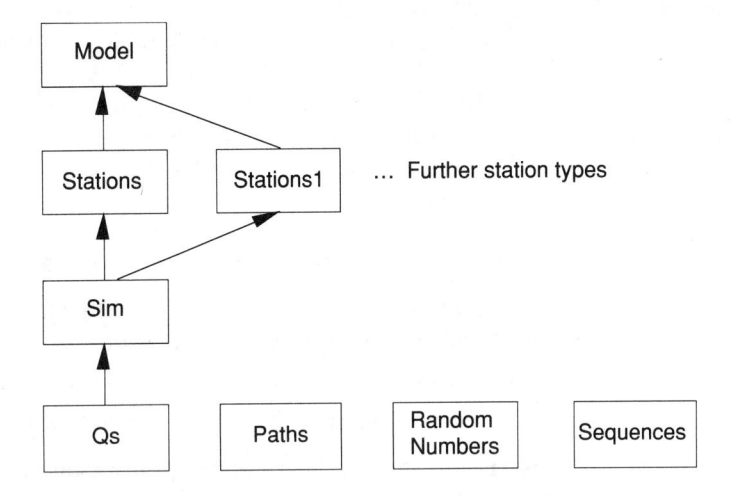

Figure 13.5 Module hierarchy (only major import relations are shown).

13.3.2 Definition of module *Stations*

According to the basic paradigm, it is the station that manages the waiting line. In particular, the station determines the customer to be served and calls its handler with a *begin service message*.

We now witness the generality of the object with a handler. There is no need to anticipate a 'begin service' method in module *Sim*. Module *Stations* simply declares a *BeginMsg* type that extends *Sim.Message* and sends a begin message to the objects that request service or are removed from the queue.

Other station types may have a need for other messages, such as a 'breakdown message.' Again, the appropriate message type is declared in the module that has the need – not in the base module.

We are now able to state the definition of module *Stations*:

```
DEFINITION Stations;
IMPORT Qs, Sim, Paths;
TYPE
    Station = POINTER TO StationDesc;
    StationDesc = RECORD
        path: Paths.Path
    END;
```

```
        BeginMsg = RECORD (Sim.Message) s: Station END;

        PROCEDURE Request(s: Station; customer: Sim.Actor);
        PROCEDURE Free(s: Station);
        PROCEDURE Open(s: Station);
        END Stations.
```

The abstract data type *Station* has three properties:

- a *path* that is used to compute statistics about the queue distribution observed at the station;
- a waiting line operating the FIFO queueing discipline (hidden);
- a server that is either busy or free (hidden).

The station sends a begin message (message of type *BeginMsg*) to the customer upon start of service. The begin message identifies the station in field *s*. The procedures defining the actions of the station are as follows:

- *Request*: The customer *customer* requests service at station *s*. The action depends on the state of the server at the time of call. If it is busy, the customer is enqueued. If it is free, it changes state to busy and starts serving *customer*.
- *Free*: Station *s* is told that the currently served customer is finished. The server is freed. If the queue is not empty, the head of the line is removed. The server changes to busy and starts serving the head of the line.
- *Open*: Initializes an instance of *s* type *Station*.

It is important to remember that *Open* does not create a station. It is the client that issues a call to NEW and passes the newly created station to *Open* for initialization. That station may be of type *Station* or an extension thereof.

13.3.3 Implementation of module *Stations*

After the preceding discussion the implementation of module *Stations* is straightforward:

```
        MODULE Stations;
        IMPORT Qs, Sim, Paths;

        TYPE
          Station* = POINTER TO StationDesc;
```

13.3 A simulation based on module Sim

```
StationDesc* = RECORD
    wl: Qs.FIFO;          (* Waiting Line *)
    path* : Paths.Path
END;

BeginMsg* = RECORD (Sim.Message) s*: Station END;

PROCEDURE Request* (s: Station; customer: Sim.Actor);
VAR msg: BeginMsg;
BEGIN
    IF s.path.n = 0 THEN  (* Server empty *)
(1) →   msg.s := s;  customer.handle(customer, msg)
    ELSE  Qs.Enqueue(s.wl, customer)
    END;
    Paths.Up(s.path, Sim.time)
END Request;

PROCEDURE Free* (s: Station);
VAR
(2) →   customer: Qs.Item;
    msg: BeginMsg;
BEGIN
    Paths.Down(s.path, Sim.time);
    IF s.path.n > 0 THEN  (* Customers are waiting *)
        customer := Qs.DequeuedItem(s.wl);
        WITH customer: Sim.Actor DO
(3) →       msg.s := s;  customer.handle(customer, msg)
        END
    END
END Free;

PROCEDURE Open* (s: Station);
BEGIN
    Paths.Init(s.path);  NEW(s.wl);  Qs.Open(s.wl)
END Open;

END Stations.
```

Notes

(1) The field *s* of the message (type *BeginMsg*) is initialized and the customer's handler called (a begin message is sent to the customer).

(2) Note that *customer* must be of base type *Qs.Item* to be compatible with the procedure *Qs.DequeuedItem*.

(3) A begin message is sent to the customer. Note the type guard that is necessary as a consequence of point (2).

13.3.4 Implementation of module *Model*

Module *Model* implements a simulation of the simple queue depicted in Figure 13.3. The goal is to gather statistics about the waiting time of customers. For that purpose, customers must be represented explicitly. Each customer keeps a time stamp that records the time of arrival. Module *Sequences* is used to gather the mean and variance of the waiting times (see Exercise 10.2).

Programming the simulation is in essence providing the handlers for customers and sources as shown in the following program text:

```
        MODULE Model;
        IMPORT Sim, Stations, Paths, Sequences, RandomNumbers, In, Out;
        TYPE
(1) →     Customer = POINTER TO CustomerDesc;
          CustomerDesc = RECORD (Sim.ActorDesc)
             ts: REAL   (* Time stamp of arrival epoch *)
          END;

          VAR (* Global state variables *)
             lambda, mu: REAL;
             s: Stations.Station;
(2) →        srce: Sim.Actor;
             w: Sequences.Sequence;

(3) →   PROCEDURE HandleCust(cust: Sim.Actor; VAR msg: Sim.Message);
        BEGIN
(4) →      WITH cust: Customer DO
              IF msg IS Stations.BeginMsg THEN
(5) →            Sim.Schedule(cust, Sim.time + RandomNumbers.Exp(mu))
              ELSIF msg IS Sim.CalendarMsg THEN
(6) →            Stations.Free(s); Sequences.Add(w, Sim.time – cust.ts)
              END
```

13.3 A simulation based on module Sim

```
           END
         END HandleCust;
```

(7) →
```
         PROCEDURE HandleSrce(srce: Sim.Actor; VAR msg: Sim.Message);
           VAR c: Customer;
         BEGIN
```
(8) →
```
           NEW(c); c.handle := HandleCust; c.ts := Sim.time;
           Stations.Request(s, c);
           Sim.Schedule(srce, Sim.time + RandomNumbers.Exp(lambda))
         END HandleSrce;
```

(9) →
```
         PROCEDURE Setup*;
           VAR c: Customer;
         BEGIN
           In.Open; Sim.Reset; Sequences.Open(w); Out.Open;
```
(10) →
```
           NEW(srce); srce.handle := HandleSrce;
           In.Real(lambda); Out.String("lambda ="); Out.Real(lambda, 10);
```
(11) →
```
           Sim.Schedule(srce, 0);
```
(12) →
```
           NEW(s); Stations.Open(s);
           In.Real(mu); Out.String("   mu ="); Out.Real(mu, 10);
         END Setup;
```

(13) →
```
         PROCEDURE Run*;
           VAR dt: REAL; q: REAL;
         BEGIN
           In.Open; In.Real(dt);
```
(14) →
```
           Sim.Simulate(dt);
           Out.String("Sim.time ="); Out.Real(Sim.time, 10);
           Out.String("    E[W]="); Out.Real(Sequences.Mean(w), 10);
           Out.String("    var[W]="); Out.Real(Sequences.Var(w), 10);
           Out.Ln
         END Run;

       END Model.
```

Notes

(1) The type *Customer* extends *Sim.Actor*. The added variable is the time stamp *ts* that is used to gather waiting time statistics.

(2) Since the source has no special state variables, there is no need to extend *Sim.Actor*.

(3) This is the handler for customers.

(4) A global type guard is required, since *cust* is of base type *Sim.Actor*. Under the auspices of this type guard, the extended fields of the customer (here *ts*) can be referenced in the handler's text.

(5) The handler is called with a message of type *Sources.BeginMsg*. This means that service may begin. The handler schedules its customer (formal parameter *cust*) in the calendar at the time the service period expires. Note that here the handler does not make use of the field *s* of the begin message. If *s* were used, a type guard would be required (see Exercises).

(6) The handler is called with a message of type *Sim.CalendarMsg*. This is a notification that the service period expired. The station *s* is freed, the waiting time is determined and added to the sequence *w*.

(7) This is the handler for the source.

(8) The handler can only be called from module *Sim* (with a calendar message). Therefore no type test is required. When called, a new customer is generated. The customer immediately requests service at station *s*. Then the source is re-scheduled to generate the next customer.

(9) *Setup* is a command that initializes a simulation run.

(10) An instance *srce* of type *Sim.Actor* is created and *HandleSource* is assigned to the field *srce.handle*.

(11) It is essential that the source be scheduled here for the first time. This triggers the whole simulation. Without it, nothing will ever happen.

(12) An instance *s* of type *Stations.Station* is created and initialized.

(13) This is a command that initiates an incremental simulation run lasting *dt* time units and printing waiting time statistics.

(14) This starts the simulation loop that is encapsulated in module *Sim*.

13.4 Summary

In this chapter, we have designed a complete simulation package using generic modules and objects with handlers. The essence is a *framework of abstract data types* that are interrelated.

We demonstrate the usefulness of the notion of the *generic module*. Extension of abstract data types exported by module *Qs* are used for the simulation calendar and for explicit representation of waiting lines. An important property of an abstract data type – the guarantee of invariants – is demonstrated. In our case, these invariants are the properties of the queueing discipline.

The notion of the event, introduced in Chapter 10, is generalized. To reflect that added generality, the type of the event is termed *Actor*. Actors are objects with a handler. The calendar, encapsulated in module *Sim*, calls the actors with a calendar message, prompting their handlers to perform the action paired with the event.

The simulation package can be extended with modules implementing various station types. The station defines a protocol such as one of the *Request/Free* pair of procedures. Of particular interest is the way the module *Stations* defines a message type *BeginMsg* and sends appropriate begin messages to customers.

Other station modules (not given in this chapter) may similarly introduce their own message types, for example, a breakdown message. The possibility of adding message types in *those modules that need to send the message*, rather than in the base module, is a particular strength of the object with a handler. Note that this flexibility is not part of the standard paradigm using classes and methods.

13.5 Exercises

13.1 [**Tandem queues**] Repeat Exercise 10.4 with the new simulation package of this chapter.

13.2 [**Stations with limited waiting room**] Module *Stations* of Section 13.3.2 allows the waiting line to become arbitrarily long. In most practical situations, however, the waiting room is limited. Add a module *StationsN* to the simulation package that reflects this limitation.

Hint: Endow the type *Station* with two queues: a *pending queue* and the *waiting line proper*. If a request is placed when the waiting line is full, the requesting actor is put into the pending queue. Upon the next departure (a call of procedure *Free*) the head of the pending queue is moved into the waiting line. Use a new message type, *AcceptMsg* say, to notify the actor when it is accepted to the waiting line.

Thus the definition of *StationsN* reads as follows:

```
DEFINITION Stations;
IMPORT Qs, Sim, Paths;
TYPE
  Station = POINTER TO StationDesc;
  StationDesc = RECORD
    path: Paths.Path
  END;
  BeginMsg = RECORD (Sim.Message) s: Station END;
```

```
              AcceptMsg = RECORD (Sim.Message) s: Station END;
              PROCEDURE Request(s: Station; customer: Sim.Actor);
              PROCEDURE Free(s: Station);
              PROCEDURE Open(s: Station; n: INTEGER);  (* n = max. size *)
           END Stations.
```

13.3 Using module *StationsN*, simulate two queues with limited waiting room in tandem. Gather statistics about the overall time a customer spends in the system. Compare results with Exercise 13.1.

13.4 [**Packet network**] Simulate a packet network like the one depicted in Figure 13.4. Assume

- M switching nodes with unlimited buffer capacity and infinite processing rate.
- N communication lines characterized by their transmission rate (in bits/s).
- R routes connecting a source node with a destination node. A route is a sequence of communication lines that are traversed sequentially. Each route has a source that generates packets.
- The parameters of a source are: (1) its arrival rate (packets/s), (2) the average size of the packet (bits). Use exponential random numbers for interarrival time and packet size.

Choose appropriate data structures to represent the network. Provide commands to initialize a configuration. Evaluate statistics of packet delay for each route and for the whole network. Determine appropriate buffer sizes at the nodes.

Provide commands to save the network configuration in a file and load it from there.

13.5 Repeat Exercise 13.4 with switching nodes of finite capacity and processors of finite speed.

14 Oberon-2

The Oberon language was designed to serve the implementation of a novel operating system using object-orientation. The major goal was conceptual elegance without sacrificing ease of programming. During the implementation of that operating system, the language was tuned towards that goal.

The latest reflection of that evolution is Oberon-2 (Mössenböck and Wirth, 1991), a slight extension that is *fully upward-compatible with Oberon*. There is one major and three minor additions. The principal one is the *type-bound procedure*. Effectively, it allows the association of procedure constants to record types. The remaining additions are

- the *for statement*, a construct expressing repetition with guaranteed termination;
- the *open array type* which is applicable to variables instead of parameters only;
- an *extended form of the with statement* simplifying conditional execution;
- a mark specifying *read-only export*.

14.1 Type-bound procedures

Objects are instances of an abstract data type whose procedures are bound dynamically. In Oberon, this dynamic binding is achieved through procedure variables that appear as fields in a record.

If we reflect on the example of the graphics editor, however, we realize, that assignments to the procedure variables are made only once – at the time the object is created. This behavior is quite typical: procedures are assigned when the object is created, and stay constant thereafter. The consequence is that *dynamic binding could equally well be based on the dynamic type of the object, rather than on its instance*. The type-bound procedure of Oberon-2 is such a language construct that associates procedures with record types, not with record instances. The advantages are twofold:

- At the time of object creation, the assignment of procedure names to procedure variables is avoided and cannot be omitted by mistake.
- The memory consumed by the procedure variables in each object is reduced.

Using type-bound procedures, the graphics object of Chapter 12 is expressed as follows:

```
TYPE
    Figure* = POINTER TO FigureDesc;
    FigureDesc* = RECORD
        next: Figure
    END;

PROCEDURE (fig: Figure) Draw*;
    ...
END Draw;

...(* declarations of procedures Clear and Mark *)

PROCEDURE (fig: Figure) Move*(dX, dY: INTEGER);
    ...
END Move;
```

The procedure fields are omitted in the definition of type *Figure*. In the declarations of the procedures *Draw*, *Clear*, *Mark* and *Move*, the formal parameter *fig*, representing the object itself, is now specified in front of the procedure name. This distinguished formal parameter is called *receiver*. Its type, *Figure*, indicates that these procedures are bound to *Figure*; that is, they are operations applicable to *Figure* objects. Compared with the Oberon implementation of the methods (Section 12.3), there is no need for a regional type guard enclosing the statement sequence of type-bound procedure. This results in a textual simplification as well as a slight run-time advantage.

Procedures *Draw* and *Move* are invoked through the call statements

    fig.Draw;   fig.Move(x, y);

In these call statements, the identifier *fig* serves two purposes: it denotes an actual parameter paired with the receiver, and its dynamic type determines which procedure is called.

Contrast this with a call of the procedure field *move* in our earlier formulation of the *Figure* object:

> fig.move(fig, x, y);

Here the two purposes are met by the two *distinct* appearances of the identifier *fig*. The first occurrence selects the operation, the second constitutes the actual parameter passing the object to the procedure.

Consider the call *fig.Draw*. If the dynamic type of *fig* is *Line* then the procedure *Draw* that is bound to *Line* is called; if it is *Rect* then another *Draw* bound to *Rect* is invoked, and so on. This mechanism is called *dynamic binding*, since the requested operation (here *Draw*) is bound to a specific procedure according to the dynamic type of the receiver.

14.1.1 Syntax and general semantics

The syntax of the procedure heading, found in Section 6.1, is augmented with a syntactic entity *Receiver* that acts as a formal parameter to the procedure as well as an indicator that the procedure is type-bound:

> ProcedureHeading =
>   "PROCEDURE" [Receiver] ident ["*"] [FormalParameters].
> Receiver = "(" ["VAR"] ident ":" ident ")".

Explicit and implicit bindings

Consider a procedure *P* bound to a type *T0*. The following declaration is said to define an *explicit binding*:

> PROCEDURE (p: T0) P(... further formal parameters ...);
> BEGIN
>   ... (* statement sequence *)
> END P;

Procedure *P* is *implicitly also bound* to all extensions $T1, T2...Tn$ of *T0*. It is possible to bind another procedure, *Q* say, to types that extend *T0*, for example to *T1*:

> PROCEDURE (p: T1) Q(... further formal parameters ...);
> BEGIN
>   ... (* statement sequence *)
> END Q;

268   Oberon-2

In this case, Q is also bound to all types that extend T1, that is T2...Tn, but not to T0. This situation is depicted in Figure 14.1.

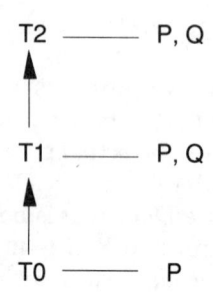

```
T2 ──── P, Q
 ▲
 │
T1 ──── P, Q
 ▲
 │
T0 ──── P
```

Figure 14.1 Type hierarchy with type-bound procedures.

Locality

Type-bound procedures are local to their record type, comparable to procedure fields. Highlighting this locality, a type with bound procedures could be visualized as follows:[1]

```
DEFINITION Graphics;
TYPE
   FigureDesc = RECORD
      next: Figure;
      PROCEDURE (fig: Figure) Draw;
      PROCEDURE (fig: Figure) Move(dX, dY: INTEGER)
   END;
   ...
```

Since it is a local entity, a type-bound procedure is uniquely defined only with the pair name/receiver-type. We adopt the notation P_T in subsequent discussions, where T is the type and P the procedure name.

Redefinition

Adding new procedures to extended types, such as Q in Figure 14.1, is not nearly as important as *redefining* the action performed by a type-bound procedure.

Assume two distinct procedures with the *same name* bound explicitly to two types T0 and T1 respectively. If T1 extends T0 then the procedure bound to T1 is said to *redefine* the one bound to T0. This relationship is depicted in Figure 14.2. Procedure P_{T1} may redefine P_{T0} only if its *formal parameters match* those of P_{T0}.

---

[1] This is the style adopted by the browser that compiles definition modules.

14.1 Type-bound procedures

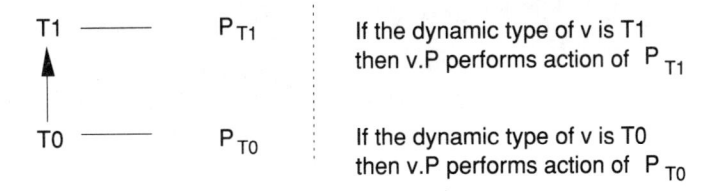

```
T1  ─────  P T1      If the dynamic type of v is T1
 ▲                    then v.P performs action of  P T1
 │
 │
T0  ─────  P T0      If the dynamic type of v is T0
                      then v.P performs action of  P T0
```

Figure 14.2 Re-definition of procedure P.

For example, consider the type *Rect*, which is an extension of *Figure*:

> Rect = POINTER TO RectDesc;
> RectDesc = RECORD (FigureDesc)
>   x, y, w, h: INTEGER
> END;

The following procedures can be declared:

> PROCEDURE (fig: Figure) Draw;
> PROCEDURE (fig: Rect) Draw;

$Draw_{Rect}$ redefines $Draw_{Figure}$.

Dynamic binding If *v* is a designator and *P* is a type-bound procedure then

> v.P

denotes the procedure *P* that is *bound to the dynamic type of v*. Note that this may be a different procedure from the one bound to the static type of *v*. If *P* has a formal parameter list, actual parameters are provided in the usual manner. The variable, designated by *v*, is passed to *P* according to the parameter passing rules.

For example, assume *rect: Figure*. Then the following are valid calls:

> rect.Draw; rect.Move(x, y);

Looking at Figure 14.2, the notion of dynamic binding may be clarified with an example:

> VAR v0: T0; v1: T1;
> ...
> NEW(v0);   (* Instance of v0 is created *)

```
            NEW(v1);        (* Instance of v1 is created *)
            ...
            v0.P;           (* Statement sequence of P_T0 is executed *)
            v0 := v1;       (* The dynamic type of v0 becomes T1 *)
            v0.P;           (* Statement sequence of P_T1 is executed *)
```

Super call

Assume that P_{T1} redefines P_{T0}. It is often useful to be able to call the redefined procedure P_{T0} from within the scope of P_{T1}. This is possible using the formulation

    r.P↑

where r is the receiver parameter of P_{T1}. In object-oriented terminology, this is known as a *super call*.

We are familiar with the notion of the super call from Section 12.4.4, where we extended module *Rectangles* to create a rectangle filled with a pattern. The type *FilledRect* is an extension of *Rect*. To draw such a filled rectangle, it is useful to use the already existing procedure $Draw_{Rect}$ to produce the wire frame and add only those statements needed to fill its interior. This leads to the following program excerpt:

```
        TYPE
            FilledRect = POINTER TO FilledRectDesc;
            FilledRectDesc = RECORD (RectDesc) pat: Pattern  END;
        ...
        PROCEDURE (fig: FilledRect) Draw;
        BEGIN
            fig.Draw↑;   (* Call to Draw_Rect *)
            ...(* Fill area within wire frame with pattern fig.pat *)
        END Draw;
```

14.1.2 Example: graphics editor

To illustrate the concepts of the type-bound procedure, we reformulate the implementations of modules *Graphics* and *Rectangles* from the example of Section 12.4:

```
        MODULE Graphics;
        TYPE
            Figure* = POINTER TO FigureDesc;
```

14.1 Type-bound procedures

(1) →   **FigureDesc*** = RECORD
       next: Figure
   END;

   Graph* = POINTER TO GraphDesc;
   GraphDesc* = RECORD list: Figure END;

   ... (* other type and variable declarations *)

   (* **type-bound procedure declarations** *)

(2) →   PROCEDURE (f: Figure) Draw*; END Draw;
   PROCEDURE (f: Figure) Clear*; END Clear;
   PROCEDURE (f: Figure) Mark*; END Mark;
   PROCEDURE (f: Figure) Move*(dX, dY: INTEGER); END Move;

   (* **procedures operating on all objects** *)
   PROCEDURE DrawAll*(g: Graph);
   VAR f: Figure;
   BEGIN
      f := g.list;

(3) →   WHILE f # NIL DO f.draw; f := f.next END
   END DrawAll;

   ... (* other procedure declarations *)

   END Graphics.

Notes

(1) No procedure variables are declared.

(2) Type-bound procedures must be declared, even if they do not define any action. Such a declaration is said to define an *abstract procedure*. It is a good idea to supply the abstract procedure with a call of the predeclared procedure HALT. If the programmer forgets to redefine one of these procedures – an obvious error – program termination results.

(3) Note the call statement: no parameter appears, in contrast to the earlier version.

Inspection of the text of module *Graphics* reveals an essential fact: the object's procedures (methods) must already be defined in the base module.

In the shape-specific modules, the methods are redefined, as can be seen in module *Rectangles*:

```
MODULE Rectangles;
IMPORT Graphics, ...;
TYPE
    Rectangle* = POINTER TO RectangleDesc;
    RectangleDesc* = RECORD (Graphics.FigureDesc)
        x*, y*, w*, h*: INTEGER
    END;
```

(1) →   PROCEDURE (rect: Rectangle) **Draw***;
```
BEGIN
    ...
END Draw;
```

...(* Declarations of Clear, Mark and Move *)

(2) →   PROCEDURE **New***(): Graphics.Figure;
```
VAR rect: Rectangle;  x, y, w, h: INTEGER;
BEGIN
```
(3) →   NEW(rect);
```
    (* obtain values x, y, w, h typically using the mouse *)
    rect.x := x;  rect.y := y;  rect.w := w;  rect.h := h;
    RETURN rect
END New;

END Rectangles.
```

Notes

(1) The receiver must be of type *Rectangle*, not, as in the previous version, *Graphics.Figure*. Therefore, the regional type-guard becomes superfluous.

(2) The result type of *New*, however, is still the base type *Graphics.Figure*, since it will be inserted into the list of graphics objects.

(3) The assignment statements initializing the procedure variables in the previous version are not needed.

14.2 For statement

A counting loop expresses the repeated execution of a statement sequence for a fixed number of times while a progression of values is assigned to an integer variable called the *control variable*. Consider the simplest case: control variable *i* is ranging over the integers $m, m + 1,..., n - 1$. In Oberon, such a loop is typically expressed with the following while statement:

> i := m;
> WHILE i < n DO ...(* some processing *) INC(i) END;

The for statement expresses this counting loops more succinctly, namely:

> FOR i = m TO n – 1 DO ...(* some processing *) END;

The for statement has the advantage of *guaranteed termination*. In particular, the common mistake to forget to increment the control variable *i* is avoided. Its EBNF definition reads

> statement = ForStatement.
> ForStatement = "FOR" ident ":=" expression "TO" expression
>   ["BY" ConstExpression] "DO"
>   StatementSequence
>   "END".

The control variable *ident* is of integer type, as are both *expression* and *ConstExpression*.

The semantics of the for statement

> FOR i := m TO n BY k DO StatementSequence END;

is expressed by the Oberon statement sequence

> i := m; temp := n;
> IF k > 0 THEN
>   WHILE i <= temp DO StatementSequence; i := i + k END
> ELSE
>   WHILE i >= temp DO StatementSequence; i := i + k END
> END;

The variable *i*, and the expressions *m*, *n* and *k* are of integer type. In particular, *m* and *n* must be assignment-compatible with *i*, *k* must be expression-compatible with *i*, and *k* must be nonzero. If *k* is not specified, it is assumed to be 1. The variable *temp* is a hidden anonymous variable. After termination of the for statement, the control variable always assumes a definite value defined by the above semantic definition.

14.3 The open array variable

From Section 8.2.4, we recall the open array parameter. The length of such an array is given by the length of the actual parameter. In Oberon-2, open arrays may be declared not only as formal (parameter) types but also as base types of pointers. In this case, the predeclared function NEW is used to create an anonymous instance of the open array on the heap. For example,

```
VAR pI: POINTER TO ARRAY OF INTEGER;
... NEW(pI, 100); ...
```

will create an anonymous integer array of length 100 and initialize *pI* to point to it.

The EBNF syntax of the array type is modified as follows:

```
ArrayType = "ARRAY" [ length { "," length} ] "OF" type.
length = ConstExpression;
```

In Oberon-2, the length specification is optional. Open arrays are restricted to formal parameter types and pointer base types.

If *T* is an *n*-dimensional open array and the variable *p* is declared as POINTER TO *T* then the corresponding predeclared function NEW has *n* + 1 arguments:

$$\text{NEW}(p, e_0, e_1, \ldots, e_{n-1})$$

where *T* is allocated with length given by the expressions e_0, $e_1, \ldots, e_{n-1}$ in the respective dimensions. A pointer to the anonymous variable is assigned to *p*. The referenced variable *p*↑ is of type *T*, and the *i*-th element of the 0-th dimension is given by the designator *p*[*i*].

The open array frees the programmer to specify maximum array bounds at compile time – often a difficult trade-off between generality and memory economy.

14.4 The Oberon-2 with statement

The with statement of Oberon provides a regional type guard. In Chapters 12 and 13, we encountered with statements in the processing of heterogeneous data structures and in the formulation of handlers.

Typically, the with statement is used in conjunction with a type test, serving as guard to avoid abnormal termination. For example, a heterogeneous list of graphics objects is processed using

```
f := list;
WHILE f # NIL DO
    IF f IS Line THEN
        WITH f: Line DO
            ...(* process line *)
        END
    ELSIF f IS Rect THEN
        WITH f: Rect DO
            ...(* process rectangle *)
        END
    ELSIF...
    END;
    f := f.next
END;
```

The Oberon-2 with statement makes the following shorthand notation possible:

```
f := list;
WHILE f # NIL DO
    WITH
        f: Line DO ...(* process line *)
      | f: Rect DO ...(* process rectangle *)
      | f: ...
    END;
    f := f.next
END;
```

The first statement sequence whose regional guard is fulfilled executes under that guard.

The EBNF syntax of the Oberon-2 with statement is

WithStatement = "WITH"
                guard "DO" StatementSequence
                {"|" guard "DO" StatementSequence}
                ["ELSE" StatementSequence]
                "END".
guard = qualident ":" qualident .

In a guard $v: T$, variable v and type T satisfies two conditions:

(1) T is an extension of the declared type of v,

(2) v is a pointer or a formal VAR parameter of record type.

The statement sequence of the first guard (in textual sequence) that is fulfilled executes. The else clause executes if no guard is satisfied. Absence of an else clause will result in abnormal program termination in that case.

To give a further example, we express the handler *HandleRect* of Section 12.5.1 using the Oberon-2 with statement:

```
PROCEDURE HandleRect(rect: Figure; VAR msg: Message);
BEGIN
   WITH
      msg: DrawMsg DO
         ...   (* draw rectangle *)
    | msg: ClearMsg DO
         ...   (* clear rectangle *)
    | msg: MarkMsg DO
         ...   (* mark rectangle *)
    | msg: MoveMsg DO
         ...   (* move rectangle by vector msg.dx, msg.dy *)
      ELSE
         ...   (* message not understood *)
      END
   END
END HandleRect;
```

14.5 Read-only export

In the design of an abstract data type, one sometimes faces the desire to make a variable visible, but in a read-only way. The requirement not to change that variable through an assignment stems from the need to guarantee certain properties or invariants of the abstract type.

An example is furnished by the type *Sequences* (see Exercises 10.2). The record field X is used to accumulate mean values through recurrence relations. To protect X, it is not exported. The client gains access to X through a function procedure *Mean*.

```
TYPE
    Sequence* = RECORD
        X: REAL;         (* the sample mean *)
        n: LONGINT       (* the number of samples *)
    END;
    ...
    PROCEDURE Mean* (s: Sequence): REAL;
    BEGIN RETURN s.X
    END Mean;
```

The use of function procedures just to protect a record field seems somewhat extravagant. Therefore Oberon-2 provides the *read-only export mark*, a minus sign "–" instead of the asterisk "*". Syntactically, the read-only export mark may appear wherever an export mark is allowed. Its proper use, however, is to protect variables and record fields from receiving assignments in client modules.

Using read-only export, the type *Sequence* will be defined as

```
TYPE
    Sequence* = RECORD
        X–: REAL; n: LONGINT
    END;
```

and the procedure *Mean* becomes superfluous.

14.6 Summary and discussion

Type-bound procedures are objects that are local to the scope of a record type. The procedures can be redefined for each extension of an object's type. The advantages claimed for type-bound procedures are summarized as follows:

(1) At the time of object creation, there is no need to assign procedures to variables, thereby eliminating the mistake of improper initialization.

(2) The objects are not burdened with memory needed for the procedure variables.

Compared with objects based on handlers, type-bound procedures are similarly efficient as procedure variables.

A possible disadvantage is that all type-bound procedures must be declared in the same module that defines the record type (abstract procedures if no action is defined).

Assuming memory sizes common in contemporary PCs, not to speak of workstations, the memory-saving argument is rarely vital.

In many practical situations, however, the two implementations can be considered equivalent, and the choice is a matter of personal preference. Since in Oberon proper the memory overhead can also be reduced greatly by means of *method suites* (for details see Wirth and Gutknecht, 1992), the addition of type-bound procedures may be viewed as a concession to the traditional object-oriented paradigm.

The for statement, the open array variable, the extended with statement and the read-only export are convenient features, reducing textual bulk and making some operations more convenient.

14.7 Exercises

14.1 Write a matrix multiplication procedure using for loops.

14.2 Repeat Exercise 12.1 (object-oriented calculator) using type-bound procedures.

14.3 Repeat Exercise 12.9 (tiny graphics editor) using type-bound procedures.

References

Mössenböck H. and Wirth N. (1991). The programming language Oberon-2. *Structured Programming*, **12**, 179–95.

Wirth N. and Gutknecht J. (1992). *Project Oberon: The Design of an Operating System and Compiler*. Wokingham: Addison-Wesley.

Appendices

Oberon report
ASCII table
Input/Output modules
Index

Appendix A
The programming language Oberon[1]

Make it as simple as possible, but not simpler
A. Einstein

A.1 Introduction

Oberon is a general-purpose programming language that evolved from Modula-2. Its principal new feature is the concept of *type extension*. It permits the construction of new data types on the basis of existing ones and provides relations between them.

This report is not intended as a programmer's tutorial. It is intentionally kept concise. Its function is to serve as a reference for programmers, implementors and manual writers. What remains unsaid is mostly left so intentionally, either because it is derivable from stated rules of the language or because it would require one to commit the definition when a general commitment appears as unwise.

A.2 Syntax

A language is an infinite set of sentences, namely the sentences well formed according to its syntax. In Oberon, these sentences are called compilation units. Each unit is a finite sequence of symbols from a finite vocabulary. The vocabulary of Oberon consists of identifiers, numbers, strings, operators, delimiters and comments. They are called lexical symbols and are composed of sequences of characters. (Note the distinction between symbols and characters).

To describe the syntax, an extended Backus–Naur Formalism called EBNF is used. Brackets [and] denote optionality of the enclosed sentential form, and braces { and } denote its repetition (possibly 0 times). Syntactic entities (non-terminal symbols) are denoted by English words expressing their intuitive meaning. Symbols of the language vocabulary (terminal symbols) are denoted by strings enclosed in quote marks or

---

[1] By Niklaus Wirth: this is a revised version of a paper "The programming language Oberon." *Software – Practice and Experience*, **18**, 671–90 (1988).

words written in capital letters, so-called reserved words. Syntactic rules (productions) are marked by a bar at the left margin of the line.

A.3 Vocabulary and representation

The representation of symbols in terms of characters is defined using the ASCII set. Symbols are identifiers, numbers, strings, operators, delimiters, and comments. The following lexical rules must be observed. Blanks and line breaks must not occur within symbols (except in comments, and, in the case of blanks, in strings). They are ignored unless they are essential to separate two consecutive symbols. Capital and lower-case letters are considered as being distinct.

1. *Identifiers* are sequences of letters and digits. The first character must be a letter.

| ident = letter {letter | digit}.

Examples include

    x   scan   Oberon   GetSymbol   firstLetter

2. *Numbers* are (unsigned) integers or real numbers. Integers are sequences of digits and may be followed by a suffix letter. The type is the minimal type to which the number belongs (see Section A.6.1). If no suffix is specified, the representation is decimal. The suffix H indicates hexadecimal representation.

A real number always contains a decimal point. Optionally, it may also contain a decimal scale factor. The letter E (or D) is pronounced as 'times ten to the power of.' A real number is of type REAL, unless it has a scale factor containing the letter D, in which case it is of type LONGREAL.

| number = integer | real.
| integer = digit {digit} | digit {hexDigit} "H" .
| real = digit {digit} "." {digit} [ScaleFactor].
| ScaleFactor = ("E" | "D") ["+" | "−"] digit {digit}.
| hexDigit = digit | "A" | "B" | "C" | "D" | "E" | "F".
| digit = "0" | "1" | "2" | "3" | "4" | "5" | "6" | "7" | "8" | "9".

Examples include

```
1987
100H          = 256
12.3
4.567E8       = 456700000
0.57712566D-6 = 0.00000057712566
```

3. *Character constants* are either denoted by a single character enclosed in quote marks or by the ordinal number of the character in hexadecimal notation followed by the letter X.

| CharConstant = """" character """" | digit {hexDigit} "X".

4. *Strings* are sequences of characters enclosed in quote marks ("). A string cannot contain a quote mark. The number of characters in a string is called the length of the string. Strings can be assigned to and compared with arrays of characters (see Sections A.9.1 and A.8.2.4).

| string = """"{character} """".

Examples include

"OBERON"   "Don't worry!"

5. *Operators* and *delimiters* are the special characters, character pairs, or reserved words listed below. These reserved words consist exclusively of capital letters and cannot be used in the role of identifiers.

+	:=	ARRAY	IS	TO
-	^	BEGIN	LOOP	TYPE
*	=	CASE	MOD	UNTIL
/	#	CONST	MODULE	VAR
~	<	DIV	NIL	WHILE
&	>	DO	OF	WITH
.	<=	ELSE	OR	
,	>=	ELSIF	POINTER	
;	..	END	PROCEDURE	
|	:	EXIT	RECORD	
(	)	IF	REPEAT	
[	]	IMPORT	RETURN	
{	}	IN	THEN	

6. *Comments* may be inserted between any two symbols in a program. They are arbitrary character sequences opened by the bracket (* and closed by *). Comments do not affect the meaning of a program.

A.4 Declarations and scope rules

Every identifier occurring in a program must be introduced by a declaration, unless it is a predefined identifier. Declarations also serve to specify certain permanent properties of an object, such as whether it is a constant, a type, a variable or a procedure.

The identifier is then used to refer to the associated object. This is possible only in those parts of a program that are within the scope of the declaration. No identifier may denote more than one object within a given scope. The scope extends textually from the point of the declaration to the end of the block (procedure or module) to which the declaration belongs and hence to which the object is local. The scope rule has the following amendments:

(1) If a type T is defined as POINTER TO $T1$ (see Section A.6.4), then the identifier $T1$ can be declared textually following the declaration of T, but it must lie within the same scope.

(2) Field identifiers of a record declaration (see Section A.6.3) are valid in field designators only.

In its declaration, an identifier in the global scope may be followed by an export mark (*) to indicate that it be exported from its declaring module. In this case, the identifier may be used in other modules, if they import the declaring module. The identifier is then prefixed by the identifier designating its module (see Section A.11). The prefix and the identifier are separated by a period and together are called a *qualified identifier*.

```
qualident = [ident "."] ident.
identdef = ident ["*"].
```

The following identifiers are predefined; their meaning is defined in the indicated sections:

ABS	(A.10.2)	LEN	(A.10.2)
ASH	(A.10.2)	LONG	(A.10.2)
BOOLEAN	(A.6.1)	LONGINT	(A.6.1)
CAP	(A.10.2)	LONGREAL	(A.6.1)
CHAR	(A.6.1)	MAX	(A.10.2)
CHR	(A.10.2)	MIN	(A.10.2)
COPY	(A.10.2)	NEW	(A.6.4)
DEC	(A.10.2)	ODD	(A.10.2)
ENTIER	(A.10.2)	ORD	(A.10.2)

EXCL	(A.10.2)	REAL	(A.6.1)
FALSE	(A.6.1)	SET	(A.6.1)
HALT	(A.10.2)	SHORT	(A.10.2)
INC	(A.10.2)	SHORTINT	(A.6.1)
INCL	(A.10.2)	SIZE	(A.10.2)
INTEGER	(A.6.1)	TRUE	(A.6.1)

A.5 Constant declarations

A constant declaration associates an identifier with a constant value.

ConstantDeclaration = identdef "=" ConstExpression.
ConstExpression = expression.

A constant expression can be evaluated by a mere textual scan without actually executing the program. Its operands are constants (see Section A. 8).Examples of constant declarations include

```
N     = 100
limit = 2*N – 1
all   = {0 .. WordSize–1}
```

A.6 Type declarations

A data type determines the set of values that variables of that type may assume, and the operators that are applicable. A type declaration is used to associate an identifier with the type. Such association may be with unstructured (basic) types, or it may be with structured types, in which case it defines the structure of variables of this type and, by implication, the operators that are applicable to the components. There are two different structures, namely arrays and records, with different component selectors.

TypeDeclaration = identdef "=" type.
type = qualident | ArrayType | RecordType | PointerType | ProcedureType.

Examples include

Table	=	ARRAY N OF REAL
Tree	=	POINTER TO Node
Node	=	RECORD key: INTEGER; left, right: Tree END
CenterNode	=	RECORD (Node) name: ARRAY 32 OF CHAR; subnode: Tree END
Function*	=	PROCEDURE (x: INTEGER): INTEGER

A.6.1 Basic types

The following basic types are denoted by predeclared identifiers. The associated operators are defined in Section A.8.2, and the predeclared function procedures in Section A.10.2. The values of a given basic type are as follows:

1. BOOLEAN   the truth values TRUE and FALSE.
2. CHAR   the characters of the extended ASCII set (0X...0FFX).
3. SHORTINT   the integers between MIN(SHORTINT) and MAX(SHORTINT).
4. INTEGER   the integers between MIN(INTEGER) and MAX(INTEGER).
5. LONGINT   the integers between MIN(LONGINT) and MAX(LONGINT).
6. REAL   real numbers between MIN(REAL) and MAX(REAL).
7. LONGREAL   real numbers between MIN(LONGREAL) and MAX(LONGREAL).
8. SET   the sets of integers between 0 and MAX(SET).

Types 3 to 5 are *integer* types, 6 and 7 are *real* types, and together they are called *numeric* types. They form a hierarchy; the larger type *includes* (the values of) the smaller type:

$$\text{LONGREAL} \supseteq \text{REAL} \supseteq \text{LONGINT} \supseteq \text{INTEGER} \supseteq \text{SHORTINT}$$

A.6.2 Array types

An array is a structure consisting of a fixed number of elements that are all of the same type, called the *element type*. The number of elements of an array is called its *length*. The elements of the array are designated by indices, which are integers between 0 and the length minus 1.

> ArrayType = ARRAY length {"," length} OF type.
> length = ConstExpression.

A declaration of the form

> ARRAY N0, N1, ... , Nk OF T

is understood as an abbreviation of the declaration

> ARRAY N0 OF
>   ARRAY N1 OF
>   ...
>   ARRAY Nk OF T

Examples of array types include

> ARRAY N OF INTEGER
> ARRAY 10, 20 OF REAL

A.6.3 Record types

A record type is a structure consisting of a fixed number of elements of possibly different types. The record type declaration specifies for each element, called a *field*, its type and an identifier that denotes the field. The scope of these field identifiers is the record definition itself, but they are also visible within field designators (see Section A.8.1) referring to elements of record variables.

> RecordType = RECORD ["(" BaseType ")"] FieldListSequence END.
> BaseType = qualident.
> FieldListSequence = FieldList {";" FieldList}.
> FieldList = [IdentList ":" type].
> IdentList = identdef {"," identdef}.

If a record type is exported, field identifiers that are to be visible outside the declaring module must be marked. They are called *public fields*; unmarked fields are called *private fields*.

Record types are extensible; that is, a record type can be defined as an extension of another record type. In the examples above, CenterNode *(directly) extends* Node, which is the *(direct) base type* of CenterNode. More specifically, CenterNode extends Node with the fields *name* and *subnode*.

Definition: A type T0 *extends* a type T if it equals T or if it directly extends an extension of T. Conversely, a type T is a *base type* of T0 if it equals T0 or if it is the direct base type of a base type of T0.

Examples of record types include

```
RECORD day, month, year: INTEGER
END

RECORD
    name, firstname: ARRAY 32 OF CHAR;
    age: INTEGER;
    salary: REAL
END
```

A.6.4 Pointer types

Variables of a pointer type P assume as values pointers to variables of some type T. The pointer type P is said to be *bound* to T, and T is the *pointer base type* of P. T must be a record or array type. Pointer types inherit the extension relation of their base types. If a type T0 is an extension of T and P0 is a pointer type bound to T0 then P0 is also an extension of P.

| PointerType = POINTER TO type.

If p is a variable of type P = POINTER TO T then a call of the predefined procedure NEW(p) has the following effect (see Section A.10.2): A variable of type T is allocated in free storage, and a pointer to it is assigned to p. This pointer p is of type P; the *referenced* variable p↑ is of type T. Failure of allocation results in p obtaining the value NIL. Any pointer variable may be assigned the value NIL, which points to no variable at all.

A.6.5 Procedure types

Variables of a procedure type *T* have a procedure (or NIL) as value. If a procedure *P* is assigned to a procedure variable of type *T*, the (types of the) formal parameters of *P* must be the same as those indicated in the formal parameters of *T*. The same holds for the result type in the case of a function procedure (see Section A.10.1). *P* must not be declared local to another procedure, and neither can it be a predefined procedure.

| ProcedureType = PROCEDURE [FormalParameters].

A.7 Variable declarations

Variable declarations serve to introduce variables and associate them with identifiers that must be unique within the given scope. They also serve to associate fixed data types with the variables.

| VariableDeclaration = IdentList ":" type.

Variables whose identifiers appear in the same list are all of the same type. Examples of variable declarations (refer to the examples in Section A. 6) include

```
i, j, k:   INTEGER
x, y:      REAL
p, q:      BOOLEAN
s:         SET
f:         Function
a:         ARRAY 100 OF REAL
w:         ARRAY 16 OF
               RECORD ch: CHAR;
                   count: INTEGER
               END
t:         Tree
```

Variables of a pointer type *T0* and VAR-parameters of a record type *T0* may assume values whose type *T1* is an extension of their declared type *T0*.

A.8 Expressions

Expressions are constructs denoting rules of computation whereby constants and current values of variables are combined to derive other values by the application of operators and function procedures. Expressions consist of operands and operators. Parentheses may be used to express specific associations of operators and operands.

A.8.1 Operands

With the exception of sets and literal constants, that is numbers and character strings, operands are denoted by *designators*. A designator consists of an identifier referring to the constant, variable, or procedure to be designated. This identifier may possibly be qualified by module identifiers (see Sections A.4 and A.11), and it may be followed by selectors, if the designated object is an element of a structure.

If A designates an array, then $A[E]$ denotes that element of A whose index is the current value of the expression E. Note that E must be of integer type. A designator of the form $A[E1, E2, \ldots, En]$ stands for $A[E1][E2] \ldots [En]$. If p designates a pointer variable, $p\uparrow$ denotes the variable that is referenced by p. If r designates a record then $r.f$ denotes the field f of r. If p designates a pointer, $p.f$ denotes the field f of the record $p\uparrow$ (that is, the dot implies dereferencing and $p.f$ stands for $p\uparrow.f$) and $p[E]$ denotes the element of $p\uparrow$ with index E.

The *typeguard* $v(T0)$ asserts that v is of type $T0$; that is, it aborts program execution if it is not of type $T0$. The guard is applicable if

(1) $T0$ is an extension of the declared type T of v, and
(2) v is a formal variable parameter of record type or v is a pointer.

designator = qualident {"." ident | "[" ExpList "]" |
 "(" qualident ")" | "↑" }.
ExpList = expression {"," expression}.

If the designated object is a variable then the designator refers to the variable's current value. If the object is a procedure, a designator without parameter list refers to that procedure. If it is followed by a (possibly empty) parameter list, the designator implies an activation of the procedure and stands for the value resulting from its execution. The (types of the) actual parameters must correspond to the formal parameters as specified in the procedure's declaration (see Section A.10).

Examples of designators (see the examples in Section A.7) include

i	(INTEGER)
a[i]	(REAL)
w[3].ch	(CHAR)
t.key	(INTEGER)
t.left.right	(Tree)
t(CenterNode).subnode	(Tree)

A.8.2 Operators

The syntax of expressions distinguishes between four classes of operators with different precedences (binding strengths). The operator ~ has the highest precedence, followed by multiplication operators, addition operators and relations. Operators of the same precedence associate from left to right. For example, x – y – z stands for (x – y) – z.

> expression = SimpleExpression [relation SimpleExpression].
> relation = "=" | "#" | "<" | "<=" | ">" | ">=" | IN | IS.
> SimpleExpression = ["+" | "–"] term {AddOperator term}.
> AddOperator = "+" | "–" | OR .
> term = factor {MulOperator factor}.
> MulOperator = "*" | "/" | DIV | MOD | "&" .
> factor =   number | CharConstant | string | NIL | set |
>   designator [ActualParameters] | "(" expression ")" |
>   "~" factor.
> set = "{" [element {"," element}] "}".
> element = expression [".." expression].
> ActualParameters = "(" [ExpList] ")" .

The available operators are listed in Sections A.8.2.1–A.8.2.4. In some instances, several different operations are designated by the same operator symbol. In these cases, the actual operation is identified by the type of the operands.

A.8.2.1 *Logical operators*

Symbol	Result
OR	logical disjunction
&	logical conjunction
~	negation

These operators apply to BOOLEAN operands and yield a BOOLEAN result.

p OR q	stands for	"if p then TRUE, else q"
p & q	stands for	"if p then q, else FALSE"
~p	stands for	"not p"

A.8.2.2 Arithmetic operators

Symbol	Result
+	sum
–	difference
*	product
/	quotient
DIV	integer quotient
MOD	modulus

The operators +, –, *, and / apply to operands of numeric types. The type of the result is that operand's type which includes the other operand's type, except for division (/), where the result is the real type which includes both operand types. When used as operators with a single operand, – denotes sign inversion and + denotes the identity operation.

The operators DIV and MOD apply to integer operands only. They are related by the following formulas defined for any dividend x and positive divisors y:

$$x = (x \text{ DIV } y) * y + (x \text{ MOD } y)$$
$$0 \leq (x \text{ MOD } y) < y$$

A.8.2.3 Set operators

Symbol	Result
+	union
–	difference
*	intersection
MOD	modulus

Sets are values of type SET. Set operators apply to operands of this type. The monadic minus sign denotes the complement of x; that is, $-x$ denotes the set of integers between 0 and MAX(SET) that are not elements of x.

$$x - y = x * (-y)$$
$$x / y = (x - y) + (y - x)$$

A.8.2.4 Relations

Symbol	Relation
=	equal
#	unequal
<	less
<=	less or equal
>	greater
>=	greater or equal
IN	set membership
IS	type test

Relations are Boolean. The ordering relations <, <=, > and >= apply to the numeric types, CHAR and character arrays (strings). The relations = and # also apply to the type BOOLEAN and to set, pointer and procedure types. x IN s stands for 'x is an element of s.' x must be of an integer type, and s of type SET. v IS T stands for 'v is of type T' and is called a type test. It is applicable if

(1) T is an extension of the declared type T0 of v, and
(2) v is a variable parameter of record type or v is a pointer.

Assuming, for instance, that T is an extension of T0 and that v is a designator declared of type T0, then the test 'v IS T' determines whether the actually designated variable is (not only a T0, but also) a T. The value of NIL IS T is undefined.

Examples of expressions (refer to the examples in Section A.7) include

1987	(INTEGER)
i DIV 3	(INTEGER)
~p OR q	(BOOLEAN)
(i + j) * (i − j)	(INTEGER)
s − {8, 9, 13}	(SET)
i + x	(REAL)
a[i + j] * a[i − j]	(REAL)
(0 <= i) & (i < 100)	(BOOLEAN)
t.key = 0	(BOOLEAN)
k IN {i .. j − 1}	(BOOLEAN)
t IS CenterNode	(BOOLEAN)

A.9 Statements

Statements denote actions. There are elementary and structured statements. Elementary statements are not composed of any parts that are themselves statements. They are the assignment, the procedure call, and the return and exit statements. Structured statements are composed of parts that are themselves statements. They are used to express sequencing and conditional, selective and repetitive execution. A statement may also be empty, in which case it denotes no action. The empty statement is included in order to relax punctuation rules in statement sequences.

> statement = [assignment | ProcedureCall | IfStatement | CaseStatement | WhileStatement | RepeatStatement | LoopStatement | WithStatement | EXIT | RETURN [expression]].

A.9.1 Assignments

The assignment serves to replace the current value of a variable by a new value specified by an expression. The assignment operator is written as ":=" and pronounced as *becomes*.

> assignment = designator ":=" expression.

The type of the expression must be included by the type of the variable, or it must extend the type of the variable. The following exceptions hold:

(1) The constant NIL can be assigned to variables of any pointer or procedure type.

(2) Strings can be assigned to any variable whose type is an array of characters, provided the length of the string is less than that of the array. If a string s of length n is assigned to an array a, the result is $a[i] = s_i$ for $i = 0, ..., n-1$, and $a[n] = 0X$.

Examples of assignments (see the examples in Section A.7) include

```
i := 0
p := i = j
x := i + 1
```

k := log2(i + j)
F := log2
s := {2, 3, 5, 7, 11, 13}
a[i] := (x + y) * (x − y)
t.key := i
w[i + 1].ch := "A"

A.9.2 Procedure calls

A procedure call serves to activate a procedure. The procedure call may contain a list of actual parameters that are substituted in place of their corresponding formal parameters defined in the procedure declaration (see Section A.10). The correspondence is established by the positions of the parameters in the lists of actual and formal parameters respectively. There exist two kinds of parameters: *variable* and *value parameters*.

In the case of variable parameters, the actual parameter must be a designator denoting a variable. If it designates an element of a structured variable, the selector is evaluated when the formal/actual parameter substitution takes place; that is, before the execution of the procedure. If the parameter is a value parameter, the corresponding actual parameter must be an expression. This expression is evaluated prior to the procedure activation, and the resulting value is assigned to the formal parameter, which now constitutes a local variable (see also Section A.10.1).

| ProcedureCall = designator [ActualParameters].

Examples of procedure calls include

ReadInt(i)   (see Section A.10)
WriteInt(j*2 + 1, 6)
INC(w[k].count)

A.9.3 Statement sequences

Statement sequences denote the sequence of actions specified by the component statements, which are separated by semicolons.

| StatementSequence = statement {";" statement}.

A.9.4 If statements

> IfStatement = IF expression THEN StatementSequence
> {ELSIF expression THEN StatementSequence}
> [ELSE StatementSequence]
> END.

If statements specify the conditional execution of guarded statements. The Boolean expression preceding a statement is called its *guard*. The guards are evaluated in sequence of occurrence, until one evaluates to TRUE, whence its associated statement sequence is executed. If no guard is satisfied, the statement sequence following the symbol ELSE is executed, if there is one.

An example is

```
IF (ch >= "A") & (ch <= "Z") THEN ReadIdentifier
ELSIF (ch >= "0") & (ch <= "9") THEN ReadNumber
ELSIF ch = 22X THEN ReadString
END
```

A.9.5 Case statements

Case statements specify the selection and execution of a statement sequence according to the value of an expression. First the case expression is evaluated; then the statement sequence is executed whose case label list contains the obtained value. The case expression and all labels must be of the same type, which must be an integer type or CHAR. Case labels are constants, and no value must occur more than once. If the value of the expression does not occur as a label of any case, the statement sequence following the symbol ELSE is selected, if there is one. Otherwise it is considered as an error.

> CaseStatement = CASE expression OF case {"|" case}
> [ELSE StatementSequence] END.
> case = [CaseLabelList ":" StatementSequence].
> CaseLabelList = CaseLabels {"," CaseLabels}.
> CaseLabels = ConstExpression [".." ConstExpression].

An example is

```
CASE ch OF
    "A" .. "Z": ReadIdentifier
```

```
        | "0" .. "9": ReadNumber
        | 22X : ReadString
    ELSE SpecialCharacter
    END
```

A.9.6 While statements

While statements specify repetition. If the Boolean expression (guard) yields TRUE, the statement sequence is executed. The expression evaluation and the statement execution are repeated as long as the Boolean expression yields TRUE.

| WhileStatement = WHILE expression DO StatementSequence END.

Examples include

```
WHILE j > 0 DO
    j := j DIV 2;  i := i + 1
END

WHILE (t # NIL) & (t.key # i) DO
    t := t.left
END
```

A.9.7 Repeat statements

A repeat statement specifies the repeated execution of a statement sequence until a condition is satisfied. The statement sequence is executed at least once.

| RepeatStatement = REPEAT StatementSequence UNTIL expression.

A.9.8 Loop statements

A loop statement specifies the repeated execution of a statement sequence. It is terminated by the execution of any exit statement within that sequence (see Section A.9.9).

| LoopStatement = LOOP StatementSequence END.

An example is

```
LOOP
  IF t1 = NIL THEN EXIT END ;
  IF k < t1.key THEN t2 := t1.left; p := TRUE
  ELSIF k > t1.key THEN t2 := t1.right; p := FALSE
  ELSE EXIT
  END ;
  t1 := t2
END
```

Although while and repeat statements can be expressed by loop statements containing a single exit statement, the use of while and repeat statements is recommended in the most frequently occurring situations, where termination depends on a single condition determined either at the beginning or the end of the repeated statement sequence. The loop statement is useful to express cases with several termination conditions and points.

A.9.9 Return and exit statements

A return statement consists of the symbol RETURN, possibly followed by an expression. It indicates the termination of a procedure, and the expression specifies the result of a function procedure. Its type must be identical to the result type specified in the procedure heading (see Section A.10).

Function procedures require the presence of a return statement indicating the result value. There may be several, although only one will be executed. In proper procedures, a return statement is implied by the end of the procedure body. An explicit return statement therefore appears as an additional (probably exceptional) termination point.

An exit statement consists of the symbol EXIT. It specifies termination of the enclosing loop statement and continuation with the statement following that loop statement. Exit statements are contextually, although not syntactically, bound to the loop statement that contains them.

A.9.10 With statements

If a pointer variable or a variable parameter with record structure is of a type $T0$, it may be designated in the heading of a with clause together with a type T that is an extension of $T0$. Then the variable is guarded within the with statement as if it had been declared of type *T*. The with statement assumes a role similar to the type guard, extending the guard over an entire statement sequence. It may be regarded as a *regional type guard*.

> WithStatement = WITH qualident ":" qualident DO
> StatementSequence END .

An example is

> WITH t: CenterNode DO name := t.name; L := t.subnode END

A.10 Procedure declarations

Procedure declarations consist of a *procedure heading* and a *procedure body*. The heading specifies the procedure identifier, the *formal parameters* and the result type (if any). The body contains declarations and statements. The procedure identifier is repeated at the end of the procedure declaration.

There are two kinds of procedures, namely *proper procedures* and *function procedures*. The latter are activated by a function designator as a constituent of an expression, and yield a result that is an operand in the expression. Proper procedures are activated by a procedure call. The function procedure is distinguished in the declaration by indication of the type of its result following the parameter list. Its body must contain a RETURN statement that defines the result of the function procedure.

All constants, variables, types and procedures declared within a procedure body are local to the procedure. The values of local variables are undefined upon entry to the procedure. Since procedures may be declared as local objects too, procedure declarations may be nested.

In addition to its formal parameters and locally declared objects, the objects declared in the environment of the procedure are also visible in the procedure (with the exception of those objects that have the same name as an object declared locally).

The use of the procedure identifier in a call within its declaration implies recursive activation of the procedure.

```
ProcedureDeclaration =
    ProcedureHeading ";" ProcedureBody ident.
ProcedureHeading =
    PROCEDURE ["*"] identdef [FormalParameters].
ProcedureBody =
    DeclarationSequence [BEGIN StatementSequence] END.
ForwardDeclaration =
    PROCEDURE "^" identdef [FormalParameters].
DeclarationSequence =
    {CONST {ConstantDeclaration ";"} |
    TYPE {TypeDeclaration ";"} |
    VAR {VariableDeclaration ";"}}
    {ProcedureDeclaration ";" | ForwardDeclaration ";"}.
```

A *forward declaration* serves to allow forward references to a procedure that appears later in the text in full. The actual declaration – which specifies the body – must indicate the same parameters and result type (if any) as the forward declaration, and it must be within the same scope.

An asterisk following the symbol PROCEDURE is a hint to the compiler, and specifies that the procedure is to be usable as a parameter and assignable to variables. (Depending on the implementation, the hint may be optional or required.)

A.10.1 Formal parameters

Formal parameters are identifiers that denote actual parameters specified in the procedure call. The correspondence between formal and actual parameters is established when the procedure is called. There are two kinds of parameters, namely *value* and *variable parameters*. The kind is indicated in the formal parameter list. Value parameters stand for local variables to which the result of the evaluation of the corresponding actual parameter is assigned as initial value. Variable parameters correspond to actual parameters that are variables, and they stand for these variables. Variable parameters are indicated by the symbol VAR, value parameters by its absence. A function procedure without parameters must have an empty parameter list. It must be called by a function designator whose actual parameter list is empty too.

Formal parameters are local to the procedure; that is, their scope is the program text that constitutes the procedure declaration.

A.10 Procedure declarations

FormalParameters = "(" [FPSection {";" FPSection}] ")"
    [":" qualident].
FPSection = [VAR] ident {"," ident} ":" FormalType.
FormalType = {ARRAY OF} qualident | ProcedureType.

The type of each formal parameter is specified in the parameter list. For variable parameters, it must be identical to the corresponding actual parameter's type, except in the case of a record, where it must be a base type of the corresponding actual parameter's type. For value parameters, the rule of assignment holds (see Section A.9.1). If the formal parameter's type is specified as

ARRAY OF T

the parameter is said to be an *open array parameter*, and the corresponding actual parameter may be any array with element type T.

If a formal parameter specifies a procedure type then the corresponding actual parameter must be either a procedure declared globally or a variable (or parameter) of that procedure type. It cannot be a predefined procedure. The result type of a procedure can be neither a record nor an array.

Examples of procedure declarations include

```
PROCEDURE ReadInt(VAR x: INTEGER);
    VAR i : INTEGER; ch: CHAR;
BEGIN i := 0; Read(ch);
    WHILE ("0" <= ch) & (ch <= "9") DO
        i := 10*i + (ORD(ch)–ORD("0")); Read(ch)
    END ;
    x := i
END ReadInt

PROCEDURE WriteInt(x: INTEGER);   (* 0 <= x < 10.0E5 *)
    VAR
        i: INTEGER;
        buf: ARRAY 5 OF INTEGER;
BEGIN i := 0;
    REPEAT buf[i] := x MOD 10;  x := x DIV 10;  INC(i) UNTIL x = 0;
    REPEAT DEC(i); Write(CHR(buf[i] + ORD("0"))) UNTIL i = 0
END WriteInt

PROCEDURE log2(x: INTEGER): INTEGER;
    VAR y: INTEGER;  (* assume x > 0 *)
BEGIN y := 0;
```

```
        WHILE x > 1 DO x := x DIV 2; INC(y) END ;
        RETURN y
    END log2
```

A.10.2 Predefined procedures

Tables A.1–A.3 list the predefined procedures. Some are *generic procedures*; that is, they apply to several types of operands. *v* stands for a variable, *x* and *n* for expressions, and *T* for a type.

Table A.1 Function procedures.

Name	Argument type	Result type	Function
ABS(x)	numeric type	type of x	absolute value
ODD(x)	integer type	BOOLEAN	x MOD 2 = 1
CAP(x)	CHAR	CHAR	corresponding capital letter
ASH(x, n)	x, n: integer type	LONGINT	$x \cdot 2^n$, arithmetic shift
LEN(v, n)	v: array n: integer type	LONGINT	the length of v in dimension n
LEN(v)	array type	LONGINT	LEN(v, 0)
MAX(T)	T = basic type T = SET	T INTEGER	maximum value of type T maximum element of sets
MIN(T)	T = basic type T = SET	T INTEGER	minimum value of type T 0
SIZE(T)	T = any type	integer type	number of bytes required by T

Table A.2 Type conversion procedures.

Name	Argument type	Result type	Function
ORD(x)	CHAR	INTEGER	ordinal number of x
CHR(x)	integer type	CHAR	character with ordinal number x
SHORT(x)	LONGINT INTEGER LONGREAL	INTEGER SHORTINT REAL	identity (truncation possible)
LONG(x)	SHORTINT INTEGER REAL	INTEGER LONGINT LONGREAL	identity
ENTIER(x)	real type	LONGINT	largest integer not greater than x

Note that ENTIER(i/j) = i DIV j

Table A.3 Proper procedures.

Name	Argument types	Function
INC(v)	integer type	$v := v + 1$
INC(v, x)	integer type	$v := v + x$
DEC(v)	integer type	$v := v - 1$
DEC(v, x)	integer type	$v := v - x$
INCL(v, x)	v: SET; x: integer type	$v := v + \{x\}$
EXCL(v, x)	v: SET; x: integer type	$v := v - \{x\}$
COPY(x, v)	x: character array, string; v: character array	$v := x$
NEW(v)	pointer type	allocate $v\uparrow$
HALT(x)	integer constant	terminate program execution

In HALT(x), x is a parameter whose interpretation is left to the underlying system implementation.

A.11 Modules

A module is a collection of declarations of constants, types, variables, and procedures, and a sequence of statements for the purpose of assigning initial values to the variables. A module typically constitutes a text that is compilable as a unit.

> module = MODULE ident ";" [ImportList] DeclarationSequence
>   [BEGIN StatementSequence] END ident "." .
> ImportList = IMPORT import {"," import} ";" .
> import = ident [":=" ident].

The import list specifies the modules of which the module is a client. If an identifier x is exported from a module M, and if M is listed in a module's import list, then x is referred to as $M.x$. If the form '$M := M1$' is used in the import list, that object declared within $M1$ is referenced as $M.x$.

Identifiers that are to be visible in client modules, that is outside the declaring module, must be marked by an export mark in their declaration.

The statement sequence following the symbol BEGIN is executed when the module is added to a system (loaded). Individual (parameterless) procedures can thereafter be activated from the system, and these procedures serve as commands.

An example is

```
MODULE Out;
(* exported procedures:  Write, WriteInt, WriteLn *)
IMPORT Texts, Oberon;
VAR W: Texts.Writer;

PROCEDURE Write*(ch: CHAR);
BEGIN Texts.Write(W, ch)
END Write;

PROCEDURE WriteInt*(x, n: LONGINT);
    VAR i: INTEGER; a: ARRAY 16 OF CHAR;
BEGIN i := 0;
    IF x < 0 THEN Texts.Write(W, "-"); x := -x END ;
    REPEAT
        a[i] := CHR(x MOD 10 + ORD("0")); x := x DIV 10; INC(i)
    UNTIL x = 0;
    REPEAT Texts.Write(W, " "); DEC(n) UNTIL n <= i;
    REPEAT DEC(i); Texts.Write(W, a[i]) UNTIL i = 0
END WriteInt;

PROCEDURE WriteLn*;
BEGIN Texts.WriteLn(W); Texts.Append(Oberon.Log, W.buf)
END WriteLn;

BEGIN Texts.OpenWriter(W)
END Out.
```

A.12 The Module SYSTEM

The module SYSTEM contains definitions that are necessary to program *low-level* operations referring directly to resources particular to a given computer and/or implementation. These include, for example, facilities for accessing devices that are controlled by the computer, and facilities to break the data type compatibility rules otherwise imposed by the language definition. It is recommended that their use be restricted to specific *low-level* modules. Such modules are inherently non-portable, but are easily recognized due to the identifier SYSTEM appearing in their import lists. The subsequent definitions are those that hold for the NS32000 implementation, but they are applicable to most modern computers. Individual implementations may differ and include definitions that are particular to the specific, underlying computer.

Module SYSTEM exports the data type BYTE. No representation of values is specified. Instead, certain compatibility rules with other types are given:

(1) The type BYTE is compatible with CHAR and SHORTINT.
(2) If a formal variable parameter is of type ARRAY OF BYTE then the corresponding actual parameter may be of any type.

The procedures contained in module SYSTEM are listed in Tables A.4 and A.5. They correspond to single instructions compiled as in-line code. For details, the reader is referred to the processor manual. v stands for a variable, $x, y, a,$ and n for expressions, and T for a type.

Table A.4 Function procedures.

Name	Argument types	Result type	Function
ADR(v)	any	LONGINT	address of variable v
BIT(a, n)	a: LONGINT n: integer type	BOOLEAN	bit n of Mem[a]
CC(n)	integer constant	BOOLEAN	Condition n
LSH(x, n)	x: integer type or SET n: integer type	type of x	logical shift
ROT(x, n)	x: integer type or SET n: integer type	type of x	rotation
VAL(T, x)	T, x: any type	T	x interpreted as of type T

Table A.5 Proper procedures.

Name	Argument types	Function
GET(a, v)	a: LONGINT v: any basic type	$v :=$ Mem[a]
PUT(a, x)	a: LONGINT x: any basic type	Mem[a] := x
MOVE(s, d, n)	s, d: LONGINT n: integer type	Mem[d]...Mem[$d+n-1$] := Mem[s]...Mem[$s+n-1$]
NEW(v, n)	v: any pointer type n: integer type	allocate storage block of n bytes, assign its address to v

Appendix B
ASCII Character set and extremal values

Dec	Hex	Char	Dec	Hex	Char	Dec	Hex	Char	Dec	Hex	Char
0	0X	NUL	32	20X	SP	64	40X	@	96	60X	`
1	1X	SOH	33	21X	!	65	41X	A	97	61X	a
2	2X	STX	34	22X	"	66	42X	B	98	62X	b
3	3X	ETX	35	23X	#	67	43X	C	99	63X	c
4	4X	EOT	36	24X	$	68	44X	D	100	64X	d
5	5X	ENQ	37	25X	%	69	45X	E	101	65X	e
6	6X	ACK	38	26X	&	70	46X	F	102	66X	f
7	7X	BEL	39	27X	'	71	47X	G	103	67X	g
8	8X	BS	40	28X	(	72	48X	H	104	68X	h
9	9X	HT	41	29X	)	73	49X	I	105	69X	i
10	0AX	LF	42	2AX	*	74	4AX	J	106	6AX	j
11	0BX	VT	43	2BX	+	75	4BX	K	107	6BX	k
12	0CX	FF	44	2CX	,	76	4CX	L	108	6CX	l
13	0DX	CR	45	2DX	-	77	4DX	M	109	6DX	m
14	0EX	SO	46	2EX	.	78	4EX	N	110	6EX	n
15	0FX	SI	47	2FX	/	79	4FX	O	111	6FX	o
16	10X	DLE	48	30X	0	80	50X	P	112	70X	p
17	11X	DC1	49	31X	1	81	51X	Q	113	71X	q
18	12X	DC2	50	32X	2	82	52X	R	114	72X	r
19	13X	DC3	51	33X	3	83	53X	S	115	73X	s
20	14X	DC4	52	34X	4	84	54X	T	116	74X	t
21	15X	NAK	53	35X	5	85	55X	U	117	75X	u
22	16X	SYN	54	36X	6	86	56X	V	118	76X	v
23	17X	ETB	55	37X	7	87	57X	W	119	77X	w
24	18X	CAN	56	38X	8	88	58X	X	120	78X	x
25	19X	EM	57	39X	9	89	59X	Y	121	79X	y
26	1AX	SUB	58	3AX	:	90	5AX	Z	122	7AX	z
27	1BX	ESC	59	3BX	;	91	5BX	[	123	7BX	{
28	1CX	FS	60	3CX	<	92	5CX	\	124	7CX		
29	1DX	GS	61	3DX	=	93	5DX	]	125	7DX	}
30	1EX	RS	62	3EX	>	94	5EX	^1	126	7EX	~
31	1FX	US	63	3FX	?	95	5FX	_	127	7FX	DEL

[1] Oberon fonts print an upward arrow "↑" instead of the caret "^".

Type T	bits	MIN(T)	MAX(T)
SHORTINT	8	−128	127
INTEGER	16	−32768	32767
LONGINT	32	−2147483648	2147483647
REAL[1]	32	−3.40282346E38	3.40282346E38
LONGREAL	64	$-a$†	a
CHAR	8	0	255
SET	32	0	31

† $a = 1.7976931348623157E308$

[1] REAL and LONGREAL values are extended one full digit beyond their represented accuracy to help in generating rounding and conversion algorithms.

Appendix C
Modules *In, Out* and *XYplane*

Throughout this book we have relied on the input/output abstractions provided by modules *In, Out* and *XYplane*. A particular implementation of these modules is given in this appendix. The modules have been tested on the original *Ceres* implementation, as well as on the Oberon system provided for IBM RS/6000, SUN Sparcstation, Apple Macintosh II and DECStation (see the list in the preface).

Module *In*

```
MODULE In;
IMPORT Texts, Viewers, Oberon, TextFrames;
VAR
    T: Texts.Text;
    S: Texts.Scanner;  W: Texts.Writer;
    beg: LONGINT;
    Done*: BOOLEAN;

PROCEDURE Put(txt: ARRAY OF CHAR);
BEGIN  Texts.WriteString(W, txt);  Texts.WriteLn(W);
Texts.Append(Oberon.Log, W.buf)
END Put;

PROCEDURE Open*;
VAR
    end, time: LONGINT;
    V: Viewers.Viewer;
BEGIN
    Texts.OpenScanner(S, Oberon.Par.text, Oberon.Par.pos);
    Texts.Scan(S);
    IF (S.class = Texts.Char) & (S.c = "↑") THEN
        (* Start input stream at beginning of selection *)
        Oberon.GetSelection(T, beg, end, time);
```

```
      IF time >= 0 THEN
        Texts.OpenScanner(S, T, beg);  Done := ~S.eot
      ELSE
        Put("No selection"); Done := FALSE
      END
    ELSIF (S.class = Texts.Char) & (S.c = "*") THEN
      (* Start input stream at beginning of text in marked viewer *)
      V := Oberon.MarkedViewer();
      IF ~Oberon.Pointer.on THEN
        Put("Pointer not visible");  Done := FALSE
      ELSIF (V.dsc # NIL) & (V.dsc.next IS TextFrames.Frame) THEN
        T := V.dsc.next(TextFrames.Frame).text;  beg := 0;
        Texts.OpenScanner(S, T, beg);  Done := ~S.eot
      ELSE
        Put("Marked viewer not a text viewer");  Done := FALSE
      END
    ELSE
      (* Start input stream after command name *)
      T := Oberon.Par.text;  beg := Oberon.Par.pos;
      Texts.OpenScanner(S, T, beg);  Done := ~S.eot
    END
END Open;

PROCEDURE Char*(VAR ch: CHAR);
BEGIN
  IF Done THEN
    ch := S.nextCh;  Done := ~S.eot;  Texts.Read(S, S.nextCh)
  END
END Char;

PROCEDURE Int*(VAR i: INTEGER);
BEGIN
  IF Done THEN
    Texts.Scan(S);  i := SHORT(S.i);  Done := (S.class = Texts.Int)
  END
END Int;

PROCEDURE LongInt*(VAR i: LONGINT);
BEGIN
  IF Done THEN
    Texts.Scan(S);  i := S.i;  Done := (S.class = Texts.Int)
  END
END LongInt;
```

```
        PROCEDURE Real*(VAR x: REAL);
        BEGIN
          IF Done THEN
             Texts.Scan(S);  x := S.x;  Done := (S.class = Texts.Real)
          END
        END Real;

        PROCEDURE Name*(VAR nme: ARRAY OF CHAR);
        BEGIN  (* Read a name such as Syntax.Scn.Fnt from input stream *)
          IF Done THEN
             Texts.Scan(S);  COPY(S.s, nme);  Done := (S.class = Texts.Name)
          END
        END Name;

        PROCEDURE String*(VAR str: ARRAY OF CHAR);
        CONST CR = 0DX;  NUL = 0X;
        VAR ch: CHAR;  j: LONGINT;
        BEGIN  (* Read blank delimited character sequence *)
          IF Done THEN
             REPEAT  Char(ch)  UNTIL ((ch # " ") & (ch # CR)) OR ~Done;
             j := 0;
             WHILE Done & (ch # " ") & (ch # CR) DO
                IF j < LEN(str) - 1 THEN str[j] := ch;  INC(j)  END;
                Char(ch)
             END;
             str[j] := NUL; Done := j # 0
          END
        END String;

        BEGIN  Texts.OpenWriter(W);  Done := FALSE
        END In.
```

Module *Out*

```
        MODULE Out;
        IMPORT Texts, Oberon, MenuViewers, TextFrames;
        VAR
          T: Texts.Text;  S: Texts.Scanner;  W: Texts.Writer;
          beg: LONGINT;

        PROCEDURE Open*;
        VAR
          x, y: INTEGER;
          menuF, mainF: TextFrames.Frame;
          V: MenuViewers.Viewer;
```

```
BEGIN
    T := TextFrames.Text("Out.Text");
    menuF := TextFrames.NewMenu("Out.Text",
    "System.Close System.Copy System.Grow Edit.Search Edit.Store");
    mainF := TextFrames.NewText(T, T.len – 200);
    Oberon.AllocateUserViewer(Oberon.Mouse.X, x, y);
    V := MenuViewers.New(menuF, mainF, TextFrames.menuH, x, y)
END Open;

PROCEDURE Char*(ch: CHAR);
BEGIN  Texts.Write(W, ch);  Texts.Append(T, W.buf)
END Char;

PROCEDURE String*(str: ARRAY OF CHAR);
BEGIN  Texts.WriteString(W, str);  Texts.Append(T, W.buf)
END String;

PROCEDURE Real*(x: REAL; n: INTEGER);
BEGIN  Texts.WriteReal(W, x, n);  Texts.Append(T, W.buf)
END Real;

PROCEDURE Int*(i, n: LONGINT);
BEGIN  Texts.WriteInt(W, i, n);  Texts.Append(T, W.buf)
END Int;

PROCEDURE Ln*;
BEGIN  Texts.WriteLn(W);  Texts.Append(T, W.buf)
END Ln;

BEGIN  Texts.OpenWriter(W);  T := Oberon.Log
END Out.
```

Module *XYplane*
```
MODULE XYplane;
    IMPORT Display, MenuViewers, Oberon, TextFrames, Input;
    CONST
        max = 32768;  replace = Display.replace;
        black = Display.black;  white = Display.white;
        erase* = 0;  draw* = 1;  (* values for parameter mode in Dot *)

    TYPE
        XYframe = POINTER TO XYframeDesc;
        XYframeDesc = RECORD (Display.FrameDesc) END;
```

```
VAR
  F: XYframe;
  bitmap: ARRAY max OF SET;
  X*, Y*, W*, H*: INTEGER;  (* location and extent of viewer *)

PROCEDURE Modify(F: XYframe; VAR M: MenuViewers.ModifyMsg);
BEGIN
  IF (M.id = MenuViewers.extend) & (M.dY > 0) THEN
    Display.ReplConst(black, F.X, F.Y + F.H, F.W, M.dY, replace)
  END;
  IF M.Y < F.Y THEN
    Display.ReplConst(black, F.X, M.Y, F.W, F.Y – M.Y, replace)
  END;
  X := F.X;  Y := M.Y;  W := F.W;  H := M.H
END Modify;

PROCEDURE Handle*(F: Display.Frame; VAR M: Display.FrameMsg);
BEGIN
  WITH F: XYframe DO
    IF M IS Oberon.InputMsg THEN
      WITH M: Oberon.InputMsg DO
        IF M.id = Oberon.track THEN
          Oberon.DrawCursor(Oberon.Mouse, Oberon.Arrow,
                                                      M.X, M.Y);
        END
      END
    ELSIF M IS MenuViewers.ModifyMsg THEN
      WITH M: MenuViewers.ModifyMsg DO
        Modify(F, M)
      END
    END
  END
END Handle;

PROCEDURE Clear*;
VAR j: LONGINT;
BEGIN
  Display.ReplConst(black, F.X, F.Y, F.X + F.W, F.Y + F.H, replace);
  j := 0;  WHILE j < max DO  bitmap[j] := {}; INC(j) END
END Clear;

PROCEDURE Open*;
VAR
  menuF: TextFrames.Frame;
```

```
    x, y: INTEGER;
    V: MenuViewers.Viewer;
BEGIN
    Oberon.OpenTrack(Display.Left, 0);
    menuF := TextFrames.NewMenu("XY Plane", "System.Close");
    NEW(F); F.handle := Handle;
    Oberon.AllocateUserViewer(Display.Left, x, y);
    V := MenuViewers.New(menuF, F, TextFrames.menuH, x, y);
    Clear
END Open;

PROCEDURE Dot*(x, y, mode: INTEGER);
    VAR k, i, j: LONGINT;
BEGIN
    IF (x >= F.X) & (x < F.X + F.W) & (y >= F.Y) & (y < F.Y + F.H) THEN
        k := LONG(y)*F.W + x;  i := k DIV MAX(SET);
        j := k MOD MAX(SET);
        CASE mode OF
            0: Display.Dot(black, x, y, replace); EXCL(bitmap[i], j)
          | 1: Display.Dot(white, x, y, replace); INCL(bitmap[i], j)
        END
    END
END Dot;

PROCEDURE IsDot*(x, y: INTEGER): BOOLEAN;
    VAR k, i, j: LONGINT;
BEGIN
    IF (x >= F.X) & (x < F.X + F.W) & (y >= F.Y) & (y < F.Y + F.H) THEN
        k := LONG(y)*F.W + x;  i := k DIV MAX(SET);
        j := k MOD MAX(SET);
        IF j IN bitmap[i] THEN RETURN TRUE
        ELSE RETURN FALSE
        END
    ELSE RETURN FALSE
    END
END IsDot;

PROCEDURE Key*(): CHAR;
    VAR ch: CHAR;
BEGIN  ch := 0X;
    IF Input.Available() > 0 THEN  Input.Read(ch)  END;
    RETURN ch
END Key;
```

Index

ABS 39, 302
abstract data structure 166, 174, 251
abstract data type 170, 174, 176, 210,
    218, 221, 230, 246, 251, 258
actual parameter 76
ADR 305
alias 72, 303
arithmetic expression 36
array 112
    abbreviated index notation 114
    assignment 115
    character array 122
    designator 113
    index 112
    length 112, 113
    loop over all elements 117
    multidimensional 113
    open array parameter 118, 301
    open array variable 274
ARRAY type 112, 287
ASCII 29, 306
ASH 302
assignment 39, 294
    array 115
    pointer 136
    procedure variable 200
    projection 193
    record 129, 191, 195
    string to character array 123, 294
    type rules 40
axiom
    of alternatives 50
    of assignment 41
    of repetition 55

base type 136, 190, 288
basic type 27, 286
binary search 120, 151
binding
    dynamic 217, 238, 269
    explicit 267
    implicit 267
BIT 305

BOOLEAN 29, 286
Boolean expression 37
browser 90
BYTE 305

C++ 238
call
    function procedure 76
    procedure variable 201
    proper procedure 66
    up-call 203
call statement 78, 295
CAP 302
case statement 52, 296
CC 305
CHAR type 29, 286
character
    array 122
    ASCII table 306
    constant 25, 283
    ordinal number 29
CHR 302
class 238
command 14, 73
comment 27, 283
compiler hints 82
CONST declaration 31, 285
constant
    character 25
    FALSE 29
    NIL 136
    number 24
    set 29
    string 25
    TRUE 29
constant expression 31
control variable 54, 273
COPY 123, 303
counting loop 54, 57

data hiding 166, 174
data structure
    abstract (or hidden) 166

Index

array 112
    binary tree 147
    dynamic 134
    heterogeneous 212
    linear list 140
    record 126
data type (see Type)
De Morgan's law 38
DEC 44, 303
declaration 30, 284
    CONST 31, 285
    forward 82
    PROCEDURE 66, 299
    TYPE 110, 285
    VAR 31, 289
declaration sequence 67
definition module 90
delimiter 25, 283
dereferencing 137
    implied 138
    nested 138
designator 33, 290
    array 113
    dereferenced pointer 138
    field of a record 129
    qualident 73
    simple 33
    with type guard 196
DIV 36
dynamic binding 217, 238, 265, 269
dynamic type 196

EBNF definition
    ActualParameters 33, 76, 201, 291
    AddOperator 33, 291
    ArrayType 112, 274, 287
    assignment 40, 294
    baseType 136, 287
    case 52, 296
    CaseLabelList 52, 296
    CaseLabels 52, 296
    CaseStatement 52, 296
    character 25
    CharConstant 25, 283
    ConstantDeclaration 285
    ConstDeclaration 31
    ConstExpression 31, 285
    DeclarationSequence 67, 82, 300
    designator 33, 73, 114, 129, 138, 196, 290
    digit 24, 282
    element 29, 38, 291
    ExitStatement 58
    ExpList 114, 196, 201, 290
    expression 33, 35, 291
    factor 33, 201, 291
    FieldList 127, 190, 287
    FieldListSequence 127, 190, 287
    FormalParameters 75, 77, 301
    FormalType 75, 77, 118, 202, 301
    ForStatement 273
    ForwardDeclaration 82, 300
    FPSection 75, 301
    FunctionCall 33, 76
    guard 198, 276
    hexDigit 24, 282
    ident 24, 282
    identdef 284
    IdentList 32, 127, 190, 287
    IfStatement 48, 296
    import 72, 303
    importList 72, 303
    integer 24, 282
    length 112, 274, 287
    letter 24
    LoopStatement 58, 297
    module 69, 303
    MulOperator 33, 291
    number 24, 282
    PointerType 136, 288
    ProcedureBody 66, 300
    ProcedureCall 78, 201, 295
    ProcedureDeclaration 66, 300
    ProcedureHeading 66, 75, 77, 267, 300
    ProcedureType 200, 289
    qualident 73, 284
    real 24, 282
    Receiver 267
    RecordType 127, 190, 287
    relation 33, 35, 291
    RepeatStatement 57, 297
    ReturnStatement 76
    ScaleFactor 24, 282
    selector 129
    set 29, 38, 291
    SimpleExpr 33
    SimpleExpression 291
    statement 42, 273, 294
    StatementSequence 42, 295
    string 25, 283
    term 33, 291
    type 110, 285
    TypeDeclaration 110, 285
    VarDeclaration 32
    VariableDeclaration 289
    WhileStatement 54, 297
    WithStatement 198, 276, 299
EBNF formalism 18
Eiffel 238
ENTIER 37, 302
example
    binary search in array 120
    copy strings 123
    factorial 81
    FIFO list 144–146
    length of a string 123

Index

linear list 140–144
matrix multiplication 118
module *Calendar* 164
module *FilledRectangles* 228
module *Graphics* 222, 270
module *IFS* (fractal fern) 92
module *In* 308
module *Model* 171, 260
module *Out* 310
module *Paths* 169
module *Qs* 247
module *RandomNumbers* 12
module *Rectangles* 223, 272
module *Sim* 252
module *Stations* 258
module *XYplane* 311
quadratic equation 79
read a file 178
search of a string in a name-list 124
search tree 147-151
write a file 178
EXCL 303
exit statement 58, 298
exponential random number 160
export mark 31, 71, 284, 303
  read-only 277
expression 32, 290
  arithmetic 36
  Boolean 37
  constant 31
  factor 33
  pointer 136
  procedure variable 200
  relation 35
  set 38
  string and character array 123
  term 32
  type compatibility rules 34
  type test 196
extension
  of pointer type 288
  of record type 288
extension (of type) 194

factor
  in expression 33
  syntactic 17
FALSE 29
file
  directory 177
  module *Files* 176
  rider 177
Files (module) 176
floating point number 28
for statement 273
formal definition
  assignment 41
  case statement 53

if statement 49
repeat statement 58
syntax 17
while statement 54
formal language 17
formal parameter 74, 299, 300
forward declaration 82, 300
function
  call 33, 76
  predeclared 39
  recursion 81
  side-effect 80
function procedure 73, 299

garbage collection 139
GET 305
global variable 70
guard 49, 196, 290, 296

HALT 42, 303
handler 230
heap 139
heterogeneous data structure 212

identifier 24, 282
  predeclared 26, 284
  qualified 72, 284
if statement 48, 296
import list 72, 303
IN 35
In (module) 88, 98, 308
INC 44, 303
INCL 303
index (array) 112
inheritance 238
input 87
  module *Files* 176
  module *In* 88, 98
input stream 98
INTEGER 27, 286
integer types 27
invariant 55, 120
IS 35
iterated function system 64

LEN 113, 302
linear search 119, 124, 143
list
  FIFO 144–146
  heterogeneous 213
  linear 140–144
list representation 153
locality
  parameter 75
  record field 127
  type-bound procedure 268
  variable 67
LONG 37, 302

LONGINT 27, 286
LONGREAL 28, 286
loop
   counting loop 54, 57
   invariant 55
   variant function 55
loop statement 58, 297
LSH 305

MAX 27, 302
mean value (of queue) 168
memory management 139
message 230, 238
method 238
MIN 27, 302
MOD 36
module 69, 303
   definition module 90
   Files 176
   In 88, 98
   Out 89, 98, 310
   SYSTEM 304
   XYplane 91, 100, 311
module hierarchy 173, 220, 256
MOVE 305

NEW 137, 274, 303, 305
NIL 136, 200
number 24, 282
numeric types 28

Oberon system 14, 95
Oberon-2 265
   for statement 273
   open array variable 274
   procedure redefinition 268
   read-only export 276
   receiver 266
   type-bound procedure 265
   with statement 275
object 218, 230, 236, 238, 265
object-orientation
   class 238
   dynamic binding 217, 238
   heterogeneous data structure 212
   inheritance 238
   message and handler 230
   message broadcast 233
   method 238
   object 230, 236, 238, 265
   procedure redefinition 227, 268
   role of module 220
   standard terminology 238
ODD 302
open array parameter 118, 301
open array variable 274
operand 32, 290
operator 25, 32, 283, 291

arithmetic 36, 292
logical 38, 291
relational (see Relation)
set 39, 292
↑ (dereferencing) 137
OR 38
ORD 302
ordinal number 29
Out (module) 89, 98, 310
output 87
   module *Files* 176
   module *Out* 89, 98
   module *XYplane* 91, 100
output stream 98

parameter
   actual 76
   array 115
   formal 74, 299, 300
   matching formal parameter list 200
   open array (ARRAY OF) 118, 301
   procedure variable 202
   receiver 266
   record 129
   substitution 78
   value 78, 295, 300
   variable (VAR) 78, 295, 300
pointer
   assignment 136
   base type 288
   dereferencing 137
   dynamic type 196
   extension 194, 288
   NEW 137, 288
   NIL 136, 288
   type guard 196, 290
POINTER type 136, 288
post-condition 41
pre-condition 41
predeclared function 302
   ABS 39, 302
   ASH 302
   CAP 302
   CHR 302
   ENTIER 37, 302
   LEN 113, 302
   LONG 37, 302
   MAX 27, 302
   MIN 27, 302
   ODD 302
   ORD 302
   SHORT 37, 302
   SIZE 302
predeclared identifier 26, 284
predeclared procedure 303
   COPY 123, 303
   DEC 44, 303
   EXCL 303

HALT 42, 303
INC 44, 303
INCL 303
NEW 137, 274, 303
procedure
  actual parameter 76
  call 66, 76, 295
  call of procedure variable 201
  command 73
  dynamic binding 217, 265
  formal parameter 74, 299, 300
  forward declaration 82, 300
  function 73, 299
  local variable 67
  NIL 200, 289
  open array parameter 118, 301
  predeclared 113, 123, 137, 302
  proper 77, 299
  re-definition 268
  recursion 81, 148
  return statement 67, 76, 77
  type-bound 265
  value parameter 78
  variable parameter (VAR) 78
PROCEDURE declaration 66, 299
PROCEDURE type 199, 289
projection 193
proper procedure 77, 299
PUT 305

qualified identifier 72, 284

random number 10, 160
read-only export 276
REAL 28, 286
real types 28
receiver 266
record 126, 129
  assignment 129, 191
  base type 190
  designator 129
  extension 190, 288
  field 287
  private field 288
  projection 193
  public field 288
  variant 198
RECORD type 127, 287
recursion
  data definition 140, 147
  procedure 81
  tree algorithms 148
regional type guard 197
relation 35, 293
    =, # (not equal) 35
    >, >=, <, <= 35
    IN (set membership) 35
    IS (type test) 35, 196

pointer 136
procedure variable 200
string and character array 123
repeat statement 57, 297
reserved word 25, 283
result-condition 41
return statement 67, 76, 77, 298
ROT 305

scope 68, 284
  global 70
  local 68
  nesting 68
  record 127
  type-bound procedure 268
scope rule 68, 284
search
  binary 120, 151
  linear 119, 124, 143
search tree 146
set
  constant 29
  expression 38
SET type 29, 286
SHORT 37, 302
SHORTINT 27, 286
side-effects 80
SIZE 302
Smalltalk-80 238
special character 25
stack 139
statement 294
  assignment 39, 294
  case 52, 296
  exit 58, 298
  for 273
  if 48, 296
  loop 58, 297
  procedure call 66, 295
  repeat 57, 297
  return 67, 76, 77, 298, 299
  while 54, 297
  with 197, 275, 298
statement sequence 42, 295
stepwise refinement 158, 250
stream 88
string 25, 283
  as ARRAY n OF CHAR 122
  terminator 122
structured programming 158
SYSTEM (module)
  ADR 305
  BIT 305
  BYTE 305
  CC 305
  GET 305
  LSH 305
  MOVE 305

NEW 305
PUT 305
ROT 305
VAL 305

term
  in expression 32
  syntactic 17
text (Oberon system) 96
token 18, 23
  character constant 25
  comment 27
  identifier 24
  number 24
  string 25
tool (Oberon system) 97
tree
  balancing 151
  binary 147-151
  n-way 154
TRUE 29
type
  ARRAY 112, 287
  ARRAY n OF CHAR 122
  assignment compatibility 40, 111, 193
  base (of extension) 190, 288
  base (of pointer type) 288
  basic 27, 286
  BOOLEAN 29, 286
  CHAR 29, 286
  conversion function 37, 302
  dynamic 196
  expression compatibility 34
  extension (of pointer type) 194, 288
  extension (of record type) 190, 288
  extremal value 27, 307
  guard 196, 197, 275, 290
  inclusion 28, 286
  INTEGER 27, 286
  LONGINT 27, 286
  LONGREAL 28, 286
  POINTER 136, 288
  PROCEDURE 199, 289
  REAL 28, 286
  RECORD 127, 287
  SET 29, 286
  SHORTINT 27, 286
  test (relation IS) 196, 293
TYPE declaration 110, 285
type-bound procedure 265

up-call 203

VAL 305
value parameter 78, 300
VAR declaration 31
VAR parameter 78, 300
variable
  control variable 54, 273
  global 71
  local 67
  of a given type 111
  open array 274
variant function 55
  of binary search 121
viewer (Oberon system) 15

while statement 54, 297
with statement 197, 275, 298
XYplane (module) 91, 100, 311